The Beggar's Benison

Beggar's Benison punch bowl, 1770s

The BEGGAR'S BENISON

Sex Clubs of Enlightenment Scotland and their Rituals

DAVID STEVENSON

Tuckwell Press

First published in Great Britain in 2001 by
Tuckwell Press
The Mill House
Phantassie
East Linton
East Lothian EH40 3DG
Scotland

ISBN 1 86232 134 5

British Library Cataloguing in Publication Data

A catalogue record for this book is available
on request from the British Library

Typeset by Koinonia, Manchester
Printed and bound by Creative Print and Design,
Ebbw Vale, Wales

Those to whom I have thought
of dedicating this book
might well be in two minds
as to whether the gesture
was a complimentary one,
given its subject

I therefore dedicate it
to its potential readers

*

'Keep them out of female sight'
Hugh Cleghorn, on
Beggar's Benison diplomas

Contents

Contents

List of Illustrations and Maps

Preface

As our own culture changes around us, so does what interests researchers in our cultural past – and what convention allows us to write about. That Scotland had two clubs in the eighteenth century, the Benison and the Wig, dedicated to the celebration of sexuality has long been known, but this has not been seen to be something worth studying, or reputable to study. Some interest was taken in the Beggar's Benison in the late nineteenth century, when it became known that obscene artefacts had survived, but understandably at that time what was published tended to be evasive and allusive, dropping hints of obscenity that might be interpreted by the learned but otherwise giving the impression that the Benison was just a rowdy gentleman's club – a bit naughty and shocking, but no more. The publication of the Benison *Records* and *Supplement* in 1892 added confusion. Publication was strictly limited, copies available by subscription only, for fear of prosecution. Moreover the material they made available was – insofar as it was seriously considered at all – greeted with suspicion. The works were so chaotically presented, and the editorial material so incompetent, that they were difficult to analyse. What they revealed about club activities was so shocking that it seemed unbelievable – surely it could not be authentic, and must be a forgery? And, anyway, the whole thing was so nasty that no scholar would wish to waste time on it. So the *Records* and *Supplement* lingered in a sort of limbo of uncertainty – historical sources, folklore, or pornographic fiction? In the late 1930s Louis Jones, an American scholar studying English clubs, stumbled on the Benison, and formed an honourable exception to the tendency to glance at the evidence, then turn aside in horror. Jones made the first serious study of the club and in terms of the context in which he wrote it is commendable. But he was limited by the fact that he was a literary historian with little knowledge of the Scottish background, and far more seriously by the fact that in a scholarly work much of what went on in the Benison was simply unmentionable. Thus the chapter he wrote on the Benison has a yawning gap at its centre. Moreover, his book on English clubs, published in America in the middle of the Second World War, had no detectable impact in Scotland.

In the sixty years since Jones wrote much has changed. The bounds of social and cultural history have expanded enormously, and the history of sex has emerged as a thriving discipline. As modern debates over sex rage it is natural that questions about how the matter was dealt with in the past now seem interesting and relevant, and not merely prurient. A sign of changing times was the republication of the *Records* and *Supplement* in 1982, with an introduction by the Scottish writer Alan Bold. The basic material for studying the Benison was now much more easily available. But Bold made no attempt at scholarly assessment of the material he reprinted, so doubts as to its reliability remained.

This is where I came in. I stumbled on a copy of the 1982 reprint in a bookshop (among remaindered books) in the early 1990s, and became fascinated by the challenge posed by the question of authenticity. I had just finished work on a study of early freemasonry, which had introduced me to the great world of eighteenth century clubs, and, I thought, it would be interesting to have a quick look at this very different club. The quick look became a longer study, as it gradually emerged how complicated the club was and how remarkably neatly it fitted into the decade of its foundation, the 1730s. It was not a freak eruption of obscenity, grotesque in soberly Calvinist Scotland, but very much a creature of its age. And it is I think a creature our age is at last ready to face, instead of shying away. But only just ready. While all nuances of hetero- and homo- sexual activity are matters of both popular debate, embarrassment and shock over auto-sexual activity still lingers. Or (lest that be interpreted as a puzzling reference to doing it in the back of the car), masturbation. It was the Benison's speciality, and that is why the taboo about studying the club has lasted so long.

Acknowledgements

The debts incurred by a historian during research and writing are many. Professor T. C. Smout, University of St Andrews, has been most helpful and encouraging. I am also indebted for information and help to Professor Robert Crawford, Dr R. G. W. Prescott, Dr Norman Reid and the staff of library Special Collections of the same university. David Brown (National Archives of Scotland), M. Y. Ashcroft (North Yorkshire County Record Office); and library and archival staff of many other institutions have also contributed their invaluable but often anonymous and unsung expertise and services. Larry Hutchison kindly made the Benison Bible available to me, and George Dalgleish helpfully introduced me to the Benison relics in the National Museums of Scotland. David Gaimster performed similar services in the British Museum, and Professor Ian Carradice in St Andrews University. David S. Howard and Peter Lole gave me the benefit of their unrivalled expertises regarding, respectively, Chinese armorial porcelain and glassware.

Shiona Airlie (formerly of the Burrell Collection), Caroline Allen (Christie's), M. Y. Ashcroft (North Yorkshire County Record Office), the Black Watch Museum, David Brown (National Archives of Scotland), A. J. Campbell, Simon Cottle (Sotheby's), Alex Darwood (of the Kilrenny and Anstruther Burgh Collection), John Gifford, Dr Tim Hitchcock, Larry Hutchison, Peter Lole, Hazel Forsyth (Museum of London), Lord Scarsdale, Michael Sharp (A. H. Baldwin & Sons) and a London private collector have also proved most helpful in hunting down references and relics. Finally, I am much endebted to my agent, Duncan McAra, for his editorial and other labours in seeing the work through to publication, and to my publishers, John and Val Tuckwell.

Abbreviations

Adam, *Political state*	C. H. Adam, *View of the political state of Scotland in ... 1788* (Edinburgh, 1887)
Anstruther, Family	A. W. Anstruther, *History of the family of Anstruther* (Edinburgh, 1923)
BBWCC	St Andrews University Library and University Collections, Beggar's Benison and Wig Club Collection. The manuscript and printed material is classified as MS 38351
BOEC	*Book of the Old Edinburgh Club*
Cockburn, 'Friday Club'	H. A. Cockburn, 'An account of the Friday Club, written by Lord Cockburn, together with notes on certain other social clubs in Edinburgh', *BOEC*, iii (1910), 105–78
CB	G. E. C[okayne], *The complete baronetage* (6 vols., Exeter, 1900–9)
CP	G. E. C[okayne], *The complete peerage* (New edn., 13 vols., London, 1910-40)
Conolly, *Eminent men*	M. F. Conolly, *Biographical dictionary of eminent men of Fife* (Cupar and Edinburgh, 1866)
DNB	*Dictionary of national biography*
Fasti	*Fasti ecclesiastiae Scoticanae* (9 vols., Edinburgh. 1915–81)
Fergusson, *Henry Erskine*	A. Fergusson, *The Hon. Henry Erskine, lord advocate for Scotland* (Edinburgh, 1882)
Gourlay, Anstruther	G. Gourlay, *Anstruther; or illustrations of Scottish burgh life* (Anstruther, 1888)
Grant, *Edinburgh*	J. Grant, *Old and new Edinburgh* (3 vols., [1880–3])
Grant, *Edin. marriages*	*Register of marriages of the city of Edinburgh, 1751–1800* (STS, 1922), ed. F. J. Grant
Grant, *St Andrews*	*The commissariot record of St Andrews: register of testaments, 1549–1800* , ed. F. J. Grant (SRS, 1902)

Abbreviations

HSL	*The history of Scottish literature*. Vol. i, *Origins to 1660*, ed. R. D. S. Jack (Aberdeen, 1988); Vol. ii, *1660–1800*, ed. A. Hook (Aberdeen, 1987)
Hutchison, 'Benison'	L. Hutchison, 'The Beggar's Benison', *Scottish Book Collector*, i (1987–9), no. 4, pp. 25–7
Jones, *Clubs*	L. C. Jones, *The clubs of the Georgian rakes* (New York, 1942)
NAS	National Archives of Scotland (formerly Scottish Record Office
NLS	National Library of Scotland
NMS	National Museums of Scotland
NRA(S)	National Register of Archives (Scotland)
OED	*Oxford English dictionary*, 2nd edn
PSAS	*Proceedings of the Society of Antiquaries of Scotland*
RCRB	*Records of the Convention of the Royal Burghs of Scotland, 1345–1779*, ed. J. D. Marwick (8 vols., Edinburgh, 1870–1918)
Records and *Supplement*	*Records of the most ancient and puissant order of the Beggar's Benison and Merryland, Anstruther*, and *Supplement to the historical portion of the 'Records of the most ancient …'* (2 parts, Anstruther [*recte* London], 1892). Though the two parts are usually found bound together they are cited separately as they have different paginations. A new edition in one volume, with preface by Alan Bold, was published in Edinburgh, 1982
Rogers, *Social life*	C. Rogers (ed.), *Social life in Scotland from early to recent times* (3 vols., Grampian Club, 1884–6)
SAUL	St Andrews University Library
Smith, 'Sexual mores'	N. Smith, 'Sexual mores and attitudes in Enlightenment Scotland', in P. G. Boucé (ed.), *Sexuality in Eighteenth Century Britain* (Manchester, 1982)
SP	J. B. Paul (ed.), *The Scottish peerage* (9 vols., Edinburgh 1904–14)
SHS	Scottish History Society
SRS	Scottish Record Society

STS	Scottish Text Society
Stevenson, *Anstruther*	S. Stevenson, *Anstruther. A history* (Edinburgh, 1989)
Stone, *Family*	L. Stone, *The family, sex and marriage in England, 1500–1800* (London, 1977)
Supplement	See under *Records* above
Williams, *Dictionary*	G. Williams, *A dictionary of sexual language and images in Shakespeare and Stuart literature* (3 vols., London, 1994)
Wood, *East Neuk*	W. Wood, *The East Neuk of Fife* (2nd edn, Edinburgh, 1887)

The East Neuk of Fife

St Andrews

SCOTLAND

Anstruther

Glasgow   Edinburgh

ENGLAND

Cambo House

Strathvithie House

Kinaldy

Balcomie Castle

FIFE NESS

Airdrie

CRAIL

Carnbee

Kilbrachmont

Pitkierie

Invergellie House

Kellie Castle

Rennyhill

KILRENNY

Balcarres House

Cellardyke

ANSTRUTHER WESTER

ANSTRUTHER EASTER

Balkaskie House

PITTENWEEM

FORTH

St Monans

St Ford (Sandford)

Elie House

OF

Earlsferry

FIRTH

0   2 miles

0   4 km

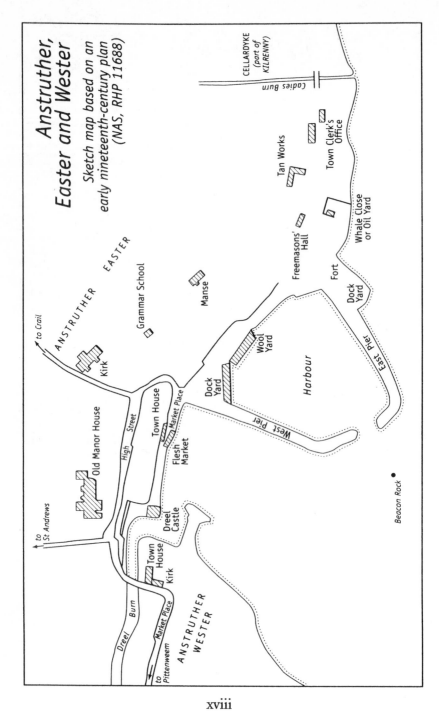

Anstruther, Easter and Wester

Sketch map based on an early nineteenth-century plan (NAS, RHP 11688)

ANSTRUTHER EASTER

to Crail

ANSTRUTHER EASTER

Kirk

Grammar School

Manse

to St Andrews

Old Manor House

High Street

Town House

Market Place

Flesh Market

Dreel Castle

Town House

Kirk

Dreel Burn

Market Place

to Pittenweem

ANSTRUTHER WESTER

Dock Yard

Wool Yard

Harbour

West Pier

Freemasons' Hall

Fort

Dock Yard

East Pier

Whale Close or Oil Yard

Tan Works

Town Clerk's Office

CELLARDYKE (part of KILRENNY)

Cadies Burn

Beacon Rock

CHAPTER ONE

The Benison:
Fabulous Foundations

From 1732 to 1836 the eastern tip of Fife in Scotland was the home of the Beggar's Benison and Merryland, a club devoted to the convivial and obscene celebration of the idea of free sex, with sidelines in its early days of support for smuggling (free trade) and distinctly subversive political sentiments. Members differed in social status, in religion and in politics, but they were bound together by the idea of a club at a meeting place in which such divisions should be ignored, and shared grievances against government – and indeed against change in general – served to unite members. Instead of reacting against the status quo with bitterness and activism, members relieved their frustrations through symbolic mockery and alcoholic defiance.

The Benison was provincial in origins, but it spawned branches in Glasgow, Edinburgh – and even St Petersburg, and it inspired the élite Wig Club in Edinburgh – which was rather more seemly than the Benison in its rituals though equally fervent in the devotion to sex. Early members of the Benison were local merchants and gentry, but later members were recruited from upper ranks of society, even reaching royalty in the person of the Prince of Wales (later George IV). The Benison and the Wig are less well known than the famous English Hell-Fire Club, but they were far longer lasting and, for the historian, have one great advantage over it. The Hell-Fire Club is only known through fragmentary references in scattered sources,

I

whereas both manuscript records and obscene artefacts survive relating to the two Scottish clubs, making it possible to reconstruct at least some of their activities in detail. Whether other such clubs existed in eighteenth-century Britain is hard to say, but it may be that the Benison and the Wig are unique not in having existed, but through records of them having survived the horrified purging of later ages. They provide a unique insight into aspects of the 'Age of Enlightenment' and while their age-old obsessions with the demands of the phallus may seem at first sight most unenlightened, there is a case to be made, especially for the Benison, that they were Enlightenment institutions, taking on board the emerging culture and ideas of the age (while protesting at some aspects of it). Clubs as institutions lay at the heart of the spread of Enlightenment, the argument that sexual activity should be embraced as pleasure and not simply procreative duty was an enlightened theme. Edinburgh might be 'a hotbed of genius' as Smollett wrote. Members of the Benison dreamed of the East Neuk of Fife as a hotbed of free sex.

Assemblies of Good Fellows

The eighteenth century was the great age of the club, an institution defined by Samuel Johnson in his dictionary of 1755 as 'An assembly of good fellows, meeting under certain conditions'. The simplicity of the definition is masterly, wide enough to embrace an extraordinary range of institutions while indicating essential parameters. A club was a gathering of people brought together by mutual enjoyment of each other's company. All were, in each other's eyes, 'good fellows'. But those involved regarded themselves as more than just informal, random gatherings of friends. Their friendship and shared interests created an institution, though it might be a very fluid one. They met voluntarily, but bound themselves by rules defining behaviour and activities, and shared the costs. A club might be born fully formed, with purpose, rules and membership laid down from the start, or it might evolve from informal meetings, gradually acquiring the trappings of 'clubship'.[1]

The word is broad enough for almost any attempt at generalisation beyond such basic points to be open to question, but some features were common. It was very rare in the eighteenth century for clubs to have their own premises like later gentlemen's clubs, providing places where members could drop in at any time to find company and leisure facilities. Instead they held pre-arranged meetings, some at first in coffee houses, but mostly in taverns, the convivial consumption of alcohol becoming almost a defining feature of club life. Meetings might be regular or irregular, frequent or infrequent. In some cases – as with the Beggar's Benison – meetings only took place once or twice a year, becoming special events in members' social calendars, annual celebrations of some particular aspect of shared friendship. The club was primarily an urban phenomenon, though sometimes in rural areas in England clubs of landowners emerged, with members meeting in each other's private houses. But such arrangements inevitably tended to divide members into host and guests, undermining the usual equality of club sociability, just as the fact of meeting in a family home placed constraints on behaviour.

Usually conviviality was the central element of the club, but frequently this was combined with the advancement of some interest or cause. Sometimes these were seriously pursued. A club might be a forum where members sought to instruct themselves in matters such as antiquities, medicine, literature, or debating skills. Some such coteries developed into learned societies, with sober discussion and lectures. Descending from high seriousness was a range of attitudes to the interests espoused by clubs, with advancement of knowledge often becoming secondary to conviviality, and perhaps no more than a pretext for meeting. In the eighteenth century as today, in golf clubs actually playing golf could be merely a preliminary to socialising. Sometimes absurd interests were joyfully proclaimed, with ridiculous club names. Identity thus established, members could proceed to build the daft myths and rituals which so much appealed to the taste of the age.

Ritual of some sort existed in nearly all clubs. It might be minimal, concerned with no more than rules of proceeding, choosing members, naming and addressing officials, or it might be highly elaborate and symbolic, as with the freemasons. Again, however, there was great variety of attitudes. Ritual might be treated solemnly, but it might equally burlesque such pomposity. Yet, even when enjoyed as ludicrous, ritual could become important in binding men together. The joy of clubs was that members were free to make what

3

they wanted of them. The form was infinitely flexible. Some appeared and disappeared with bewildering rapidity, but others lasted for generations.

Men had of course in previous ages often formed informal, voluntary groups for socialising and other activities, but the rise of convivial clubs into being a major feature of British society began in the coffee houses and taverns of London after the Restoration of monarchy in 1660. The Puritan restraints of the previous era had been removed, and meeting just for sociable pleasure was increasingly regarded as acceptable and not mere sinful idleness. The example of the libertine Charles II and his court indicated that worldly enjoyment had official sanction, and it seemed that relaxed sociability (and indeed sexual immorality) was symbolic of loyalty to the restored monarchy, demonstrating rejection of a repressive past. There did however, survive a whiff of the subversive about the word 'club'. Clubs which were purely interested in hedonism might be harmless, but those in authority found it difficult at first to accept that letting organisations emerge which discussed serious, and even topical, matters without the blessing or supervision of church or state was not dangerous. Private gatherings in clubs could be concerned with political issues, and were therefore potentially subversive. A different fear about clubs was expressed by many moralists. They were shocking and deeply dangerous because they took men out of their families, the natural forum for sociability, and were all too often blatantly devoted to earthly enjoyment, distracting men from higher things.

The fact that in spite of lingering suspicion clubs were allowed to thrive and become widely accepted in the eighteenth century indicates an increasingly 'open society,' with the state disinclined to interfere in private life, the churches still longing to do so but too divided and weak to be effective. However fears that men gathering together in clubs might be a threat to morals or political stability never disappeared. The great century of clubs was thus also the great century of mistrust of clubs. In the first half of the eighteenth century there was much worry about Jacobite clubs,[2] though many of the groups to which the name 'club' was attracted were nebulous gatherings of disgruntled drinkers. Even after the Jacobite threat faded, suspicions that for men to gather together was for them to conspire together remained, and such attitudes seemed ultimately to be justified by the coming of the French Revolution. Political clubs with revolutionary ideologies briefly flourished before being suppressed. 'Clubship' in general lost its attraction for many through fears of such contamination. Some clubs closed, many that survived went through a generation of decline. Even freemasonry, that vast organisation of lodges that constituted a highly successful network of clubs and counted royalty and aristocrats among its members, came under suspicion, and the foundation of new lodges was forbidden. Both the Benison and the Wig Club show signs of decline in the 1790s.

Nonetheless, in general the concept of clubs as innocent forums for sociability came to prevail. The decline of religious constraints and a relatively tolerant secular regime were essential preconditions for the rise of the clubs. The social changes underlying the movement may be seen in terms of increasing urbanisation and the growing strength of the middle ranks of society – growing both in numbers and in wealth (and therefore leisure), increasingly secularised (though without questioning underlying religious beliefs), increasingly educated, and with widening interests. The middle ranks – from successful craftsmen through merchants to professional men and officials – dominated most clubs, though country gentlemen and aristocrats played a leading part in some. Central to many clubs was an acceptance of a limited suspension of social hierarchy in the name of convivial brotherhood. Alcohol blurred social distinctions. A craftsman like Gavin Wilson, shoemaker in Edinburgh, was a member of the Cape Club, a remarkably large and amorphous club, and so was the earl of Haddington. The nobleman clearly did not feel his membership was derogatory to his status. But other clubs were much more limited socially. Haddington was also a founder of the Wig Club, and in its records Wilson appears as an artisan commissioned to make objects for ritual use. The idea of his becoming a member would have been absurd. The Cape was unusually wide ranging socially, the Wig was unusually narrow. A narrowness is seen also in clubs associated with certain professions – medicine and law, or with intellectual interests in philosophy or antiquities. They might not be consciously socially exclusive, but the shared knowledge and interests that bound members together often implied leisure and/or specialised education.

One of the joys of the club for many men was the opportunity to escape from the constraints and responsibilities of family and household. Full advantage was often taken of the absence of the restraining influence of women, whether mothers, sisters, wives or daughters, on talk and behaviour. In the ideal club you were in the company of fellows with whom you could behave with a freedom not found elsewhere. Your choice might be for fairly decorous company, or for the outrageous, or by belonging to several clubs you could indulge a range of sociable tastes. The essentials were that you choose your own company and parameters of behaviour with a liberty not obtainable in any other institution – and the absence of women and children was central to exercising such freedoms. In the eyes of some, however, even among the educated and secular-minded, the very fact that clubs provided forums for exclusively male sociability was damaging to society. William Alexander, a Scottish physician, produced a *History of women* (1779) which argued the point. Men could not be trusted on their own, and one of the main functions for which nature intended women was to act as civilising influences on men. If men were to achieve their full potential for civilisation, they needed the company of women (though they could have too much of it, in which case they became effeminate). Without women, men declined into 'roughness of behaviour and slovenliness of person'. Alexander did not specifically attack clubs, but concentrated his wrath on the English custom of women withdrawing from table after dinner, leaving the men on their own. Men often showed impatience if their ladies were slow in withdrawing, 'which is a certain indication, that they either want to debauch themselves with liquor, or indulge in those indecencies of discourse, which the company of women always restrains'. In France things were handled far better: the ladies did not withdraw, and conversation and enjoyment in such mixed company was superior. He had a point, for in clubs as well as after dinner at home, as Alexander suggested, the main advantages taken of male exclusivity were to get drunk and talk dirty.[3]

At dinner, the ladies withdrew from the men. Through clubs, the men removed themselves from women to tavern or other meeting place. But though this decreased socialising between the sexes, it also, paradoxically, in some respects paved the way for the emergence of institutions advancing sociability between the sexes outside the family. Once the shock of unsupervised male sociability in clubs had been absorbed, it was easier for the idea of voluntary social institutions including women to be accepted as well. In Scotland the church fought a long delaying action, but as the eighteenth century passed, middle and upper class women were accorded places in the explosion of sociability. Assemblies, dances, balls, concerts and theatre emerged, creating a world of socialising outside home and family for women as well as men. At first such activities were strictly supervised to preserve the proprieties, but not by outside authority. Instead internal officials were appointed to regulate conduct, to placate the Presbyterian conscience and maintain decorum. Nonetheless, what the church long condemned as 'promiscuous dancing' gradually became accepted. It is hard to imagine such developments taking place without the previous victory of the male clubs. But if this mixed-sex sociability in some ways followed the example set by the clubs, another perception was that it was the evils of the all-male clubs that made mixed sociable bodies acceptable, even desirable, as they formed a more seemly alternative, with women performing their civilising role.

In the emerging networks of voluntary social institutions, men had it both ways. The company of women at assembly or concert when they felt like civilising female presence, exclusive male company when they tired of such restraint. And often, as William Alexander feared, the major motive for fleeing the company of women was to be free to talk about them. This could be restrained to the respectable – in terms of language if not alcohol. Toasting or 'raising the ladies' was common, a beauty-competition held in the absence of the contestants, with the winner being the lady whose champion could drink most toasts without slumping into unconsciousness. But talking and singing about the ladies in terms of respect and admiration often led on to bawdiness and obscenity, considerations of beauty and love giving way to raw sex. There is of course nothing surprising or novel in men having such obsessions, and combining idealising women with regarding them as products for consumption, but clubs did give men additional opportunities to talk convivially about their own fantasies and prowess and deeds. In anecdotes, boasts, verse and song they celebrated women – from a male perspective. There was, after all, no more universal a topic, no more common an interest which could bind members together than shared lust for the female.

Ancient Genesis and Medieval Monks

Like many a club with mock pretensions to importance, the Beggar's Benison felt an urge to create grandiose origin myths to support its claims, to validate its rituals, and to be enjoyably ludicrous. In some more serious clubs there was a danger of, in time, coming to take myths of ancient origins to be literally true. Some freemasons really came to believe in ancient freemasonry. But for many the legends of origins were seen as symbolic rather than historical, and for some the legends were fun more than anything else. In the case of the Benison it was clearly felt that to have merely one foundation myth would indicate poverty of imagination. Consistency was boring.

Many famous families laid claim to fanciful pedigrees starting with the Creation. After all, every one was descended from Adam and Eve, so constructing a family tree was simply a matter of filling in the names of the intervening generations. Similarly the Creation was a favourite starting point for club inventiveness – nobody could go further than that in mock-heroic claims. Archbishop Ussher's calculation of 4004 BC was widely accepted as the date of the Creation of the world, but the freemasons found calculation somewhat easier if they rounded the figure down to 4000. Thus in their dating system anno lucis (AL), the year of light, was simply the AD date plus 4000 (for example, 1765 AD + 4000 = 5765 AL). The Beggar's Benison copied this system from the masons. Their justi-fication for claiming to be coeval with the Creation was obvious. Once you had Adam and Eve, you had sex. The glorious reign of the phallus began, so that was metaphorically the date of the Benison's creation. But not even the most fervent member really believed that the Garden of Eden had been located in Anstruther, or that Adam had been a native of the East Neuk of Fife.

As well as cheerful claims to the utmost antiquity more specific and local mythological backing was thought appropriate. The Beggars took a passing glance at the Middle Ages, speculating about the deeds of randy monks of the priory on the Isle of May (which had later moved to Pittenweem). As staunch Protestants, members took it for granted that supposedly celibate Catholic monks were sex-mad, and masturbation was regarded as a monastic speciality. The name of the island that the monks had roamed added a double bonus. It bore a girl's name, which was also the name of the month specially associated with spring and fertility.

The confused body of Benison mythology also included reference to a medieval lord – or even earl – of Anstruther who earned the nickname Fisher Willie because of his zeal in developing the fishing industry. Though it is not specifically stated, the implication is that he too was somehow a founder of the Benison. But the only example of the activities of Fisher Willie celebrated within the Benison suggests that it was not fishing that won him immortality – or rather that he was a fisher of women rather than fish. A verse supposedly recited by the earliest known 'sovereign' of the Benison, John McNachtane, told of the exploits of 'Earl Willie,' depicting the earl seducing May – the Isle of May, which symbolised the female sex:

> *May* was not like other lasses, –
> From twelve her breasts swell'd in a trice;
> Firm they were as two cupping-glasses,
> Just like peaches, dainty and nice.

And so on. The Isle of May was Venus arising from the waves, and Fisher Willie was eventually married to her – by, appropriately, the prior of Pittenweem.[4] The reference to Venus added classical allusion to the biblical and medieval, but looking at the stark cliffs of the Isle of May, which from some angles give it the shape of a whale, it takes some effort of imagination to see it as Venus, but no doubt drink and unfocused lust helped.[5]

The King and the Beggar Maid

For their main myth, however, the Beggars settled on something more modest chronologically, inventing a tale set in the early sixteenth century.

Motifs in folklore are often common to very different cultures, and the 'king goes in disguise among his people' motif is known from Russia to Arabia – and to Scotland. Here it became attached to King James V, forming an interesting contrast with his reputation for brutality.[6] James found little favour among historians, one referring to 'the revulsion with which he must be regarded', another to his

9

being 'probably the most unpleasant of all the Stewarts.'[7] But in popular lore he was to be remembered as a man who liked to wander among his people incognito, socialising and listening to their opinions, and, in fact as well as tradition he was notorious for bedding women of all ranks with promiscuous zeal, making him an ideal royal patron for the Beggar's Benison.

James had became king in 1512, at the age of one year. As he grew up the regent, his step-father the earl of Angus, 'was accused of deliberately encouraging the young king in a precocious career of vice'[8] – the idea being that a youth who developed an obsession with sexual indulgence would show little interest in government, and therefore leave the exercise of power in Angus's hands. If there was such a plot, it was only partly successful. James did indeed pay undue (but what is due?) attention to sex, but kept a close watch on government as well. He was chided in verse for his licentiousness by David Lindsay of the Mount, poet and herald. In one poem several characters discuss the king's reputed conquests, mentioning girls in Stirling, Linlithgow – and one in Fife:

> Bot, schir, I knaw a maid in fyfe,
> Ane of the lustiest wanton lassis.[9]

Possibly, but no more than that, the lusty wanton lass in Fife was the inspiration for the 'beggar maid' of the Benison myth associated with the king.

In reply the king, also in verse, jeered at Lindsay for lack of activity in Venus's work. The poet felt it necessary to protest that he had had plenty of affairs in earlier years – and then, having thus boasted his past manhood, he proceeded to seek credit for his present morality as well. He had repented

> That euer I did Mouth thankles so persew

The 'mouth thankless' was a term for the vagina that appealed to early Scottish poets.[10] The king's own conduct, continued the courtier-poet, was deplorable. He pulled no punches:

> Thoucht ye rin rudelie, lyke ane restles Ram,   *run*
> Schutand your bolt at mony sindrie schellis   *shooting; shells (vaginas)*
> …
> For, lyke an boisteous Bull, ye rin and ryde   *run*

| Royatouslie lyke ane rude Rubeatour, | *riotously; libertine* |
| Ay fukkand lyke ane furious Fornicatour. | *fucking* |

...

On Ladronis for to loip ye wyll nocht lat.[11]   *whores; leap; not stop*

In thus denouncing his sovereign Lindsay must have known he was quite safe: the young king gloried in his sexuality and its expression. For the courtier-poet to call the arrogant royal stud a bull and a ram was flattery. To the men of the Benison, two centuries later, the reign of James V had been a golden age. A king who had set an example of sexual licence, and had lived in an age when bawdy was an element which was included comfortably within the 'high' literature of the court, sounded like a dream come true.

The stories of James revelling in disguise mostly rest on oral traditions, unsatisfactory sources for the historian.[12] But one documented incident indicates that in reality as well as a myth he had a taste for disguise and exploitation of the advantages of observing while remaining himself unobserved. In 1536 he journeyed to France, to arrange his marriage. The proposed bride was Marie of Vendôme, but James,

> indulging his taste for chivalric adventure, disguised himself as a servant in order that he might view his prospective bride incognito. However, the quixotic gesture backfired spectacularly when, finding Marie ugly, hunchbacked, and not at all to his taste,

James insisted on a change of bride.[13] The chivalry of the episode is hard to detect: it sounds more like a calculated act to make sure that he was not committed to a bride unseen. This known incident of James assessing candidates for his bed in disguise gives a measure of plausibility to the stories of his bucolic philanderings in Scotland, and eastern Fife was a plausible setting for some of these tales, for the king and court frequently stayed at St Andrews or at Falkland Palace. Often in legend James is portrayed as wandering in the guise of a beggar, and the poems 'The Gaberlunzie Man' and 'The Jolly Beggar' were believed to celebrate his exploits in that role.[14] But he was also reputed at times to have called himself 'the gudeman of Ballengeich', indicating a man of humble status but not poverty.[15] The association of the term with royalty became deeply established. In the mid-seventeenth century the term was used as code for Charles I.[16] A century later it was current in Jacobite circles to refer to another royal exile, Prince Charles Edward.[17] More widely, the memory of James V was kept alive by stories of his hearty enjoyment of the basic pleasures of life.[18]

> And wha can match the fifth King James
> For sang or jest?[19]

In the Beggar's Benison myth, one day James V in his 'king as commoner' guise came to the Dreel Burn, the boundary between the two little burghs of Anstruther Easter and Anstruther Wester in the East Neuk. He hesitated because he didn't want to get his feet wet (hardly a heroic moment). In such crises, it is said, it was customary to call on the services of poor women, who would wait by un-bridged streams for this purpose: 'By easy adjustment of their garments, they waded across streams, bearing the men upon their shoulders'.[20]

A beggar lass was duly waiting, and carried the king over the burn. James then gave her a gold coin for her services, and in return she gave him her thanks in the form of a blessing or 'benison:'

> May your purse naer be toom   *never; empty*
> And your horn aye in bloom.   *always*

Here the Benison taste for double entendre reveals itself. At first sight this may be a blessing on the king's wealth (the gold in his purse) and hunting horn, but behind this lies the blessing of his testicles (in the purse of the scrotum),[21] and his erect ('in bloom') penis. The implication is clearly that the beggar lass had granted the king more than aquatic transport: she was rewarded with gold for sexual favours.

The two-line version of the 'benison' quoted above is in Scots, but more commonly, as a toast or motto, the club used a shorter, anglicised version:

> May Prick nor Purse never fail you.

Different wording, but the same sentiments. It is possible that the Beggar's Benison picked up the blessing from oral traditions of James V, but the only written reference to it known before the club was founded in 1732 comes not from Fife but London, where it appears as a 'cant' – the vocabulary of the criminal underground –

term. A pamphlet printed in 1728, catering for the taste for sensational accounts of criminals, related the crimes and adventures of one James Dalton. This petty criminal specialised in purse-snatching, mugging, robbing coaches, 'biting' (cheating) whores, and infiltrating gatherings of 'mollies' (homosexuals). On one occasion a coach held up by Dalton and his gang contained an actor and a 'Lady of Pleasure'. On his money being demanded, the actor launched into a harangue about the poverty of his profession. He was so poor that he had had to work out a careful budget before venturing out even for a frugal night with a whore. Now he was being further humiliated. He, a man who often played an emperor on the stage, would 'be forc'd to go to Bed without either his Mistress or his Supper' if he was robbed. The thieves were entertained by this dramatic performance, 'being Lovers of the Sport which was going forward' (sex). They let the actor keep his money so he could have his whore, and sent him on his way

> wishing his — [prick] and Purse might never fail him.[22]

Quite possibly the blessing was an old one – for a beggar to give a man a combined blessing on his two most important possession, money and genitals, sounds good business practice – but the chronological coincidence of the blessing making its first known appearance in 1728 and it becoming the Benison club motto in the 1730s suggests that the Benison had picked up the blessing from English sources, and produced a suitably 'ye olde' Scots version of it to suit it to the adventures of James V. Calling it a 'benison' rather than a blessing had added advantages. Dr Johnson in his Dictionary says the word 'is not now used, unless ludicrously', so this semi-archaic word added to the Benison both an air of antiquity and a comic touch. Even better, where the word did linger on in Scottish usage, in popular song, it usually referred to the sexual favours – from a kiss onwards – that a woman might grant a man.[23]

Thus the 'Beggar's Benison' was a most suitable title for a club devoted to sex. The words indicated the sexual favours of women in general, blessed gold and genitals, and referred to the specific encounter of James V and the beggar maid. The members of the Benison saw themselves as the heirs of the disguised king who had fornicated his way through Fife. For them, James was an archetypal figure of sexual fantasy, of masculine roving and enterprise, of blithe acceptance that sex was pleasure. And they saw themselves as kings like him, for they too were rulers, by right of the phallus.

The King over the Water

The Beggars enjoyed playing with symbolism, half seriously, half wittily. The king and the beggar maid story is most superficially a simple anecdote of James V's wandering in disguise. Beneath that lies the story of a sexual encounter. Dig deeper, and there are subversive political allusions – so well hidden that they have been overlooked in the past.

When the Beggar's Benison was founded in 1732 less than a generation had passed since the Jacobite rising of 1715 and the abortive attempt of 1719. Beneath surface calm and acceptance of the Hanoverian dynasty, which had succeeded to the British thrones in 1714, Jacobite sympathies were strong in Scotland. Longing for the restoration of the old Stuart dynasty, dethroned in 1688–9, was widespread, though ineffectual. Pledges of support for the cause were exchanged among friends and contacts were maintained with Jacobite exiles on the Continent. Symbolic rituals evolved whereby Jacobites at once revealed and veiled their loyalties. Even in the presence of opponents, support for the cause could be covertly indicated. Drinking a loyal toast to the crown might outwardly be a toast to the Hanoverians George I or II, but by passing their toast glasses over water in a glass or jug on the table, Jacobites symbolically converted their toast into a pledge to the 'king over the water,' the exiled Prince James Edward, in their eyes King James VIII and III.[24] Intellectually this might be little superior to a child arguing that if you have your fingers crossed when making a promise it is not binding, but to frustrated Jacobites it was meaningful. Genuine intrigue and this sort of sentimental Jacobitism created a mystic, allusive mythology, with the king over the water as one of its most enduring images.

The lyric poetry and song of Jacobite allegory presents the political issue in the guise of romantic yearning, a seeking and finding of true love. Scotland is seen as a girl searching for true love (legitimate authority) by seeking out and submitting to a figure representing the

Stuart dynasty. Often the girl (Scotia, Caledonia) is represented as a Lowlander who rejects unworthy suitors but at last finds true love with the Highland Laddie – the Stuart cause. Sometimes the Lowland lass is admitted to have been faithless in the past, straying from true love (loyalty), but returning to her 'true identity after yielding to the Highland patriot'.[25] Conveniently, of course, being female, the girl in recognising her true destiny becomes subservient. Stuart royal power over Scotland is male power over the female. Grieving Scotland seeks happiness and at last finds love through loyalty and submission. Country and dynasty are reconciled, and the assumption is, will live happily ever after. This is the romantic, acceptable face of the erotic Jacobite vision, giving a powerful emotional charge to a political ideology. Sentimental, nostalgic lyric bathed political loyalties in a warm glow of the sensual. The beggar maid myth of the Benison parodies this with cheerfully iconoclastic enthusiasm – but in a coded form.

The Benison story tells of a Stuart[26] king who for a time is without his legitimate royal authority (James V was in disguise). He is stranded, separated by water from where he wants to be. He is then carried to where he wishes to be, 'over the water' by the beggar maid. The story then ends not with romantic love but with a sex for gold exchange. Benison bawdy has thus appropriated the lyric Jacobite fantasy and stripped it naked, substituting raw sexual reality. A beautiful girl representing Scotland? Make her a beggar maid, emphasising the poverty of mis-governed Scotland – and parodying the element in the 'Highland Laddie' myth that stressed that he identified with its ordinary folk.[27] The beggar maid in helping the disguised king over the water and having sex with him does so because she wants cash payment, not because she is 'Scotia' idealistically helping her true sovereign back to his thrones and then submitting to his male authority.

Interpreted in this way, it seems at first sight that the Benison's beggar-maid story is anti-Jacobite. In place of idealisation of the exiled dynasty is the message that it is simply after sexual gratification. But explaining the tale simply as a crude Hanoverian joke does not work, because James V, the substitute for the Stuart pretender, was the Benison's hero. He was rightful king, and his sexual opportunism was something was to be admired. Thus the Benison-Jacobite story is politically ambiguous, and examination of the club's membership reveals why (see Chapter 6). Both Jacobites and Hanoverians were members. They met basically through personal friendship – and obsession with sex – and it might have been thought expedient to ignore politics altogether for fear of causing impossible tensions. But these men were not political activists, and their commitment to their causes was not blind. They were malcontents who found in the Benison a safe forum for expressing their frustrations in semi-comic, coded forms. All could agree that Scotland was badly governed under the Hanoverians, and Jacobites, though they believed that legitimacy demanded that the Stuarts should be restored to the throne, could concede that that dynasty had contributed to its own downfall by its policies. Moreover, both Hanoverians and Jacobite members had imbibed from the libertine atmosphere of the Restoration monarchy of the last of the Stuarts (Charles II and James VII and II) a robust belief in the legitimacy of the pursuit of sexual pleasure. The many satires that had depicted the royal power of the promiscuous Charles II as essentially phallic power had been digested and appreciated.

Out of this men of different political inclinations had devised a mock historico-political myth. Successful monarchy was successful sexual adventure. James V was a hero through his open embracing of sex as central to life and rule, an attractive figure compared with the Hanoverians George I and George II, with their outward pretence of piety combined with mistresses kept out of the public eye. Politics was a mug's game. Better concentrate on the more personal satisfactions of sex (or sexual fantasy), and confine potentially disruptive political discussion to playing with the connections of sexual and political power. Disillusioned Jacobites as well as Hanoverians could laugh cynically at the idealisations of Jacobite propaganda, of suffering but loyal Scotland and the gracious Stuart saviour who would return to claim her, rule her and bring peace and prosperity. Out of half-bitter, tipsy laughter there emerges a bawdy version of Jacobite idealism. None of this wishy-washy stuff about the suffering exile and love, but a beggar girl and the buying of sex.[28] There is superb bathos in the Benison's setting of the 'king over the water' idea. The English Channel is reduced to the Dreel Burn, Britain and France to the two Anstruthers, a nobly suffering exiled king to one who didn't want to get his feet wet. Here is myth of a golden Stuart past that could unite malcontent Hanoverians and Jacobites in joyous smutty fun, with a glorious send-up of the rival propaganda versions of Scotland's past.

That there is no direct evidence for this 'Jacobite' interpretation of the beggar maid story is not surprising, for (like mainstream Jacobite talk of the Highland Laddie and Scotia) it was deliberately allusive rather than explicit. One possible objection to the Jacobite inter-pretation might be that, if the Benison wanted a sexually voracious hero-king to play with in their convivial stories, surely they would have chosen the promiscuous Charles II, far closer in time and far better known, for the role. But distance made James V safe. No-one would be likely to fear subversion if it leaked out that a club revered his memory, but Charles II had been the second last of the Stuart kings, and his absolutist and pro-Catholic tendencies had done much to lead to the overthrow of the dynasty. A club dedicated to Charles II, even if the dedication was ribald, might well be seen as a guise for Jacobite activism. Moreover, even the tolerant Jacobite and Hanoverian members of the Benison might have found it hard to talk of the controversial (especially as the persecutor of Presbyterian dissidents) Charles II without acrimony. Moreover, Charles II had been Stuart in blood but anglicised, and had ruled from England, whereas James V had lived in an idealised golden age when Scotland had been independent and before the Reformation had brought religious conflict to divide the country.

The obliging maid in the Benison myth was a beggar primarily because she represented Scotland, notorious for poverty. But there was possibly another inspiration. John Gay's *Beggar's Opera* was first performed in London in 1728 and soon became hugely popular, not least because there was concealed within it political satire attacking the government of Sir Robert Walpole. Was an echo of this, the using of beggars to hide political meanings, in the minds of the malcontents who created the Beggar's Benison just a few years later?

The Colony of Merryland

The Beggar's Benison is usually known as just that, but the club's full title was the Order of the Beggar's Benison and Merryland.

Merry had long been a word with meanings relating to sex and bawdy. 'Merry May' was not an amusing time of year but a breeding time. Shakespeare has Ophelia chide Hamlet for being 'merry' when his talk got risqué. *The Merry Wives of Windsor* were not merely comic.[29] Charles II, the 'Merry Monarch', was noted for promiscuity rather than humour. Robert Burns was to use 'merry' frequently. His illegitimate child was 'Sweet fruit o monie a merry dint'. 'Her cunt's as merry's mine' says one girl of another who had expressed disapproval of the former's fornication. Bawdy combinations including merry abounded. A 'merry-bout' meant sex; a 'merry-legs' was a whore, a 'merry-maker' a penis.[30] Merryland was a relative latecomer, and indeed only once had its use been noted before the Beggar's Benison was founded. In 1652 an English newspaper had referred to a ship on the Thames, which was being used as a brothel, as a floating ark of pleasure 'bound for Merryland'.[31] Merryland was a fantasy land of sexual pleasure and, more specifically, the female body. The word seems thereafter to disappear until it was used by the Benison in 1739. Then, for a few years beginning in 1740, 'merryland' became prominent in English pornography, which featured 'a whole series of strange publications consisting of descriptions of female anatomy in terms of elaborate topographical metaphor, complete with shrubs, hillocks, vales and grottoes'.[32] First was *The potent ally; or succours from Merryland* ([London], 1740). Thomas Stretzer's *A new description of Merryland. Containing, a topographical, geographical, and natural history of that country* also first appeared in 1740 (under the pseudonym 'Roger Phequewell'), and reached a fourth edition by 1741, a tenth by 1742. In 1741 two editions of *Merryland displayed*, also by Stretzer, appeared. In 1743 was added *A short description of the roads which lead to that delightful country called Merryland* to these ingenious inquiries. Merryland had clearly become a hot word in pornographic circles, but the attempt to produce an ambitious series of engravings, a *Complete set of charts of the coasts of Merryland* went beyond the bounds of acceptability. The plates were seized and destroyed,[33] and thereafter pornographers tired of this topographical obsession.

Merryland died of over-exposure, though some of these works were reprinted several times later in the century. Only, it seems, on Beggar's Benison membership diplomas did the word survive. Superficially, the fact that the Benison was using the term 'Merryland' immediately before it suddenly emerged as fashionable in published English pornography might seem to make plausible to argue that the

English authors involved borrowed the term from the Benison, but this would almost certainly be incorrect.. It is more probable that the word remained in use in England between 1652 and 1740 unrecorded, then winning favour by writers for a few years. It may also have been in use in Scotland, but the fact that works of pornography are known in a number of cases to have been circulated in manuscript before publication makes it quite possible that the Benison picked it up in unpublished English pornography in the 1730s. This might seem to suggest an unlikely close link between provincial Fife and English pornographers, but such a link undoubtedly existed, for the Benison had read a manuscript of *Fanny Hill* long before publication (see Chapter 2). Someone in the Benison had access to unpublished English pornographic material.

'Merryland' was the female territory the Beggars lusted after, and their obsessions with the Isle of May, the merry month, doubtless made them especially fond of the conceit. More widely, Benison members feasted their imaginations on the East Neuk, with its coastline full of caves and crannies. Further, 'merryland' may well have had another resonance, obliquely (and therefore safely) recalling merry Charles II and the libertine era he had presided over. Charles had visited Dreel Castle in Anstruther in 1651, so could claim local credentials. Bring back the Stuarts and restore the proper cultivation of Merryland?

Notes

1 For clubs in Britain as a whole see R.J. Morris, 'Clubs, societies and associations,' in *The Cambridge social history of Britain, 1750*, vol. iii, ed. F.M.L. Thomson (Cambridge, 1990), 395–443; J.C. Ross, *An assembly of goodfellows. Voluntary associations in history* (Westport, Conn., 1976); and P. Clark, *British clubs and societies, 1580–1800. The origins of an associational world* (Oxford, 2000). Clark's comprehensive book unfortunately appeared too late for its arguments to be fully considered in writing the present work. Much of the interest in Scottish clubs has, been concentrated on the more high-minded institutions: see N.T. Phillipson, 'Culture and society in the 18th century province: The case of Edinburgh and the Scottish Enlightenment,' in *The University in Society*, ed. L. Stone (2 vols., Princeton, 1975), ii, 407–48 and D.D. McIlroy, *Scotland's age of improvement. A survey of eighteenth century literary clubs and societies* (Washington State, 1969). For other clubs see Cockburn, 'Friday Club', 105–78; A. Clark, 'An old Edinburgh club' [the Luggy Club],

BOEC, xxxi (1962), 43–51; J.B. Sutherland, 'An Eighteenth Century Survival: the Wagering Club,' *BOEC*, ii (1909), 149–66; R. Chambers, *Traditions of Edinburgh* (1st edn. Edinburgh, 1824; the 1868 edition has been used), 138–58; Grant, *Edinburgh*, iii, 122–6. See also, J. Strang, *Glasgow and its clubs: or glimpses of the condition, manners, characters and oddities of the city* (3rd edn, Glasgow, 1864).

2 M.G.H. Pittock, *Poetry and Jacobite politics in eighteenth-century Britain and Ireland* (Cambridge, 1994), 292–7.

3 W. Alexander, *The history of women* (3rd edn, 2 vols., London, 1782: 1st edn 1779), i, advertisement & 475, 486, 493–4.

4 *Records*, 15–16; *Supplement*, 66–7. Fisher Willie's name may contain a double-entendre. A fisherman is a predator, therefore Fisher Willie stands for predatory penis, which fits perfectly with the Beggars' obsessions. See Williams, *Dictionary*, iii, 1536, for some early examples of 'will' etc. meaning penis. Some of the wording in the verse McNachtane recites raises suspicion that it may have been composed towards the end of the Benison's existence rather than in its earlier days.

5 G. Legman, *The horn book. Studies in erotic folklore and bibliography* (London, 1964 & 1970), 142–3 wished to add the Knights Templar and the Druids to the Benison's ancestry, an exercise in myth-making rivalling those of the club's own founders in fertility of imagination.

6 P. Burke, *Popular culture in early modern Europe* (London, 1978), 152.

7 Gordon Donaldson and Jenny Wormald, quoted in J. Cameron, *James V. The personal reign* (East Linton, 1998), 329.

8 C. Bingham, *James V, king of Scots, 1512–1542* (London, 1971), 90–9.

9 D. Hamer (ed.), *The works of Sir David Lindsay of the Mount* (4 vols., STS, 1931–6), i, 46 & iii, 57.

10 Williams, *Dictionary*, i, 919.

11 Hamer, *Lindsay*, i, 103; iii, 117; Bingham, *James V*, 98.

12 Many of these stories are to be found in J. Paterson, *James the fifth: or 'the gudeman of Ballangeich': his poetry and adventures* (Edinburgh, 1861).

13 C. Edington, *Court and culture in Renaissance Scotland. Sir David Lindsay of the Mount* (Amherst, Mass., 1994), 33, 101.

14 Bingham, *James V*, 95–6.

15 See D. Stevenson, 'The gudeman of Ballengeich', *Folklore and the historian*, ed. D. Hopkin (Folklore Society, 2001, forthcoming).

16 *Lauderdale papers*, ed. O. Airy, ii (1885), 50; D. Stevenson, *Revolution and counter revolution in Scotland* (London, 1977), 96.

17 E. Charlton, 'Jacobite relics of 1715 and 1745', *Archaeologia Aeliana*, new series, vi (1865), 34; P.K. Monod, *Jacobitism and the English people, 1688–1788* (Cambridge, 1989), 329.

18 See note 15 above.

19 James Beattie, 1768, quoted in R. Fergusson, *Poems*, ed. M.P. McDiarmid (2 vols., STS, 1954–6), i, 143.

20 Rogers, *Social life*, i, 219. It may be, in fact, that the story that it was customary for women to do this is based on the Benison myth.

21 See Williams, *Dictionary*, iii, 1116–19 for purse as scrotum.

22 E. Partridge, *A dictionary of catch-phrases* (London, 1977), 145, citing *A genuine narrative of all the street robberies committed since October last by James Dalton...* (London, 1728), 26–7.

23 D. Herd, *Ancient and modern Scottish songs, heroic ballads, etc.* (reprint, 2 vols., Edinburgh, 1973), i, 204; ii, 43, 99. Herd's collection first appeared in 1776, but most of the songs date from much earlier. The poet Allan Ramsay included 'benison' in his list of Scottish words which needed an 'Explanation' in an appendix to his *Tea table miscellany* (4 vols., Edinburgh, 1724–37). Robert Burns never used the word.

24 The 'over the water' theme in Jacobite propaganda appears early, but the toast derived from it may be late. It appears as practised by Fielding's drunkenly raucous Squire Weston in *Tom Jones* (London, 1749), who holds his glass over the water-filled wine-glass cooler while drinking to 'The King'. It is said that after the coronation banquet of George III in 1760 finger-bowls were banned from royal banquets (until 1905) as some guests were suspected of using them seditiously during the loyal toast, G.B. Hughes, *English, Scottish and Irish table glass* (New York, 1956), 307; Monod, *Jacobitism and the English people*, 305–6n.

25 M.G.H. Pittock, *Poetry and Jacobite politics in eighteenth-century Britain and Ireland* (Cambridge, 1994), 135–43.

26 Strictly speaking James V was not a 'Stuart' but a 'Stewart,' the change to the former (French) spelling only coming under his daughter, Mary Queen of Scots.

27 See Pittock, *Poetry*, 57, 58, 93 for this theme.

28 These generalisations about the early Benison are supported by information and analysis which follows in chapters 2 and 4–7 below.

29 R. Burns, *Poems and songs*, ed. J. Kinsley (3 vols., Oxford, 1968), i, 100; ii, 903.

30 E. Partridge, *A dictionary of slang and unconventional English* (3rd edn, London, 1949), 517; Williams, *Dictionary*, i, 879.

31 Williams, *Dictionary*, ii, 874.

32 P.J. Kearney, *A history of erotic literature* (London, 1982), 53. The brief Merryland craze perhaps owed something to *Erotopolis: The presents state of bettyland* (1684) which gave a social and geographical description of this female territory, R. Thompson, *Unfit for modest ears. A study of pornographic, obscene and bawdy works written or published in England in the second half of the seventeenth century* (London, 1979), 190–4.

33 Kearney, *Erotic literature*, 55–9; P.J. Kearney, *The private case. An annotated bibliography of the erotica collection in the British (Museum) Library* (London, 1981), items 1758, 1750; D. Foxon, *Libertine literature in England, 1660–1745* (New York, 1965), 16–18. Foxon, 16n, argued that the Benison use of the word must be related to Stretzer's publication. Less happy is his comment that the word was 'clearly a pun on Maryland,' for this seems highly unlikely. Rogers,

Social life, ii, 417n (copying Fergusson, *Erskine*, 149n) suggests that the word 'Merryland' was adopted 'in allusion to' the ballad The Jew's Daughter. This seems absurd. The 'Mirry-land toune' of the ballad is a corruption of 'Lincoln town,' the alternative title of the ballad being 'Hugh of Lincoln,' and the grim theme of the ballad (supposed Jewish ritual murder) has nothing to do with the sensual merryland of the Beggars. F.J. Child (ed.), *The English and Scottish popular ballads* (5 vols., New York, 1956), iii, 234.

CHAPTER TWO

The Benison:
Records and Relics

The *Records* and *Supplement*

The Beggar's Benison existed for just over a century, from 1732 to 1836, but most of the surviving evidence about its activities and interests relate to the 1730s. Thereafter, trying to write the history of the Benison is a matter of piecing together a thin scattering of written references, the evidence of relics used in rituals, and much in the way of later anecdotes about the club. As time passed, the actual sexual activity which featured in the club's rituals, for which there is evidence in the 1730s, may have been replaced by ritual containing symbolic or parodic enactment, as membership widened and sensibilities changed. Nonetheless, the surviving relics prized by the club indicate that to the end it remained concerned with the convivial celebration of male sexuality with a degree of obscenity that could be found in few if any other institutions. The 1730s members doubtless regarded themselves as bold defiers of conventions, but by the 1830s the obscenity that had once been brave and exciting seemed tawdry and antiquated. It was an embarrassing left-over from a past age of coarse and deplorable manners, surviving incongruously in an era in which fashion favoured respectability and decorum. The Benison, already probably moribund, was dissolved, appropriately, just a few months before the Victorian age dawned.

At this point, 1836, it might have been expected that a determined effort would have made to eradicate all traces of the club. Evidence that such an institution had once existed cast a most unwelcome light on the standards of immediately preceding generations – and indeed of surviving members. But though there was indeed much destruction of evidence, this was tempered by a degree of lingering nostalgia for a past sociability which was remembered as having been enjoyable, even though in retrospect it seemed shocking. Most of the written records which survived were lost or destroyed, but some scraps were retained, and there was almost certainly at some point a degree of re-writing of records concerning the crucial matter of what went on in the early and most robustly obscene days of the Benison. Probably several people were involved in the 'editing' that produced the written material which survives in printed form, and its reliability is not easy to assess. But confidence that the obscenity revealed in this written material is not later salacious invention is provided by the remarkable artefacts used in Benison activities which survive in metal, glass and pottery, providing startlingly explicit proof of the club's dedication to the phallus. How they were allowed to survive when so much of the written record was suppressed is a mystery.

Even before the Benison was dissolved in 1836 it had lost many of its records and relics. At one point Andrew Johnstone, of Johnstone Lodge, Anstruther, had refused to surrender the box which contained the club's possessions. Legal action is said to have been taken by the club in the 1820s to regain it and its contents,

> a great quantity of which, well known, were stolen, scattered, or burnt. Several MS. books were pilfered and destroyed by the various Officials from time to time, viz., Minutes, Songs, Toasts, Bon Mots, Pictures, and one renowned Wig worn by the Sovereign composed of the Privy-hairs of Royal courtesans.[1]

Among the items lost were 'All Notes and Memoranda' from 1738 to 1806 and 'Sederunt Book, Journal and Cash Book' covering 1739 to 1823.

The key figure in both the preservation and the piecemeal destruction of the remnants of the records of the Beggar's Benison that survived until 1836 was Matthew Forster Conolly. Born in 1789, he was the son of an Irishman, Daniel Conolly who had settled in the East Neuk of Fife as overseer of the coal and salt works at Pittenweem.

Later Daniel became owner of the Golf Hotel in Crail through a 'lucky accident' (whatever that may mean), and he became very much a stalwart of the local establishment – treasurer of the little burgh of Crail and a founder-member of the Crail Golfing Society. Matthew Conolly was appointment burgh clerk of Anstruther Easter in 1811 and of Anstruther Wester in 1812. He retained these offices for over sixty years, until his death in 1877. At an unknown date he joined the Beggar's Benison, and at the time of its dissolution he was its 'interim recorder,' or secretary. In later years he could have claimed (had he dared) to be the last surviving member of the long defunct sex club, as well as the longest-serving clerk of a royal burgh in Scotland.

Conolly's office as recorder made him the natural guardian of the Benison's records and relics when the society dissolved, and his longevity meant that they remained in his hands for over forty years. It seems extraordinary that he did not destroy everything as compromising relics of distant obscenity, but perhaps he felt a sense of responsibility for the items entrusted to him. Moreover, he was an avid local historian, and in several books sought to preserve knowledge of the Fife he had known in his youth (though without ever mentioning the Benison). His instinct was to preserve, and he seems to have dithered with his hoard, in the end destroying some but not all of the manuscript material. It might have been expected that a priority would have been destroying the most blatantly obscene material, the phallic relics, yet they survive.

A further complication is that Conolly evidently destroyed some records only after copying them – or partly copying them. When in 1892 some fragments relating to the Benison were published, it was said they had been taken from 'a mutilated Scrap-book' drawn from original sources – but that even the scrapbook had eventually been burnt by Conolly.[2] Yet he made careful provision for the preservation of the remaining Benison material after his death. About £70 of club funds remained in his hands, and he bequeathed this, through an intermediary, to a good cause. The money was donated to the school of East Anstruther. By a coincidence that seems like a joke in bad taste, it was decided that the money would be used to fund prizes for 'two co-equal girls'.[3] Thus the funds of the Benison, partly used in the past to pay young girls to display themselves naked to members, were distributed to schoolgirls. Unintended and ironic compensation for past exploitation.

The papers and relics were left by Conolly to his son-in-law, the Rev. Dr. J.F.S. Gordon. An Episcopalian priest might seem an inappropriate choice of legatee, but Gordon (1821–1904) was a noted antiquarian and historian, who had published several valuable works on the medieval church in Scotland.[4] His first post, in 1842, had been as a curate to Bishop David Low, who had been for many years a member of the Benison and lived in Pittenweem in the East Neuk. It was presumably during his short stay in Pittenweem that Gordon had met Conolly's daughter. Perhaps Conolly, himself an Episcopalian, had sought advice from Gordon on what to do with the Benison legacy, and Gordon had argued that the relics should be preserved as being, by that time, items of antiquarian interest, however obscene. Certainly Gordon showed no embarrassment about his most un-ecclesiastical inheritance.

By the mid-nineteenth century, however, the once notorious Beggar's Benison had been almost entirely forgotten – though a tourist guide of 1861 mentioned the club as once having been the 'favourite club of the claret and brandy carousing lairds' and as having acted with 'the want of refinement characteristic of the age'.[5] By 1866 the words *Beggar's Benison* were innocuous enough to be used as the title of a novel which had nothing whatever to do with the club, both author and readers being unaware of the words having obscene connotations.[6] But the club began to emerge from this obscurity in 1879. In *Notes and Queries* a correspondent, signing himself 'Orc', inquired what the objectives of the Beggar's Benison's as a society had been. That 'Orc' (evidently the Rev. J.B. Craven, an Episcopalian priest in Kirkwall and distinguished historian of the church in Orkney) was reluctant to identify himself may suggest that he already had some idea that the club had been disreputable.[7] J.F.S. Gordon responded promptly, stating that the Benison had been a club for collecting 'facetiae' – a learned word for the obscene or pornographic. He also revealed that he had inherited the club's property from Conolly.[8]

Gordon's disclosure that he held the Benison legacy sparked off antiquarian interest. Alexander Fergusson in 1882 and Charles Rogers in 1884 published accounts of the Benison, both acknowledging

Gordon's help in giving them access to the relics.[9] But both were of course very limited in what they could reveal in print. They hinted at the disreputable, indicating fascinated shock at the goings-on of past generations, but did not go much beyond that. Then, in 1892, came the publication of the *Records of the Most Ancient and Puissant Order of the Beggar's Benison and Merryland, Anstruther,* along with a separate *Supplement* and photographs of many of the relics.[10] On these works, totalling in all about 120 pages of 'records' and editorial commentary, all later writings on the Benison have been based. They do not form a happy foundation for scholarship. The arrangement is chaotic, the information given often consists of random snippets, the editorial contributions often wander into complete irrelevance and are sometimes self-contradictory. A healthy first reaction is to trust nothing. With a commentary containing much inflated assertion but little reference to sources, and some obvious factual errors, the safest thing to do might seem to be to walk away. And this is what most investigators have done. Vague generalisations have been made about the Benison, based on the 1892 publications, often with warnings that the material was not necessarily reliable, but with no attempt investigate it. Even when the publications were reprinted in 1982, a new introduction made no attempt to assess whether the material was trustworthy. Only Louis Jones, an American historian working in the late 1930s, made a serious scholarly study of the Benison, and his work too was constrained by the conventions of his time, making it impossible for him to mention masturbation, which was central to the club's rituals.[11]

Who it was that compiled the 1892 publications remains a mystery. Publication did not take place in Anstruther, as the title pages asserted, but in London. The publisher was one J. Lewis, 174 Wardour Street – and Wardour Street lies in the heart of Soho, still a centre of British commercial sex. Lewis was clearly wary of the laws relating to pornography, and he published the *Records* on subscription only. Copies were not for sale to the public, he stressed on the subscription form, and publication (at two guineas) was only being undertaken 'at the request of many of the Nobility and Antiquarians of Scotland'. This bombastic statement indicating widespread support from respectable people is just as much to be believed as the claim that Anstruther was the place of publication. Nominally the subscription only covered the *Records*. What was regarded as the most obscene material was reserved for the *Supplement*, and copies of it (including, evidently, the illustrations) were to be distributed free to subscribers, but only if they filled in and returned a special application form. Thus, if legal problems arose, Lewis could claim that he had not sold the *Supplement*, even by subscription. He had merely given it to individuals who had specifically asked for it. As a last resort, the address given on the subscription form was not his own, but that of a second-hand bookseller.[12]

The first suspect as editor and initiator of these publications must be J.F.S. Gordon, for the Benison papers and relics were still in his hands in 1892. But it is hard to believe that this scholarly, capable writer could have produced such an appallingly incompetent, disorderly heap of material and believe it worth publication. The most likely scenario is that Gordon gave access to the Benison materials to someone, with or without the intention that they be prepared for publication, who then made a mess of preparing them for the press. It is quite possible that Matthew Conolly had tried to work up a sort of history of the Benison, and had left a chaos of notes on the subject, and that these were cobbled roughly together after his death with some additional editorial matter and sent off to the press. It might be added that though Conolly was the author of several books, they show very limited literary ability.[13] He had much anti-quarian knowledge, but could seldom sustain a subject for long without meandering off into the marginally relevant and becoming scrappy and rather chaotic. If he was like that in works polished for publication, perhaps the *Records* and *Supplement* reveal what his draft work could be like.

Others, however, must have had a part in preparing whatever material Conolly left and seeing it into print. It may be that some part was played by the Rev. Charles Rogers – a Church of Scotland minister thus joining the Episcopalian J.F.S. Gordon in the Benison saga. Rogers was a well-known antiquarian, and he had been one of the first to exploit Gordon's Benison material in print, in 1884. Rogers also had relevant local knowledge, having been brought up at Dunino, just north of Anstruther. He was an intelligent, energetic, and ambitious man, but wayward and frustrated. He wrote much on historical topics, but tended to produce too much too fast, resulting in some publications that were scrappy and slapdash. But though these characteristics recall the disastrous editing of the *Records* and *Supplement*, in fairness it should be said that Rogers's limitations as an editor are never nearly so gross as the incompetence displayed in these works. Moreover, he died in 1890, two years before they were published. Conceivably he left some notes which were then worked on by whoever finally prepared the works for the press. Certainly there was some contact between Rogers and this final editor of the *Records*, for the work includes an anecdote told by him, inserted after his death.

The most sensible approach to the quagmire of the *Records* and *Supplement* is to start with the documents embedded in the publications which seem most reliable, through the existence of corroborating evidence, before tentatively approaching the more dubious of the supposed sources and the commentary.

The Diploma and the Code

The Benison membership diploma provides a solid foundation.[14] Many original diplomas issued to members survive containing virtually identical wording. The earliest of these original diplomas which can now be located is dated 1746, but there is a reference to a diploma dated 1739 having once existed.[15] As will be seen below, the diploma is closely linked to the club's code of institutes, which is dated 1739, and that may be accepted as the date at which both documents were adopted by the Benison.

The diploma is in mock-solemn style, with ludicrous bombast and word-play used to produce sexual double-entendres. The sovereign guardian of the order (supereminently beneficent and superlatively benevolent), out of regard for the happiness and prosperity of the inhabitants of the celebrated territory of Merryland, and for encouraging trade, manufacture and agriculture in that delightful colony, admits a new member to the Benison by signing a diploma for him. The diploma authorises members to enjoy Merryland as their dominion. But first, the sovereign has had to be satisfied of the candidate's 'inclinations, as well as sufficient abilities' (his interest in sex and ability to perform). Satisfaction having been given, the bold adventurer is constituted a knight companion of the Beggar's Benison and Merryland 'with our full power and Priviledges of Ingress, Egress, and Regress from and to and to and from all the Harbours, Creeks, Havens, and Commodious Inlets' of the extensive territory, at his pleasure, without payment of any tolls or taxes. The sexual innuendoes are obvious.[16] Free or fair trade was free exploitation of sexual opportunities, though (as will emerge) free trade in its own right was also a Benison obsession, the Beggars' ideal of fair trade being trade free from restrictions – in other words, smuggling. Only one significant deviation from the standard diploma text has been noted: one copy limits the rights of 'free trade' to sixty years, in mockery of the shortness of human life and libido.[17]

It has already been suggested that the use of the word 'Merryland' indicates the influence of English pornography on the Beggar's Benison. So too does the phrase 'Ingress, Egress, and Regress' in the diploma. An English publication of 1734, purporting to denounce pornography but doing it with so many salacious examples that its intended market was clearly not the pious, gave what was supposed to be the sort of letter a drunken noble would give to a friend, granting him access to his mistress's services.

Dear Molly,
On sight hereof permit the Bearer, to immediately enter a Pair of Holland Sheets with you; let him have Ingress, Egress and Regress to your Person.[18]

This fantasy of free access clearly appealed to the Beggars.

The *Records* describe the club diploma as a 'travesty of a Ship's License'[19] compiled by John McNachtane, the reputed founder of the Benison, or his clerk Nathaniel Murray. As an obscene parody of an official document it belonged to a long-established minor literary *genre*, dating back on the continent at least to the sixteenth century – an example from about 1530, relating to a fictitious law case, is described as bearing 'a truly remarkable phallic ornament or seal'.[20] Immediate inspiration possibly came from erotic French clubs. The *Régiment de la calotte* (Regiment of the skull-cap) issued mock *brevets* and *lettres patents*, though with emphasis on satire rather than obscenity',[21] while the 'Order of Felicity' helpfully produced a glossary of nautical terms providing a 'secret or metaphorical language'.[22] The idea of a whole language of sexual euphemism based on a single specialised vocabulary – topographical, nautical, commercial or military – clearly had a strong attraction. Indeed, it may well be that the founders of the Benison had specific knowledge of *l'ordre herma- phrodite, ou les secrets de la sublime félicité*, to give the club its full title ('hermaphrodite' simply means that both sexes were admitted to membership). Members of the order sought safe haven in 'Ile de Félicitié,' and spoke of sex as entering the port of happiness. A male initiate of the order swore not to interfere in any harbour in which a member of the order was at anchor, and a female initiate not to receive any strange ship (man) in her harbour if a ship of the order was already at anchor there. The word-play hardly needs explaining, and since dropping of the anchor in harbour meant sexual conjunction, the order's symbol was an anchor.[23] As will emerge below, the Benison's badge was to feature an anchor and a phallus.

The code of institutes of the Benison, as signed on 14 September 1739, is only known through the text in *Records*,[24] but it is so similar in style to, and consistent in content with, the diploma that there is little doubt as to its authenticity. Moreover, as will be shown in chapter six, the thirty-two signatories whose names appear at the end of the code constitute a highly plausible and coherent list of members for that date. The code is pervaded by the same sort of tipsy, mock-solemn tone as the diploma. It reads like a foundation document, forming a new organisation, though in fact it represents the revival or reorganisation of a club dating from 1732.

The signatories of the code announce that they have constituted themselves a 'Collective body' known as 'The Most Ancient and Puissant Order of Beggars Benison and Merryland'. Members agree to support and maintain each other in the delightful territories of Merryland, and to extend fair trade and legal entry, and prevent as much as possible 'a preposterous and Contraband Trade too frequently practised'. The society is founded on the principles of 'Benevolence, Charity and Humanity', and only those possessing such character- istics will be made knights of the order. Members must also be of 'undoubted worth, untainted honour, integrity, and candour, and detestors of litigiosity'. None will be admitted who have been convicted of cowardice, or even suspected of being capable of ingratitude, malice, slander or anything infamous.

Three officials are to be appointed: a sovereign guardian, a remembrancer acting as his deputy, and a recorder, though the last of these might also appoint a deputy or clerk. In addition to Anstruther Easter, the seat of the club, the four neighbouring royal burghs of the East Neuk (Anstruther Wester, Crail, Kilrenny and Pittenweem) were to send representatives to meetings. This woffle of rather drunken, hearty men having a bit of fun, like the diploma disguises sex as free trade and legal entry, but not in a way seriously intended to fool anyone. The denunciation of 'preposterous and Contraband Trade' shows the limits of the Benison's willingness to advocate sex free from conventional fetters. Members wanted to make it clear that they abhorred sodomy, which was 'preposterous' in the literal meaning of 'inverted in order,' and hence 'contrary to nature; monstrous, perverse'. There seems no reason to doubt that the repugnance was genuine, though no doubt the fear of the death penalty which sodomy might incur was also present. The fact that 1726–30 had seen a brief purge in England of homosexual brothels or 'Molly Houses' and a number of executions for sodomy may have been in the minds of the drafter of the institutes.[25]

The code declares allegiance to benevolence, charity and humanity. All good 'modern' qualities to claim – enlightened, secular, rejecting the rigidities and fanaticisms of the past. The names of remembrancer and recorder for officials are notable. Both were English legal terms, introduced to the Scottish administration only after the Union of Parliaments of 1707. They are used here not through zeal for anglicisation but as absurd pompous terms. Similarly, the inflated title 'code of institutes' for this short exercise in double-entendre is intended to be ridiculous.

Bawdy Talk, Bawdy Verse, Bawdy Song

The diploma and code of institutes solemnly declare the Benison to be a brotherhood devoted to good fellowship and advocating sexual freedom – or at least the indiscriminate satisfaction of male lust and fantasy.

Some idea of the general tone of the Benison meetings can be derived from the *Supplement*, which contains a considerable amount of material recording the sort of talk that was common. For some of this the only provenance is the editor's dubious blessing, but one of the main segments can be linked to a manuscript known to have existed in the 1890s. The 'Dinner Sentiment, Bon-Mots, Toasts Etc. collected from Scraps written in Ink and Pencil, dated from 1732 to 1820'[26] were copied into a book, probably by Matthew Conolly. This was in J.F.S. Gordon's collection, though it has now disappeared.[27]

The material is pretty commonplace. Much was part of the sort of popular and predictable repertoire of bawdy which had been around for generations – or centuries. But a few poems and jokes are attributed to specific authors who were members of the Benison, and there are a few local references. These contributions may have some claim to originality, though the basic themes of bawdy have a large degree of timeless obviousness. The Beggars dined and drank in an atmosphere of happy obscenity, delighting themselves with how shocking they were being. The air was full of sexual innuendoes ranging from basic crudity to some quite ingenious and witty efforts. In small doses the material can be quite entertaining, but it is wearisome in bulk. Dreel (the castle in which, nominally at least, the Beggar's met) becomes military drill, to be employed in 'drilling' 'our *Merry Island*' leading to the battle honour '*Mons Veneris*'. Toasts are drunk to 'The Beggar's Benison, – the Ramrod Corps'; 'Firm Erection, fine Insertion, Excellent distillation, no Contamination'; and 'Three qualities in a proper Woman: – Well-hipped, well-breasted, easy mounted'.[28] Occasionally, a quotation from Shakespeare or Pope, or a reference to Ovid, seeks to raise the tone. The 'merryland' obsession with the female body as territory recurs frequently. It could be new and exotic: Botany Bay (discovered in 1770) was hailed in verse as discovered and seduced by Adam, amidst much laboured metaphor.[29] Or it could be local. 'The Ainster [Anstruther] Lassie' fills her creel or fishing basket (euphemism for vagina) with 'a fine big Silver Eel'.[30] 'Let us often gaze on the varied inspiriting Nooks of our East Neuk in the Town o' Maggie Lauder,' extolled the laird of Cambo in one of his elaborate toasts. In another, he lauded 'the mutual capacity of the chiefest and greatest of all *natural Art*', which was could be studied through the great examples of their forefathers Abraham, Solomon and David: 'onwards, upwards, and downwards, *To and Fro*'.[31] Occasionally anecdotes unrelated to sex slip in. When the laird of Innergellie called for sheep's heads for supper, Cambo seconded the motion: 'present company always excepted, *Sheeps' Heads for ever*'.[32]

Scots in the eighteenth century had something of a patriotic obsession with sheep's heads and other outlandish dishes that could be relied upon to appal the English.

Interest in local tradition did not exclude irreverence. Maggie Lauder was well-known as an Anstruther girl depicted in a seventeenth century poem which recorded her love for a piper. The Benison, typically, deflated the romantic image:

> Bonnie Maggie, Braw Maggie, Bonnie Maggie Lauder!
> She pisht upon the puir folk and farted on her faither![33]

Edification is seldom to be found in the Benison, and the schoolyard is often near at hand. Other 'Poems Recited at Meetings'[34] are also predictable, though sometimes slightly more elevated in tone. Two are attributed to members of the society, Colonel Alexander Monypenny and John McNachtane. The latter, as already noted, tells of 'Earl Willie' and his marriage to May. In the poem there also occur the lines

> Ah! 'Lose no opportunity',
> Is the motto of the Knight's medal,

referring to one of the surviving relics of the club.

In their repertoire of ribaldry the Beggars included poking fun at a rather different Anstruther convivial club. The masonic lodge of St Ayle (No. 95) was founded in 1764, and the Beggars' gleeful response was 'The Lady Freemason'. Masonic ritual, terminology and tools become the target for coarsely entertaining double-entendres. The lady in question becomes an 'Entered Apprentice', but eventually wins the contest for sexual domination. She becomes Master, and then, when she is 'mounted astride him', 'Says he, you're enrolled; you are now "Royal Arch".'[35] This was doubtless a local composition, but other material was copied. *The Oeconomy of love* by the eccentric Scottish physician John Armstrong (who wisely had his work published anonymously) proved a fruitful source of titillation.[36]

Finally, the *Supplement* peters out with brief lists of riddles, proverbs and lewd biblical references, carrying on the same themes of delight in being naughty about the celebration of sex.[37] Local references apart, none of this material is unusual in its obscenity. The eighteenth century saw the publication of dozens of books of songs, jests and toasts to entertain men as they drank in taverns, private houses or clubs, the predominant themes being patriotic (British), romantic, and directly or allusively obscene. To quote just two examples of toasts out of many hundreds, *The frisky songster* (1756) recommended the generalised 'Girls lecherous, kind and willing', while *The hearty fellow* (1770s?) was more specifically, though allusively, genital – 'The mouth that never had the tooth-ache'. In written, sung and spoken obscenity, the Beggar's Benison's repertoire was pretty run of the mill stuff.

The Benison Lectures

The Beggars were happy hedonists. They revelled in their sexuality, but, occasionally at least, they tried to treat sex as a matter for serious study. Self-improvement was involved in many clubs, and the Benison was no exception. Talks on sex were given to spread accurate information. Perhaps they also calmed any twinges of conscience at the club's obsessions through making it seem that interest in sex was an enlightened striving for knowledge. As with much of the material in the *Supplement*, the argument in favour of the authenticity of the lectures is that they seem highly appropriate and plausible – and why would anyone bother to forge them?

The texts of two of these talks survive. The first was given by James Lumsdaine in 1753.[38] He talked on 'The Act of Generation'. John McNachtane had cited the motto from one side of a Benison medal in a poem. Lumsdaine took the motto from the other side as his text.

'Be fruitful and multiply.' But this can't have been nature's only intention in equipping man with sexuality, Lumsdaine argued, for the sexual urge continued even after one had multiplied. Indeed, if men tried to stop being sexually active after having families, they would be left with 'living plagues' – strong sexual drives with no outlet, causing anguish and wasting a capacity for intense enjoyment. Nature has given us 'this exquisite endowment', and it becomes us to enjoy the great gift with thanksgiving – but with caution to avoid procreation when it is not wanted. Contraception in other words. Withdrawal, use of 'French Letters' or condoms and other methods are described. Ensuring that unwanted conceptions do not take place is argued to be central to love-making. Men should not be thoughtless brutes or beasts in satisfying their desires. Contraception would prevent people having larger families than they could easily support, women with health problems would not need not endanger themselves by having children, and there would be no illegitimate births. The 'sexual embrace should be independent of the dread of a conception which blasts the prospects of the female'. All very responsible, but hovering in the background of such worthy sentiments without being made explicit is the thought that effective contraception makes it a lot easier to entice girls into bed. In his talk Lumsdaine also shows some knowledge of current debate over the process of conception. He specifically rejects the centuries-old belief that both male and female produced 'seminal fluid' during intercourse, which mixed to bring about conception, and relies on the scientifically more accurate theory of the egg in the female. It was to be nearly seventy-five years before mammalian eggs were isolated to provide direct proof of the hypothesis, but many investigators were already confident of their existence.

Lumsdaine's little speech displays an enlightened 'joys of sex' rationalism, anatomically detailed and informed by the studies of physicians, but stressing humanity. The second of the Benison Lectures to survive considered 'The Male Organs of Generation' and was read 'at the Conference, St Andrew's Day, 1813.'[39] It is attributed to 'M.D.' – which presumably indicates that the speaker was a doctor of medicine. The genitals are described with medical precision – though defining 'the best shape [of penis] for deflowering a virgin' seems unnecessary. Masturbation is depicted as very common in both sexes, and as not harmful: the prevailing idea that it led to insanity is dismissed. In most cases in which women are labelled as 'barren' it is the man who is responsible. On conception 'M.D.' accepts the existence of eggs, but mentions the mingling of seminal fluids as something that 'it has been supposed' may possibly produce conception without them. By the time the speaker reached the habits of hermaphrodite snails and other such exotica he may have lost his audience's attention, but in general stance the 1813 doctor and Lumsdaine in 1753 have much in common in the way of a rational, humane and factual approach to sex. The physician is rather more technical in approach than the amateur, though he does try to lighten the tone with a joke. If 'lecherous King Solomon' was puzzled by 'the way of a man with a maid' he must have been a pretty slow learner, for he had a thousand concubines.

Two fragments of lectures contain a careful anatomical description of the female genitals and some additions to M.D.'s essay on the male genitals. These essays and notes were doubtless not just delivered as lectures but kept for reading by later members – and would have provided in some respects sounder and saner short courses in sex education than was likely to be easily available elsewhere.

The Proceedings of the Benison, 1733–1738

So far deciding on the reliability or otherwise of the contents of the *Report* and *Supplement* has not been a major problem. The documents have had elements of external validation, and are in themselves consistent and plausible.

The 'Notes' which record club meetings between 1733 and 1738 are a very different matter.[40] Their provenance is unknown. As they stand in the *Supplement* it is not clear whether they are supposed to be transcribed from an original manuscript, or notes assembled from other original sources. Moreover, the activities on which the notes concentrate attention are not mentioned in the Benison 'documents' so far discussed. That girls were hired to be the subject of close anatomical examination and dance naked may be regarded as within common norms for male behaviour, and the immediate inspiration may, yet again, have come from English sources. In the late seventeenth and early eighteenth centuries 'posture girls' were popular there, hired to adopt ingenious poses and display their genitals.[41] But the Benison notes also record activities that are much more unusual. New members of the Benison are described as being initiated by masturbating in front of existing members; and sometimes all members masturbated together as a sociable activity (though solitarily – every man to his own penis – not mutually); and they compared phalluses. Here the obscenity may seem so extreme, the activity so bizarre (at least for adults rather than experimentally minded adolescents), that initial doubts as to whether the notes describe actual events or the inventive fantasies of someone involved in the 1892 publications are inevitable.

The following extracts indicate the tone of these brief notes. In 1734

18 assembled, and Frigged upon the Test Platter. The origin and performance were discussed. The Platter was filled with Semen, each Knight at an average did not 'benevolent' [donate] quite a horn spoonful.

A 'horn' spoonful was clearly appropriate. In 1737: '24 met, 3 tested and enrolled. All frigged', the test being ritual masturbation. The fullest account of the viewing of naked girls concerns the Candlemas meeting of 1734:

> One Feminine Gender, 17, was hired for One Sovereign, fat and well-developed. She was stripped in the Closet, nude; and was allowed to come in with her face half-covered. None was permitted to speak to or touch her. She spread wide upon a Seat, first before and then behind; every Knight passed in turn and surveyed the Secrets of Nature.

A very clinical and decorous coming out of the closet. Later in the year 'Betty Wilson, 15, was hired, but a bad model and unpleasant.' On other occasions the events were more agreeable. In 1735 'a girl of 15 appeared nude for a few minutes', and was satisfactory enough to be booked for the next meeting. In 1736: 'Jane Bowman behaved well; 'a capital form of humanity.' In 1737 'Two girls, 16 and 17, posed, exhibited, and danced nude.' Still it seems, no touching or talking to the girls, but the action had moved on from static postures to dancing. Are these real events of the 1730s or, as sometimes has been suspected, steamy late Victorian fantasies?

The editorial commentary in the *Supplement* is little help in deciding on the authenticity of this material. It ignores the masturbation and is confused on the matter of the girls. It first seems to dismiss the possibility of something so shocking on practical grounds: 'Owing to the sparse population of the small Burgh wherein it [the Benison] originated, there was no supply of wenches, even if such had been in demand'. Yet on the very next page the editor regales readers with an anecdote he had heard from Charles Rogers. When Rogers was fourteen he had been present at a wedding in Dunino at which his father James Roger (it was Charles who added an 's' to the family name) had officiated as parish minister. As the happy couple left the church, a girl in the crowd shouted out, referring to the bride 'Ah! ah! that's the Bitch that shewed her hairy C[unt] and A[rse] to the gentlemen of the Beggar's Benison for Five Shillings'. One of those marriage-day incidents that it is hard to live down. In fact Rogers only reached the age of fourteen in 1839, three years after the Benison had dissolved, but the anecdote could be true in essentials nonetheless. The *Supplement* editor solemnly assures readers that this anecdote is the only evidence of 'a stark exhibition' having taken place in the Benison – [42] but then a few pages later prints the notes on 1732–8 with repeated accounts of 'stark exhibitions'.

On the more crucial (to the understanding of what went on in the Benison) matter of ritual masturbation, the *Records* are much more forthcoming than the *Supplement*. The writer (possibly a different person from the editor of the *Supplement*) describes the Benison initiation ceremony in full. The sovereign presided over the meeting, at which members wore their sashes and medals. The remembrancer placed the test platter on a high stool or altar in the middle of the room. The novice was 'prepared' in a closet by the recorder and two rembrancers 'causing him to propel his Penis until full erection'. He then came out of the closet, a fanfare being provided by 'four puffs of the Breath Horn,' and placed 'his Genitals on the Testing-Platter', which was covered with a folded white napkin. 'The Members and Knights two and two came round in a state of erection and touched the novice Penis to Penis.' A special glass with the order's insignia on it was then filled with port and a toast drunk to the new member, and, in a brief parody of a church service, he had to read aloud an 'amorous' passage from the Song of Solomon and comment on it. Investment with sash and medal followed, as the sovereign and other members intoned the benison or blessing: 'May Prick nor Purse never fail you'.[43] It is notable that this version of the initiation does not state that the initiate had to masturbate to orgasm, only that he had to prove capacity to achieve erection. Here, it may be, is a clue to the way in which the extreme obscenity of early Benison ritual was toned down over time, ejaculation having been replaced by erection as proof of manhood.

Whatever the details, there is no doubt that central to the early Benison was the provision by members of physical proof of sexual capacity (as is documented in the membership diplomas). Several toasts and injunctions provide additional evidence. 'Before we break up for the season, let us each show the best Articles for propagating Truth' suggests mass exposure. 'At our initiation into the Beggar's Benison, when the Sough [breath] Horn sounds, we have warning to view the motions of the Tested.' 'We all admire the Transformation-scenes exhibited at each initiation of our several novices, for the nonce, until they reappear at next installation. Again they vanish, till, at next opportune sederunts, new lights appear, which, year by year, become the brighter for the more frequent and careful snuffing.' This sententious stuff appears to date from the 1750s or earlier.[44] Finally, there is the explicit evidence of the 'test platter' (described below). It is true that it dates from the 1780s rather than the 1730s, but the inscription and graphic genital engravings on it are strong additional evidence of the fact that initiation to the Benison involved the candidate in a display of sexual capacity.

Such supporting evidence suggest that the notes on the 1733–8 meetings have truth in them, but it does not prove that they are actual notes on meetings as written by a contemporary. Leaving aside the sensational parts of their contents, they do not ring true simply as a historical document. It is highly likely that anyone wishing to keep a systematic record of meetings would have used the form of conventional minutes (like those of the Wig Club), starting with the date and a *sederunt* (a list of the names of members present). But not only do the *Records* state that all early formal minutes were lost, the notes themselves are not structured as minutes. They are simply headed 'Lammas,' 'Candlemas' and 'St Andrew's Day,' plus the year. Simple for a forger, sloppy for a clerk. Total numbers present are given, but no names (except for those of a few girls). Not even the sovereign is named. Moreover, virtually all the entries are sensational – masturbation, naked girls, a few tipsy disputes between members. Formal minutes (as anyone who has ever attended a committee meeting knows) are usually boring, and leave out the juicy bits. The main point of minutes is to record decisions rather than activity or debate. In the Notes the emphasis is reversed. It could of course be argued that these are informal notes by a member whose interest lay precisely in the sensational bits. But there is a bit of a feeling of 'too good to be true' about the notes. Moreover, both the first and last entries in the notes raise suspicions of different sorts.

The first entry might indicate that a playful hoaxer is giving a hint that all is not well. The Notes are to turn out to be primarily concerned with obscene behaviour. But the opening entry, for St Andrew's Day 1733, reads –

16 present. The engendering of Toads; The menstruation of Skate; and The gender of an Earthworm. *Arcana* shown. Chambers shut in the usual form by our Sovereign.

It is as if the teasing writer knows his reader will expect hot stuff – and then fobs him off with the sex lives of toads, skate (menstruating fish?) and worms. Then, next entry, slap bang, the real thing: well developed naked girl emerging from closet and being examined. The panting reader has not been cheated after all.

The last entries raise different doubts. Apart from these Notes, absolutely nothing is known about the Benison before the 1739 reorganisation which produced the diploma and the code of institutes. But the final entries in the notes provide a perfect lead-in to the events of 1739 – perhaps, again, too perfect. In 1737 'Rules were submitted by Mr Lumsdaine for future adoption'. The following year 'Several members got combative, when stricter Regulations were passed in order for proper and subordinate behaviour in all time coming. A Seal and Diploma were drafted'. The End – the future mapped out. Rather too neat?

No absolutely certain conclusion about the notes is possible. However, the likelihood seems to be that the later Benison had only scraps of records dating from before the 1739 organisation. But these scraps and club tradition provided evidence that masturbation and naked girls had been central features of the Benison in the 1730s, so someone has concocted the Notes from them to show what the early Benison had been like – or was believed to have been like.

Fanny Hill in Merryland

There is just a single item of factual information in the 1733–8 Notes that can be checked against independent evidence in seeking to judge their reliability. At first sight it seems to prove that a forger is at work, yet on closer examination it indicates the exact opposite, providing a persuasive argument that the compiler of the Notes really did know something about what went on in the Benison in the 1730s. On St Andrew's Day 1737, after two 'nymphs' had exhibited themselves, 'Fanny Hill was read'.

Has a forger made an obvious blunder? John Cleland's celebrated work of pornography was not published until 1748–9, and was then called *Memoirs of a woman of pleasure.* The title *Fanny Hill* was only substituted in later editions. In trying for a touch of verisimilitude, has a forger instead destroyed his credibility? *Fanny Hill* could not have titillated the Beggars in the 1730s. But such a conclusion is premature, and historians must be grateful for the fact that Cleland was prosecuted for his part in the publication of *A woman of pleasure*, for it provoked him into writing about the circumstances in which the book had been written.

> The plan of the first Part was originally given me by a young gentleman of the greatest hopes that ever I knew, (brother to a nobleman now Ambassador at a foreign Court) above eighteen years ago, on an occasion immaterial to mention here.

What he was doing was indicating that someone else was involved in writing the book who had eminent relatives who would be furious to see his name dragged through the courts in a sordid obscenity case. The threat is implicit: if I am prosecuted I will reveal information embarrassing to the establishment. However, in the context of the Benison what is important is that Cleland's threat reveals that the manuscript Fanny Hill had been drafted in about 1730 – and indeed, drafted in India, for he had then been in the service of the East India Company in Bombay.

Thus there is no impossibility about Fanny Hill being read in Anstruther in 1737 in a manuscript version. Possibly it is significant that John Cleland's father was a Scot. William Cleland had served as one of the five commissioners who constituted the board of customs in Edinburgh from 1713 to 1723, when he moved to another administrative post in England, and kinship might have provided a link through which a manuscript version of Fanny Hill reached the East Neuk. However the assertion that John Cleland was probably related to Robert Cleland, merchant in Crail and a signatory of the Benison institutes of 1739 is no more than wishful guesswork.[45]

John Cleland produced a pornographic work designed to be free of vulgar or coarse words – and therefore, of necessity, full of euphemisms and double entendres, words and phrases with sexual connotations made clear by their context but in themselves inoffensive. The words thus employed have a wide range of primary meanings, but almost inevitably a fair number were topographical. In the text of

Fanny Hill geographical features such as landscapes, avenues, clefts, hillocks and crevices are featured. Indeed the very title, a colloquial translation of *mons veneris*, provides an allusion to classical topological / anatomical usages. The merryland craze dealt similarly in euphemisms, but confined them almost entirely to topography. The Beggar's Benison in its 'official' documents (the code of institutes and diploma) shows the influence of both these precedents, but adapts them to its own circumstances. The coastal situation of the club was emphasised in the topographies described, and the vocabulary of trade and commerce was adopted to signify active male working on the passive female landscape. Perhaps coincidence, but perhaps Cleland's pornography without naughty words, circulating in manuscript, helped inspire both the Benison and the merryland craze.

In one instance, the Benison may have borrowed directly from Cleland, to help refer euphemistically to a subject which needed careful treatment. In the first edition of *A woman of pleasure* Cleland had included a description of a homosexual encounter. It was evidently shock at this passage in particular that led to his arrest, and it was omitted in later editions. In Cleland's euphemistic language, sodomy had been referred to as 'a project of preposterous pleasure'.[46] It has already been noted that the institutes similarly use 'preposterous' to denote homosexuality. This usage was so unusual that it has evidently never found its way into dictionaries,[47] and though it does occur elsewhere in the obscene literature of the period,[48] it seems likely that the Benison was borrowing from Cleland, adding its own commercial twist by making sodomy a 'preposterous Contraband Trade'.

Medals and Seals

The Beggar's Benison, it may be assumed, once had a hoard of written pornography, bawdy and obscenity from the age of *Fanny Hill*, acquired for the entertainment of members. Whether the manuscript of Fanny Hill was kept or passed on is unknown, and the copies of Ovid's *Art of love* and (much later) of Byron's *Don Juan* possessed are lost – or perhaps it was copies owned by members which were read at meetings. Of the Benison's written sources of sexual inspiration only the club Bible survives. From it appropriate texts 'were freely *anatomised*'.[49] As well as pornographic words the Benison had a stock of graphic pornography, the lost 'Pictures' mentioned in the *Records*.[50] Until the mid eighteenth century visual pornography available in Britain was almost entirely imported, but it seems to have been readily available in London by the late seventeenth century.[51] A club which had acquired written pornography from England would presumably have had little trouble in getting hold of such engraved material. As the great majority of copies of historical indecent literature and illustration have been lost, destroyed by guilty and apprehensive owners or shocked families, the fact that that the Benison hoard should have disappeared is no surprise. What is amazing, as already indicated, is that other forms of highly indecent material have been preserved.

Sexually explicit objects, whether intended as titillating works of art or crude symbols, are rarely referred to. In British contexts at least, survival is almost unknown.[52] As with pornographic prints and paintings, such items were usually imported. This is doubtless true of the indecent snuff boxes which were known by the late seventeenth century as conversation pieces. Archbishop Paterson of Glasgow was said by his enemies to have owned one, either painted with sexual postures or phallic in shape. Even if the accusation was no more than hostile propaganda, the fact it was thought meaningful to accuse him of having one indicates that such things were known to be in circulation. An English source refers to 'a sweet bawdy snuff-box' in 1696, and phallic or obscenely painted ones are mentioned shortly thereafter.[53] A 1725 work refers to fans and snuff boxes painted with 'undecent postures'.[54] The English 'Hell-Fire Club', the Medmenham Monks, in the 1750s had 'special wine cups made in an unusual shape',[55] which may be assumed to have been obscene, though the conflicting assertions that they were 'shaped like horns' (phallic, presumably, rather than hunting) and 'silver cups in the form of a woman's breasts' seem to owe more to invention than evidence.[56]

Indecent watches and playing cards are known, but a few phalluses of English provenance[57] are evidently the only obscene artefacts known to survive from seventeenth or eighteenth-century Britain which have any resemblance to the Beggar's Benison and Wig Club materials.[58] All show a primary interest in the crudely symbolic and (except for some of the medals) little concern for artistic merit.

The official insignia of the Benison were the medals, worn round the neck on collars or sashes at meetings. The relative restraint of most of their subject matter suggests that they represented the public face of the club. Naughty and suggestive but not downright obscene, they could indicate to non-members the club's dedication to sex without being grossly indecent. This may be why a theme included on what was evidently the earliest of the club's medals was quickly abandoned. It was too explicit to be shown in public without being regarded as offensive.

On one side of this early medal design the theme is 'decent.' Though it depicts two naked figures holding hands, the male gesturing to invite the female to withdraw with him into a bower, the legend makes it respectable. 'Be Fruitful & Multiply' identifies them as Adam and Eve. Thus nudity is sanctioned by the context of the Garden of Eden, and no one could object to an encouragement to copulation which is taken from the word of God. The contrast with the other side is extreme, and the intention must have been to shock. The legend consists of the benison of the beggar maid, 'May Prick and Purse Never Fail You'. A woman figure sits with her legs spread wide in lewd invitation. With one hand she holds aloft a purse, With the other, she points to the genitals of a man who stands beside her. Purse and prick. While at one level the figures may represent James V and the beggar-maid, the hound that runs behind the man suggests he is to be recognised as Adonis – in which case the scene is a crude caricature of the theme of Venus and Adonis.

On one side of the medal sex is a divine injunction to procreative sex, on the other sex as something bought and sold with a liberty free from moral restraint. As if to add to the joke, while Adam and Eve are naked but innocent, the woman and her customer are clothed but lewd. Only two examples of this early medal design survive, in different sizes.[59] Perhaps the larger was for the sovereign, the smaller for other members. It is tempting to link the abandonment of the design, indicating that it was thought wise to be more discreet, to the reform of the club in 1739.

The second standard design for medals also features two sexual encounters. Adam and Eve remain, with the same legend as before, while on the other a naked or partially draped (there are several variants of the medal) female figure reclines asleep in the foreground, tended by Cupid, while a male figure approaches her from behind, armed with a spear and accompanied by a hunting dog. 'Venus and Adonis' – if that is indeed what is depicted on the medals described above, have cleaned up their act and become 'respectable' artistic images, and while the legend 'Lose no Opportunity' is clearly suggestive, the crudity of the Benison motto has disappeared.[60] As John McNachtane refers to this as the medal motto, some of these medals must have been in use by 1773, the year of his death.

Well-known classical and religious allusions were in part for public consumption. Artefacts to be displayed only inside the club were a very different matter, and rampant phallicism reigned. On the medals, even in the soon-abandoned beggar maid scene, sex was depicted in a context of whole human bodies, but the other relics reduce it to basic physical essentials, the genitals. The club symbol or badge was the phallus, though occasionally vulva are depicted. Members celebrated the phallus as their true sovereign.

Seven Benison seals are known. Impressions of four survive on club diplomas, all dominated by the phallus (here defined as the complete male genitals with erect penis). Three small seals are relatively simple in design. One reads: 'Anstruther Beggar's Benison 1732', with 'Love's Cave' faintly interlineated (the cave, in the Benison's fantasy merryland, being of course female), while the second proclaims 'May Prick nor Purse Never Fail You. B.B.A. 1732'. The third small seal reads 'Sight Improves Pleasure B.B.A.,' and makes clear what is meant by the legend by showing a heart with vulva within it. The dates in these legends are not those of manufacture – there would be little point in dating a brass seal matrix in this way as it would be intended for use over many years. Rather they commemorate the year of the Benison's foundation. The fact that all three seals define the institution as not only the Benison but as the Anstruther Benison (B.B.A.) indicates that they date from the 1750s or later, as in was in that decade that an Edinburgh branch was founded, making distinction between the two bodies necessary.[61]

None of these small seals are found attached to diplomas, so their purpose is unknown, but four larger seals exist attached to diplomas on ribbons. The earliest (on a diploma dated 1746) displays a horizontal phallus across the centre, with a small bag suspended from it by a ribbon, and an anchor below it. Along the phallus are the words 'Beggar's Benison'. Only one impression is known, and the seal looks incomplete, the space above the phallus being left empty. Moreover its dating is dubious – the diploma also bears a text dated 1750.[62] Nonetheless this is evidently the first time that the two main elements of the Benison's 'coat of arms' or badge appear. The phallus needs little explanation – though the symbolic significance of the bag needs separate discussion below. The anchor was the coat of arms of Anstruther Easter, but may also have carried for the Benison the meaning given it by the French Order of Felicity as a euphemism for having sex.

This phallus and anchor seal was the prototype for a pair of seals adopted in the 1750s. In one a large anchor stands behind the horizontal phallus, while in the other the anchor stands above the genitals, while below is a castle and the words *Nisi Dominus Frustra*.[63] The castle and motto were the symbols of Edinburgh, and the anchor is placed above the castle to indicate that the Edinburgh branch of the Benison, which had now emerged, was subordinate to Anstruther. The 'Edinburgh' seal is found first on a diploma dated 1755, and though no copy of the 'Anstruther' version is known before 1763 this may be put down to accidents of survival, for the two are clearly designed as a pair.

The last of the Benison seals not only brought a new intricacy of symbolism, but a modern reference. The seal commemorated a particular event, the building of a lighthouse on the Isle of May in 1816.[64] 'Rectus 1816 Ins[ula] Mai' reads the inscription. The classic shape for the lighthouse which evolved in the eighteenth century was of course splendidly phallic, and, given the place the Isle of May held in Benison lore, the idea of having that female merryland surmounted by such a building must have been stimulating. Unfortunately, the lighthouse commissioners did not considered the needs of the Benison fantasists, and produced a most un-phallic construction, much more to the taste of Sir Walter Scott than the Beggars – a little Gothic castle with battlements and a low tower carrying the light.

Whoever conceived the new seal was undaunted. Symbolically, lighthouses were phallic, so the seal shows a proper free-standing tower-lighthouse on the Isle of May, and to hell with reality. It is truly, phallic, 'rectus' – upright or erect. However, such simple symbolism was not enough for the designer. The lighthouse is depicted with a cleft at its base, representing the vulva. Male and female genitals are combined. Even this was not enough. On each side the lighthouse is faced by pelicans, like heraldic supporters on a coat of arms.[65]

Test Platter and Breath Horn

For ritual purposes the most important of the Beggar's Benison arte-facts were the test platter and the breath horn. The platter is an ordinary pewter domestic plate, but a legend on the rim proclaims it to be the property of 'The Beggar's Benison, Anstruther, 1732', while round the bowl is engraved the biblical reference to 'The Way of a Man with a Maid.'[66] In the centre appears a penis (again with the purse attached), symbolically depicted inside vulva, with the inscription 'Test Platter'. Thus its use is clear. This was – in fact or in ritual simulation – the dish on which initiates displayed their phalluses, and perhaps onto which they and other members ejaculated while masturbating. Just in case this was not sufficiently obvious, at some point a crudely scratched inscription on the underside of the platter asserts obscenely how 'many a six inch prick in full bloom' had performed on it.[67]

Helpfully, two makers marks also appear stamped on the underside. 'Graham and Wardrop' reveals the dish was made after 1774, when these two men qualified in their craft in Glasgow. By great good fortune for the historian trying to date the object their firm was highly unusual in that it often added a sort of advertising stamp to its wares. The firm evidently specialised in sales to the American Colonies, and sent them good wishes through a stamp showing a merchant ship under full sail with legends like 'Success to the British Colonies.' Then the unfortunate business of American independence made an advertising re-launch advisable. 'Success to the United States of America' was substituted, and this duly appears on the stamp on the test platter. Thus its manufacture is pushed forward to 1783 or later.

The novice is said to have been accompanied to the test platter with 'four puffs of the Breath-Horn'.[68] Horn music was obviously appropriate. The silver-plated instrument bears a legend in a diamond-shaped panel enclosed in vulva. No phallus was necessary, as the horn already was one. The breath of the horn in this sense was presumably semen, the puffs simulating ejaculation. The legend reads 'My breath is strange', followed by references to passages in the *Book of Leviticus* relating to ritual washing after sexual intercourse.[69] However, the quotation itself is from *the Book of Job* (xix, 17): 'My breath is strange to my wife, though I intreated for the children's sake of mine own body'. This Authorised Version translation is obscure, and the Douai Bible (the English translation used by Roman Catholics) is no clearer: 'My wife hath abhorred my breath, and I entreated the children of my womb'. Neither the Job nor the Leviticus texts seem entirely appropriate to the Beggars' proceedings, and it may be that what attracted the Beggars to talk of strange breath was that the word 'strange' has sexual connotations in the Authorised Version of the Old Testament. Consorting with 'strange women' is repeatedly denounced, but made to sound distinctly alluring: 'For the lips of a strange woman drop as an honeycomb, and her mouth is smoother than oil'; 'Thine eyes shall behold strange women, and thine heart shall utter perverse things'.[70] More widely, 'strange woman' had come in English to indicate a prostitute. Maybe adding strangeness to breath as semen added somehow to the naughtiness.

Punch Bowls and Wine Glasses

Turning from examination of ritual objects designed to accompany masturbation to ones designed for social drinking brings respite in that at least the purposes the latter were put to are more acceptable. But no relief from genitals. Indeed it brings them in full colour paint instead of chaste engraving.

At least five Benison punch bowls of Chinese porcelain survive. Three date from about 1775, and may have been part of the same order sent to Canton. Two of them belonged to Benison members, while the other belonged to the club itself. On the outside of the club bowl, two floral bouquets alternate with two Benison badges, with splendid gold legends announcing the club's name on a broad dark blue band, with the 'Anstruther' phallus and anchor inside it. A bow of pink ribbon tops these medallions, and one also appears on the inside, at the bottom. An identical bowl is at Kedleston Hall in Derbyshire, the home of the Curzon family. Nathaniel Curzon (later 2nd Lord Scarsdale) was admitted to the Benison in 1775.[71] The third in this group of bowls descended in a Yorkshire family of Wentworths, and was probably the property of Sir Thomas Wentworth (5th baronet). The bowl is part of a whole service of Wentworth armorial porcelain, and the Benison badge appears on the inside. But on the outside it is replaced by the coat arms of the Wentworth family.[72] It is a remarkable indication of the attitude of an aristocrat to membership of the Benison that the club's badge should thus be displayed alongside the arms which proclaimed the family's honour and antiquity. No doubt the bowl was only produced on special occasions, but it was a deliberate affront to conventional values. Libertinism and and lineage are proclaimed side by side, and perhaps the design also provided a joke: Wentworth's guests (after the ladies had withdrawn) would have had to drink deeply before the level of the punch fell low enough for them to see, as if in a drunken vision, the obscene Benison badge leering up at them from the depths. Two other Benison bowls are known to exist, but their whereabouts are unknown.[73]

From the bowls, members of the Benison ladled their punch into their glasses. Three Benison wine glasses survive, and can be dated to the 1770s by their fashionable enamelled decoration. They all bear the badge of the Edinburgh Benison, with the anchor of Anstruther over the castle of Edinburgh, separated by a cheerfully colourful phallus.[74]

Pandora's Box and the Benison Bible

The artefacts belonging to the club were stored in a large wooden chest adorned with a brass plaque depicting vulva and inscribed 'Pandora's Box for Champions Bold. Open Sesame. Beggar's Bennison, Castle of Dreel, Anstruther'. The earliest use of the phrase 'open sesame' (here crudely referring to more that just the box lid) recorded in the *Oxford English Dictionary* come in the 1780s, and this suggests an approximate date for the box.[75] Pandora was, in classical mythology, the first and most beautiful of women, and with a name meaning 'all-giving' she naturally aroused the attention of pornographers, though the gifts released from her 'box' were both evil and good – in the most crude interpretation, sexual joy and venereal disease.[76] She had been the subject of the frontispiece of *A new description of*

Merryland in 1740, and this or a similar pornographic use of her name may have given the Beggar's Benison and Merryland inspiration to name the chest in which they hoarded their smutty goodies after her.[77] At some time the brass plate had been unscrewed from the lid, and thereafter it was kept within the box. Matthew Conolly or one of his predecessors had evidently decided that keeping a plain locked wooden box was more discreet than having one proclaiming obscenity.

Even the Beggar's Benison copy of the Bible did not escape genital decoration.[78] The keyhole on the brass hasp which locks it lies at the centre of two sets of engraved vulva crossed at right-angles (guess what the 'key' to open the lock would be?) with the legend 'Lignum Scientiae. Boni & Mali,' referring to 'tree of knowledge of good and evil' in the Garden of Eden – a biblical citation echoing of the classical theme of good and evil in 'Pandora's Box'. Perhaps the toast 'Love's key-hole'[79] helped inspire the design.

The Bible, an edition published in Edinburgh in 1744, may be the earliest of the surviving Benison relics, but according to an inscription (1820s or later) on the title page it was presented by Thomas, 6th earl of Kellie (1756–81). As he was not born until 1732 he could not have presented the Bible until many years after publication. A good deal of messing about at the back and front of the Bible has taken place, some blank pages being torn out, others inserted. Some of the entries on the pages now present are said to have been copied from loose scraps and fragments found in Pandora's Box – attempts at bawdy wit are mixed up with miscellaneous anecdotes about sex and obscene inanities. Notations in the text of the Bible are occasional and predictable. 'The way of a man with a maid' naturally receives attention. A degree of scholarly knowledge of genitalian history is however shown by some notes. The text 'put, I pray thee, thy hand under my thigh'[80] leads the annotator to comment that the Douai translation reads 'testicles' rather than 'thigh'. But, the manuscript note insists, the truly accurate translation is 'Take hold of my Genitals'. This, it is explained, shows how the genitals had once been regarded as objects not of libertinism but of veneration as the instruments of procreation. An oath said while holding the genitals of the man you were swearing it to was the most binding of all promises.

A final feature of the Benison Bible presents problems. Copies of twenty-nine coats of arms of leading Scottish nobles, cut from some reference work on the peerage produced around 1800, are glued to the back of the title page. Presumably the intention was to suggest that they were all members of the club.

Phallicism and the Benison Relics

That the men who made up the membership of the Beggar's Benison, obsessed with the demands of their libidos, should have taken the phallus as their symbol is hardly surprising, for it had been an obvious symbol since humans first evolved such things. It has been repeatedly suggested since the eighteenth century that phallicism lies at the roots of all religions, and it has been said that 'Phallicism, however interpreted, would seem to be of central importance in any society, ancient or modern, eastern or western'.[81] Most obviously, the phallus stood for male libido, but it also stood for domination and assertion. The Greeks and others used phallic stones as boundary markers, a practice ultimately descended from male primates displaying on the edges of their territory. In cults featuring the phallus the worshippers often adopted submissive or 'female' behaviour, reflecting the behaviour of male primates who wished to avert attack by a dominant male by showing acceptance of his status.[82]

However, the phallus also had a range of less threatening connotations. It was a symbol of fertility and procreation, and was thus of central relevance to women as well as men. The theme of fertility made it symbolic of any increase or profit, and therefore of all commerce. It was a potent charm to avert the evil eye. And, of course, it was the obvious symbol of sexual pleasure. It could also symbolise female as well as male sexual desire (or at least a male artists interpretation of what it was – or should be).

References in literature, both ancient and modern, to the phallus as a symbol were plentiful, and easily available as inspirations to Benison members. In English Restoration verse, for example, genitals of both sexes are sometimes described as engaged in combat virtually independent of their owners,[83] and equations of the phallus with political power were commonplace. Perhaps significantly, nearly all the English phallic verses published in the first half of the eighteenth century appeared in the decade before the Benison was founded, so there was no shortage of inspiration for the Beggars' adoption of it. If inspiration veiled in the respectability of Latin was required, the ancient collection of highly obscene verses on Priapus, the phallic god, was easily available, having been edited by one of the greatest of classical scholars, Joseph Scaliger (d.1609), as well as the obscene poems of Martial, Catullus and others.

For graphic or sculpted depictions also the Benison would have found inspiration in the classical past, supposedly superior in civilisation to the modern world. On Greek vases the phallus played its natural role in scenes of sexual activity, and detached phalluses often lived lives of their own. Free-range phalluses scuttled around on legs, phallus-birds strutted proudly, winged phalluses flew past. Often they accompany scenes of women engaged in various tasks, and seem to indicate women's thoughts about sex – the equivalent of the cartoon bubble that says 'thinks ...' These are not threatening or dominating images. Modest in dimensions, they sometimes seem like domestic pets. In one scene a flourishing crop of phalluses grows in a garden, with a woman carefully watering them. But the phallus could, escaping the confines of vases, be much more assertive, and vast in scale, as in the avenue of stone phalluses on the Island of Delos.[84]

The almost playful phallus of the Greek vase was only occasionally used by the Romans, but the image of the phallus was nonetheless very common. Again it played its role in paintings of sexual activity, and a number of gods were, at least in some of their roles, depicted with erect penises. Statues of Priapus, the ugly little god with a vast phallus, commonly stood in gardens. Genuinely venerated as a guardian of crops, he nonetheless was the constant subject of ridicule in verse because of his grotesque endowment. The secrets rites of Bacchus/Dionysus celebrated the phallus as well as wine, in the age-old combination of sex and alcohol. As a detached entity, a carved or painted phallus could be a votive offering to a god, and most commonly it was deployed as a charm to avert the evil eye and thus ensure good luck. It could form an amulet, worn to protect an individual, or appear, carved or scratched or painted, on walls in the street or at entrances of houses. There was no perception of obscenity or even directly of sexuality in it. The phallus was simply an important, and entirely benign, item in a wide repertoire of accepted symbols. However when one phallus proclaims *Hic habitat felicitas*, 'here dwells happiness',[85] double-entendre is doubtless deliberate: happiness dwells in the house on whose wall the phallus is depicted, but happiness also in the sexual role employment of the symbol.

How much would it have been possible for members of the Benison to have known of the use of the phallus as a symbol in ancient civilisations is hard to assess. Little about Greek usages would have been accessible, but Roman obsessions with carved phalluses could be traced in the publications and collections of antiquarians. Indeed shortly before the Benison was founded, Scotland produced its own Roman phallus, a stone carving intended as a votive offering. After its discovery it came into the hands of Sir John Clerk of Penicuik, the foremost Scottish antiquarian and collector of his day. The piece was regarded as notable enough to be described in print in 1732 – 'a remarkable *Priapus* or fallus' – though the accompanying illustration is utterly fatuous as the engraver has added a large leaf covering the phallus, the only feature that makes the stone of interest.[86]

Quite possibly the Benison knew of the Penicuik phallus, for one of its leading members was acquainted with Clerk and shared his antiquarian interests. On one occasion at least (1741) he corresponded with Clerk on the subject of Roman antiquities, in a letter that indicates that they were on familiar terms.[87] This was Robert Lumsdaine of Innergellie. In 1739 he is listed as a member of the Beggar's Benison, and from 1752 until his death in 1761 he was sovereign of the Edinburgh branch of the club. His eldest son, James, became sovereign of the main (Anstruther) Benison in 1773 and remained in office for nearly half a century, dying in 1820. A scenario of Lumsdaine having visited Sir John Clerk's collection, been impressed by the Roman phallus, and using it as respectable ancient authority to cite in urging the Benison to adopt the phallus as a symbol is attractive – but highly speculative. Moreover, it would not explain the most notable features of the way the Benison used the phallus as a symbol.

This is partly a matter of orientation. In both Greek and Roman carvings depicting phalluses, they are usually shown as vertical. In the Benison badge the phallus is horizontal – and it has a bag or purse suspended from it. The purse-phallus association is explained at one level by the 'king and the beggar-maid' story: sex paid for in gold and the blessing on prick and purse. But there is much more to it than this, for there was one particular type of invocation of the phallus in Roman culture in which the phallus did often appear horizontal, did have objects hung from it, and was associated with a purse or bag.

In shops bronze phalluses were suspended from chains in a horizontal position, often with little bells hanging from them. These *tintinnabula* were good-luck charms like the carved vertical phalluses on house walls, and they specifically invoked Mercury as god of commerce. A *tintinnabulum* in a shop would, it was hoped, lead to business success. Mercury is best known as the messenger god, with his winged helmet, sandals and caduceus (winged staff entwined with serpents) as his attributes. Passing messages was essential to all sorts of commerce, and indeed all sorts of human transaction. He facilitated love affairs through presiding over the making of assignations – and indeed could come to be seen as a procurer, a pimp-god arranging commercial deals in sex. As the god of commerce as opposed to communication in general Mercury's symbols were often a phallus and a purse, both in different ways symbolising profit.[88] A remarkable wall painting at Pompeii depicts Mercury holding a pair of scales and weighing his vast phallus against a purse.[89]

The phallus and purse were the symbols not only of sexual encounters that were commercial in the sense of monetary payment being involved for services rendered. More generally, sex was commerce in the sense of being a mutually advantageous exchange. Sex brought not just physical satisfaction but the creation of profit in the form of children. Through sex men went forth and multiplied, the ambition of anyone engaged in trading. The sex-commerce equation can already be seen in Greek art. In scenes of sexual activity on Greek vases a purse is often depicted as a courtship gift of man to woman, or is simply alongside scenes of heterosexual activity, indicating the exchange the encounter involved.

The Benison badge depicts the phallus and bag of Mercury, which are also the prick and purse of the beggar-maid's blessing. Having invoked the Garden of Eden, Medieval monks and James V in their mythology, the inventive Beggars have now summoned up a classical god as their patron. The realisation of this immediately throws light on the what otherwise seems the rather odd coupling of the club's twin obsessions, free sex and free trade. Mercury as the facilitator of trade was the natural patron of smugglers, and through his phallus and role as facilitator of sexual encounters a most appropriate patron for free sex. The game in the Benison diploma and code of institutes of pretending to disguise sex by referring to it in terms of trade, while really standing for both, simultaneously becomes a play with the cult of Mercury. The Benison badge it not just the crude obscenity that it appears at first sight, but an appeal to ancient religion. The appeal was not of course a matter of belief, but of symbolic meaning. Mars was often short-hand for war, Venus for love, and so on. To the Benison Mercury stood for sex and smuggling. That he had inherited from Hermes, his Greek predecessor, the reputation for being essentially benign and un-warlike (rare qualities in divinities) and for being a trickster were perhaps added attractions.

How certain is the identification of the Benison badge with attributes of Mercury? Two difficulties need to be pointed out. One is that while Mercury's horizontal phallus often had bells hung from it, there appear to be no known examples of his bag or purse being thus attached. However, two full-figure Mercuries from Pompeii come close (one painted, one bronze), by depicting the god holding his bag against his phallus, making the direct sex/trade connection in a way similar to the Benison badge.[90] It is plausible to imagine the Benison developing the symbolism a little, tying phallus and purse together to indicate that sex and trade are not just linked but inextricably bound together. The other difficulty in accepting that the Benison badge derives from the invocation of the Mercury in the *tintinnabula* is chronological. The *tintinnabula* are known mainly from the excavations that began at Pompeii in the mid-eighteenth century. The Benison's earliest known use of the badge dates from 1755, and this is too early for any knowledge of discoveries at Pompeii to be plausibly argued to have reached Anstruther. However, 'obscene' Roman antiquities had been attracting the interest of collectors and scholars since the Renaissance,[91] and it is conceivable that Robert Lumsdaine had travelled on the Continent and studied antiquities there (virtually nothing is known of his life beyond his Benison interests), and had seen relevant artefacts.

Mercury/Hermes, the trickster-god, has, moreover, a final trick in store which makes the argument for his identification as the patron of the Benison overwhelmingly. In one of his bewildering variety of roles, he was the god of masturbation – and the philosopher who claimed this position for him is unique in having used masturbation to demonstrate a philosophical point. The conclusion seems inescapable that some early member of the Benison's classical studies had brought him to the works of the Greek writer of the first century AD, Dio Chrysostum. One of Chrsysostum's discourses or orations was devoted to the fifth century BC philosopher, Diogenes, who had sought to cast off what he saw as the slavery of social convention and the distortions of civilisation, and lead the simplest of lives, devoted to practical good. He believed that all natural functions should be performed in public. Money and power he despised. Competitive pursuit of sexual partners was destructive, the thing that cost men the most trouble and the most money. All this was unnecessary, for he himself 'found Aphrodite everywhere, without expense'. When challenged, he demonstrated what he meant by masturbating. Then, speaking to this text, he argued that the prolonged horrors of the Trojan War could have been diverted if men instead of feuding over Helen of Troy had dealt with their demanding libidos in his way. 'Make love, not war' would have not made sense to Diogenes, for conflict was inherent in love. 'Masturbate for peace,' however, could well have been his slogan.

On the origins of masturbation Diogenes said 'in a joking way' that 'this sort of intercourse was a discovery made by Pan'. The half-goat god of shepherds, the son of Mercury / Hermes, had been devastated by the desertion of his mistress Echo, which deprived him of a sexual outlet. 'Hermes took pity on his distress [and], since he was his son, taught him the trick. Pan, when he had learned his lesson, was relieved of his great misery; and the shepherds learned the habit from him.'[92] Shepherds, often leading solitary lives in the mountains with their herds for months at a time, were in particular need of the technique.

The Beggars conceived of themselves as followers of Diogenes, beneficiaries of Mercury's gift to humanity. They masturbated 'in public' – at least before as large a public as it was possible without being arrested – both to demonstrate their contempt for the artificial conventions that distorted society and to gain sexual release in a way that was cheap and did not cause rivalries and tension. In their bitterness at the society they lived in, they like Diogenes found in rejection of sexual convention a symbol of a much wider rejection of established values. But whereas for Diogenes masturbation was the complete answer to the distractions of the libido, the Beggars continued to dream the dream of willing women. Diogenes would have laughed at this folly, but a philosopher who could laugh instead of rage at human folly was just what the Benison needed.

Diogenes's alleged foray into the theology of masturbation established Hermes / Mercury as the patron deity of the practice, and of the Benison. A remarkable public, though disguised, symbol hinting at this survives. A few miles from Anstruther Robert Lumsdaine, antiquarian and leading member of the Benison, dedicated his house to Mercury. He had bought the estate of Innergellie in about 1730. In 1740, the year after the Benison had reorganised itself through the drafting of its code of institutes and diploma, he built a substantial new house, Innergellie House. Its entrance-front has recently been described as 'a remarkable display of master mason's gothic',[93] a phrase suggesting a rather provincial style devised by a local craftsman rather than a professional architect. The most remarkable feature of this front, however, is not gothic but classical, and should not be interpreted as an oddity of provincial design but as a feature mischievously stipulated by the owner.

Above the door of Innergellie House Lumsdaine's coat of arms is carved, a common (though by that time rather old fashioned) way of announcing ownership. Walking under it, one entered the domain of the Lumsdaines. But above the arms stands a statue of Mercury. To place another symbol above the family arms was extremely rare, and declares dedication to and subordination to whatever was symbolised. This is shown by the only other instance in Scotland of thus capping family arms at the main entrance of a house. Huntly (then Strathbogie) Castle in Aberdeenshire was blown up in 1594 as a reprisal for the Gordon family's continued commitment to Catholicism after Protestant Reformation. But the Gordons were undeterred. The castle was rebuilt, and in a elaborate heraldic doorway the family coat of arms was submissively surmounted by the royal arms. But then they in turn were defiantly surmounted by Catholic religious symbols. It was an affirmation that this was a castle of the king and the marquis of Huntly, but they in turn were subservient to a Catholic God.[94]

Robert Lumsdaine chose to invoke a pagan god as his domestic patron rather than Christian faith. Obviously he could not display Mercury-as-phallus-with-bag, the guise that he takes in Benison symbolism, nor as Mercury-with-prominent-phallus, as in many ancient depictions, so the god appears in his 'respectable' messenger-god guise with winged helmet and caduceus. In this form he is perfectly reputable. Eyebrows would indeed be raised by the statute, but not because it was Mercury but because of its position. It was no doubt dismissed as a harmless eccentricity of the owner (added to by the fact that it was made of lead, a material usually reserved for statues used as garden ornaments). Only Lumsdaine's cronies in the Benison would enjoy the joke, that the entirely respectable image was disguise for the god of masturbation, of the commerce of sex and free (smuggled) trade. More than two and a half centuries later, Lumsdaine's little trick with the trickster-god still works. Displaying the clean but meaning the obscene, Mercury still gazes over the fields of Fife.

With the 1816 'Lighthouse' seal inspired by the Isle of May the Benison abandoned their horizontal phallus for a vertical one. Clearly the lighthouse theme made this necessary, but again the Benison called upon antiquity to give added value to a symbol. Here the mythology is not classical but Hindu. In Hinduism the god Shiva is usually worshipped in the form of a *lingam*, a phallic pillar often standing on vulva (*yoni*) as a base. On many *lingam*, the *yoni* is shown as a cleft on the side of the phallus, as on this seal. The message is that the genitals of the two sexes form a single whole, which represents the totality of existence. Though in earthly representations the *lingam* of Shiva has to be represented as finite, there is in reality no spatial limit to it. The Benison is indicating the ultimate in phallic boasting. This bizarre mixture of civil engineering and Eastern philosophy as an explanation for the lighthouse seal leaves the supporting pelicans on the seal to be interpreted. Perhaps they are drawn from Christian symbolism. In medieval legend the pelican pecks its breast so its chicks can feed on its blood. This came to symbolise sacrifice by parents out of love for offspring, and the pelican was therefore sometimes used as a symbol of Christ's sacrifice, the shedding of His blood for mankind. In the seal it may be that the pelicans are sustaining life as represented by the phallus, holding it upright. And, of course, the phallus is itself a sustainer of life – and so indeed is a lighthouse. When it came to symbolism the Beggars were lacking in high seriousness but not in ingenuity. As will be seen when the Wig Club is discussed, its phallicism was much more straightforward than the Benison's. It played with mock foundation myths, but a phallus was never more than a blunt reference to libido, with no fooling around with allusions to Mercury or Shiva.

The Lure of the Phallus

Eighteenth-century fascination with the phallus as a symbol was not confined to the Benison and the Wig. The interest taken in 'obscene' ancient artefacts since the Renaissance has already been mentioned. Usually, as with the two Scottish clubs, discretion ensured that such interests did not cause scandal, for pushing them into the public domain could be risky. A scandal of the 1790s must have brought home to the clubs the extent to which they were playing with fire. The incident arose from a discovery made in 1781 by the British envoy to the kingdom of Naples, William Hamilton (who had not yet achieved eminence among cuckolds in British history through his wife's affair with Horatio Nelson). In the church of the remote village of Isernia he found wax replicas of penises (erect and otherwise), which were commonly given as votive offerings. The church was dedicated to the physician saints Cosmas and Damian, and the afflicted made offerings of models of the parts of the bodies that required cures. St Cosmas had come to be regarded as particularly effective in dealing with problems of the male genitals, and above all with impotency – most of the penile offerings were made by women whose husbands had failed to make them pregnant. In the context of medieval religious practices there was nothing remarkable about this. The penises symbolised a desire for healing of the organ, and there was nothing obscene about them in the minds of the peasants who offered them. In some parts of southern Italy, indeed, similar practices continued into the later twentieth century. But to eighteenth-century sensibilities, the Isernia offerings seemed totally unacceptable. Greek and Roman phalluses, pagan in context and sterilised by antiquity, were one thing, modern Christian ones quite another. The ecclesiastical authorities quickly intervened and suppressed such offerings when their existence was publicised by Hamilton.[95]

The envoy however was excited by his find, for both antiquarian and sectarian reasons. He was a zealous seeker after antiquities, and thought he had found a survival of an ancient cult. Moreover, he shared the common Protestant belief that in many respects Catholicism was based on corrupt pagan practices. The Isernian relics 'proved' not only that Catholicism contained remnants of paganism, but shockingly that it contained survivals of the obscenely phallic cult of Priapus. In reality of course in Isernia there was no priapic celebration of the potency and power of the male genitals; on the contrary the offerings were intended to help restore performance which was lacking.[96]

Hamilton wrote an account the discovery, using his Protestant interpretation of them as evidence of the pagan roots of Catholicism, and in 1786 this was published along with a work by another English antiquarian, Richard Payne Knight, on the worship of Priapus. It was Knight's contribution to the joint work that was to cause scandal. He went much further than Hamilton in a number of respects. He showed what was regarded as an undue enthusiasm for his subject, even hinting at recognition that the subject was not merely of earnest scholarly interest but entertaining, and whereas Hamilton exploited the Isernian finds to discredit Catholicism, Knight indicated that all Christian faith had phallic elements in its origins. Finally, Knight's work was richly illustrated with phallic images from a number of cultures, including a heap of Isernian penises – Hamilton had conveniently presented some to the British Museum (with an instruction 'keep hands off' indicating his own bawdy humour).[97]

The book was sponsored by the Society of Dilettanti, a club of rich aristocratic Englishmen dedicated to classical studies which had sidelines in ritual, fancy costumes, libertinism and atheism. All members had to have visited Italy, and it was widely accepted that the Grand Tour made by young gentlemen that culminated there provided a sexual education as well as the study of antiquities. Sir Francis Dashwood, creator of the 'Hell-Fire' Medmenham Monks of the 1750s, was prominent in the society, and members were suspected of gathering evidence from the classical past to justify their inclinations towards sexual promiscuity.[98] By appropriate coincidence, the Dilettanti Society had been founded in 1732, the same year as the Beggar's Benison. Compared to the Beggars' raucous celebration of the phallus, the Dilettanti's interest was rather more scholarly, though the report that a wax phallus was 'laid on the table at their solemn meetings'[99] indicates that the organ was regarded as more than a detail in ancient art. The wax phallus may indeed have been from Hamilton's collection, for the society was intrigued and perhaps mischievously delighted by Hamilton's finds and the priapic thesis of Payne Knight (also a member of the Dilettanti).[100]

There was no attempt to keep Payne Knight's book secret, but as copies were distributed to members and not sold publicly it was some years before it was widely enough known for enraged reaction to emerge. The delay did not work to Knight's advantage. Possibly reaction in 1786 would have been limited, but by 1794, when the scandal broke, horror at the excesses of the French Revolution had led to strong reaction in favour of conventional religion and morality. For the Dilettanti to be spreading phallic mischief in the name of classical studies was now regarded as debauchery and subversion. Condemnation of Knight was extreme and universal.[101]

The episode is indicative both of the growing interest in priapism and other ancient cults in the eighteenth century and of potential hostile reaction to it. The Dilettantis and the Beggars had in common a seizing on ancient cults as justifications for free sex. Payne Knight presumably never knew of the Benison, but would have been fascinated by it. A French scholar working in the same field, however, came across the club, and leapt to exactly the same conclusion that William Hamilton had done on making his discovery at Isernia. Here was proof that a form of the ancient cult of Priapus lingered on. Jacques Antoine Dulaure had somehow came into possession of an old Benison diploma. His conclusion was that

> One finds in England, and the officers of the navy offer an example, remnants of this cult [of the phallus] in the form of a mysterious society, called *the Most Ancient and Most Puissant Order of the Beggar's Benison and Merryland*, of which in 1761 Sir Louis Chamber was the grand master. The seal of this society shows, as the principal piece, a *Phallus* well characterised: above is an anchor, and below a fortress. One does not know why this society, of which I have a diploma in front of my eyes, and which wishes for the prosperity of industry, commerce, manufactures, and freedom from customs duties and other dues, takes for its symbol a formerly sacred symbol, today so indecent. That is the secret of the initiates.

The Frenchman was thus bewildered by his discovery of the Benison. His grasp of idiomatic English was insufficient for him to discern the double-entendres in the diploma which lightly disguised the fact that it was as much about free sex as free trade. He noticed the castle and anchor on the seal, though understandably without realising that they symbolised Edinburgh and Anstruther – and he took the anchor to indicate that the Benison had a naval connection. But he overlooked the association of the bag with the phallus that might have told him that the connection between the sexual connotations of the phallus and a text devoted to free trade was commerce, the realm of Mercury.[102]

Another half century, and another writer showed recognition of the possible relevance of the Benison to debate on phallic cults, but did so in a deliberately obscure way. Charles Rogers used a word that had never appeared in a dictionary to describe the Benison's activities: they were 'Isernian'. He stood in the long tradition of belief that things obscene should be referred to in such terms that that only the highly educated (and therefore, it was presumed, incorruptible) could understand, for here only readers who had been swatting up on phallic studies would have been able to understand his coded reference to the fact that the Benison's activities were phallic.[103]

Notes

1 *Records*, 8, 10; *Supplement*, 16.

2 *Records*, 8.

3 'Copy of Sir Walter Scott's diploma. Musomanik Society, Anstruther,' *Scottish Notes and Queries*, vi (1892–4), 44; *Records*, 8.

4 W.J. Anderson, 'J.F.S. Gordon and his contribution to the history of Scottish Catholicism,' *Innes Review*,' xvi (1965), 18–26.

5 H. Fairnie, *The Fife coast from Queensferry to Fifeness* (Cupar, [1861]), 180–1. See also A. Campbell, *Notes by the way; a descriptive, historical and biographical account of Fife and Kinross* (Ayr, [1880s?]), 30.

6 *The Beggar's benison: or, a hero without a name. A Clydesdale story* (2 vols., London, 1866). The BL catalogue and the *DNB* attribute authorship to George Mills.

7 *Notes and Queries*, 5th series, xii, 48 (19 July 1879). The identification of Craven with 'Orc' is based on the fact that in 1897 he was to write to J. Macnaught Campbell, who then had possession of the Benison relics 'B.B. I shall be glad to hear from you in regard to this.' Cryptic, but it seems that Craven the Orc was trying to acquire the relics for himself: BBWCC, 5 Aug 1897, Craven to Campbell.

8 *Notes and Queries*, 5th series, xii 98 (2 Aug. 1879).

9 Alexander Fergusson, *The Hon. Henry Erskine, lord advocate for Scotland* (Edinburgh, 1882), 144–54; Rogers, *Social life*, ii, 412–18.

10 *Records* and *Supplement* (2 vols., Anstruther, 1892). The two parts are usually bound together as a single volume, and a reprint, with a preface by Alan Bold (Edinburgh, 1982) treats the two as a single work. However, as the two items have different paginations they have been cited separately below.

11 L.C. Jones, *The clubs of the Georgian rakes* (New York, 1942), 175–201, 205–9, 230–4.

12 BBWCC, Correspondence between J. Macnaught Campbell and J. Lewis, 1892; Jones, *Clubs*, 206. The address 174 Wardour Street was occupied by a tailor, a boot and shoe factor, and a second-hand book seller. The last seems the most probable as Lewis's 'front.' *Post Office London Directory, 1893*, 709. P.J. Kearney, *The private case. An annotated bibliography of the erotica collection in the British (Museum) Library* (London, 1981), 220 states that the *Records* were printed 'apparently by Leonard Smithers, in London.'

13 *Biographical dictionary of eminent men of Fife* (Cupar and Edinburgh, 1866); *Fifiana: or, memorials of the East of Fife* (Glasgow, 1869).

14 *Records*, 6–7.

15 For known copies of the diploma see Appendix 2.

16 The equation of free trade and free sexual access also appears, generations later in the designation of open-crotch knickers: they were referred to as being of the '"free trade" pattern,' J. Barke and S.G. Smith (eds.), *The merry muses of Caledonia*, ed. (London, 1959), 31.

17 Edinburgh City Library, Y DA1820 G44 (Accession no. 70638A). The diploma text printed in Rogers, *Social life*, ii, 417 omits some passages of the standard text, but this is probably simply the result of Rogers censoring some of the most explicit double entendres.

18 Quoted in V.L. Bullough, 'Prostitution and reform in eighteenth-century England,' R.P. Mccubbin (ed.), *'Tis nature's fault. Unauthorised sexuality during the eighteenth century* (Cambridge, 1987), 63.

19 Records, 7–8

20 G. Legman, *The horn book. Studies in erotic folklore and bibliography* (London, 1964 & 1970), 209.

21 I. Disraeli, *Curiousities of literature* (New edn, 2 vols., London, 1863), ii, 269–70, citing *Recueil pièces du regiment de la calotte* ('L'an de 'ere Calotine 7726' [Paris, 1726])

22 Legman, *Horn book*, 208, citing Jean Hervez [Raoul Vèze], *Les sociéties d'amour au XVIIIe siècle* (Paris, 1906), 176–205. J.E.S. Tuckett, 'L'Ordre de la Félicité', *Ars Quatuor Coronatorum*, xxxiii (1920), 82–111.

23 Hervez, *Les sociéties*, 182–3, 189, 193, 204.

24 *Records*, 2–6.

25 E.J. Bristow, *Vice and vigilance. Purity movements in Britain since 1700* (London, 1977), 29–30.

26 *Supplement*, 16–32.

27 BBWCC, letter from Gordon to J. Macnaught Campbell, 18 Oct 1897.

28 Legman, *Horn book*, 187, 441, alleged that toasts very similar to those of the Benison were current (1960s) in the 'Horseman's Word,' a secret society of Scottish farm-workers.

29 *Supplement*, 71–3, reprinted in A. Bold (ed.), *The bawdy beautiful. The Sphere book of improper verse* (London, 1979), 34–5. As the verses refers to convicts transported to Botany Bay they must date from 1787 or later.

30 *Supplement*, 63–4, reprinted in Bold, *Bawdy beautiful*, 4–5.

31 *Supplement*, 23–4, 71–3.

32 *Supplement*, 23.

33 *Supplement*, 22.

34 *Supplement*, 57–80.

35 *Supplement*, 61–2.

36 *Supplement*, 60, 77–80.

37 *Supplement*, 82–91.

38 *Supplement*, 45–52.

39 *Supplement*, 33–43,

40 *Supplement*, 13–16.

41 Williams, *Dictionary*, ii, 1077–8.

42 *Supplement*, 5–7.

43 *Records*, 9–10.

44 *Supplement*, 20, 24.

45 Epstein, *Cleland*, 69–71, 219. The 'young gentleman' who acted as assistant pornographer in the production of *Fanny Hill* was Charles Carmichael, a younger brother of John, 3rd earl of Hyndford, who was a leading diplomat of the age: see D. Stevenson, 'A note on the Scotsman who inspired Fanny Hill', *Scottish Studies Review* (2001), 39–45.

46 Cleland, *Fanny Hill*, ed. Wagner, 194.

47 Williams, *Dictionary* records no usage of the word with a sexual meaning. However in the mid sixteenth century 'preposterous venus' had been used to describe the homosexual activities of native Americans. But this usage quickly died out, and it most unlikely that Cleland was aware of it. J. Goldberg, *Sodometries. Renaissance texts and modern sexualities* (Stanford, 1992), 182, 279n.4.

48 See the reference to 'base prepost'rous Venery' in *Almonds for parrots: or, a soft answer to a scurilous SATYR call'd, St James's Park, with a word or two in praise of condoms* (London, 1708), 4.

49 *Records*, 10.

50 *Records*, 8.

51 Thompson, *Unfit for modest ears*, 176–87.

52 Thompson, *Unfit for modest ears*, 182, describes as 'visual' a description of indecent statues, but these are imaginary statues fantasised in a pornographic work.

53 Williams, *Dictionary*, i, 36.

54 *A supplement to the Onania* (London, 1725), 169.

55 John Wilkes was entrusted with buying the cups, but he failed to pay the silversmith's bill for £20, Jones, *Clubs*, 129, citing *Public Advertiser* 29 Oct. 1772.

56 G.D.K. McCormick, *The Hell-Fire Club. The story of the amorous knights of Wycombe* (London, 1958), 122; F. Dashwood, *The Dashwoods of West Wycombe* (London, 1987), 39. I am grateful to Peter Lole for these references.

57 One, owned by the Dilettanti Society, is mentioned later in this chapter, two ceramic examples in Chapter 9. Though not directly parallel to the Benison and Wig material, some extremely obscene eighteenth-century tiles from a fireplace in an upper room of a London pub, the Old Cheshire Cheese, are relevant, as in all probability the room was used for the meetings of clubs which appreciated such bawdy decoration: M. Henig and K. Munby, 'Some tiles from the Old Cheshire Cheese, London', *Post-Medieval Archaeology*, 10 (1976), 156–9 and plates 21–2. I am grateful to Hazel Forsyth for this reference.

58 See Chapter 9 below for the Wig Club artefacts.

59 Appendix 3, nos. 1.1–1.2.

60 Appendix 3, nos. 1.3–1.7.

61 Appendix 3, 3.1–3.3.

62 Appendix 3, no. 3.3.1.

63 Appendix 3, nos. 3.4–3.5.

64 *Records*, 17, 18–19, is correct in stating that the duchess of Portland owned the Isle of May in 1816, but is wrong in claiming that her father, General John Scott of Balcomie, was sovereign of the Benison at the time. He had died forty years before, in 1775.

65 Appendix 3, no. 3.6.

66 *Proverbs*, xxx, 19.

67 Appendix 3, no. 4.1.

68 *Records*, 9.

69 Appendix 3, no. 5.1.

70 See *Proverbs*, ii, 16; v, 3, 20; vi, 24; xx, 16; xxii, 14; xxiii, 27, 33.

71 I am grateful for the expertise of David Howard on this point. Eighteenth century aristocratic habits can linger surprisingly long. Lord Scarsdale, who died in 2000, was wont to surprise guests at Kedleston Hall when he 'retired behind a 3 ft screen in the drawing room where he kept a … urinal, which he used whenever the urge came upon him,' *The Times*, 18 Aug 2000.

72 Appendix 3, nos. 6.1–6.3. David Howard tells me that he has come across a punch bowl decorated with an obscene illustration of the lower half of a female body, with the initials 'AFC,' perhaps denoting an unknown club. Here too the joke effect may be intended – gradual revelation of the obscene.

73 Appendix 3, nos. 6.4–6.5.

74 Appendix 3, nos. 7.1–7.3. Among the relics are also glasses shaped as phalluses

(Appendix 3, nos. 16.1, 16.2) but as these are specifically mentioned in Wig Club minutes they are assigned to it rather than the Benison.

75 Appendix 3, nos. 11.1, 11.2.

76 Williams, *Dictionary*, ii, 990–1.

77 Kearney, *History of erotic literature*, 56–7.

78 Appendix 3, no. 8.1.

79 *The buck's merry companion* (1760s?), 143.

80 *Genesis*, xlvii, 29.

81 G.S. Rousseau, 'Sorrows of Priapus,' *Sexual underworlds of the Enlightenment*, ed. R. Porter and G.S. Rousseau (Manchester, 1987), 123. For a cheerful introduction to the subject see J. Kirkup, 'Phallic worship: Some personal meditations on a sacred theme,' in A. Bold, *The sexual dimension in literature* (London, 1982), 145–62.

82 W. Burkert, *Homo Necans. The anthropology of Ancient Greek sacrificial ritual and myth* (Chicago, 1983), 58, 69.

83 Thompson, *Unfit for modest ears*, 121–3.

84 J. Boardman & E. La Rocca, *Eros in Greece* (London, 1978), 46–9, 157; M.F. Kilmer, *Greek erotica on Attic red-figure vases* (London, 1993), 193–7; J. Boardman, 'The Phallos-Bird in Archaic and Classic Greek art,' *Revue Archéologique*, ii (1992), 227–42.

85 C. Johns, *Sex or symbol. Erotic images of Greece and Rome* (Austin, Texas, 1982), 62–75; M. Grant, *Erotic art in Pompeii* (London, 1975), 108–9.

86 J. Horsley, *Britannia Romana* (London, 1742); Johns, *Sex or symbol*, 21.

87 NAS, GD18/5056.

88 Grant, *Erotic art*, 134–5, 138, 140–1, 155; Johns, *Sex or symbol*, 52–4, 67–70.

89 Johns, *Sex or symbol*, colour plate 6. This well-known painting is usually interpreted as Priapus, but the association of purse and phallus and the caduceus beside the figure make it clear that it is Mercury.

90 Grant, *Erotic art*, 134–5, 155.

91 G. Carabelli, *In the image of Priapus* (London, 1996), 24–6.

92 *Dio Chrysostom*, i (Loeb Classical Library, 1932), 259–61; P. Borgeaud, *The cult of Pan in Ancient Greece* (Chicago, 1988), 77; M. Foucault, *The history of sexuality* (3 vols., 1976–84; Eng. trans., New York, 1978–86), iii, 140.

93 J. Gifford, *Buildings of Scotland. Fife* (London, 1988), 247.

94 W. Douglas Simpson, *Huntly Castle, Aberdeenshire* (Edinburgh, 1960), 15.

95 The fullest account of the Isernia discoveries is in Carabelli, *In the image of Priapus*, 1–18, 53–5. In 1996 the British Museum put the Isernia phalluses – or what was left of them – on public display, carefully reconstructed: I. Jenkins & K. Sloan, *Sir William Hamilton and his collection* (London, 1996), 238–9.

96 There is, however, one possible link between the pagan past and the cult at Isernia. Cosmas and Damian had lived in the forth century, but saints of the same name were often conflated, and this may have happened with Cosmas. Another saint of that name (twelfth century) had been bishop of Aphrodisia –

The book of saints. A dictionary of servants of God canonized by the Catholic Church (6th edn, London, 1989), 139. It is conceivable that the idea of St Cosmas being connected with a place dedicated to goddess of love led to belief that he would be particularly effective in cases of impotency

97 M. Clark and N. Penny (eds.), *The arrogant connoisseur: Richard Payne Knight, 1751–1824* (Manchester, 1982), 50.

98 S. West, 'Libertinism and the ideology of male friendship in the portraits of the Society of Dilettanti', *Eighteenth-Century Life*, xvi, no. 2 (1992), 81, 84, 88, 95–100; I.H. Cust, *History of the Society of Dilettanti* (London, 1914), 4–5, 25–6; R. Trumbach, 'Erotic fantasy and male libertinism in Enlightenment England, in L. Hunt, *The invention of pornography. Obscenity and the origins of modernity, 1500–1800* (New York, 1993), 273–9; Carabelli, *In the image of Priapus*, 65–7.

99 G.S. Rousseau, 'The sorrows of Priapus,' *Sexual underworlds of the Enlightenment*, ed. R. Porter and G.S. Rousseau (Manchester, 1987), 123.

100 W. Hamilton & R.P. Knight, *An account of the remains of the worship of Priapus lately existing at Isernia, in the kingdom of Naples ... To which is added*, a discourse on the worship of Priapus and its connection with the mystic theology of the ancients (London 1786); Trumbach, 'Erotic fantasy,' 279–81.

101 Carabelli, *In the image of Priapus*, 72, 84, 88; Johns, *Sex or symbol*, 24–6.

102 J.A Dulaure, *Histoire abrégée de differens cultes* (2nd edn.; 2 vols., Paris, 1825), ii, 299. Chambre Lewis (Dulaure's 'Louis Chamber') was grand master of the Edinburgh branch of the Benison.

103 Rogers, *Social life*, ii, 417. The book by Hamilton and Knight dealing with Isernia had been reprinted in 1861, but still its circulation was very limited, it being produced by a publisher specialising in high-class obscenity. Rogers, avid writer of missionary pamphlets and works on Scottish history, clearly had wide tastes when it came to reading.

CHAPTER THREE

Enlightened and Unenlightened Sex

The previous two chapters have dealt with the Beggar's Benison's mythologies, symbolism and sexual activities. The club emerges as advocating – in fantasy at least – a cheerful sexual hedonism. Responsibility for consequences should be accepted, but basically sex is pleasure, and talking and reminiscing and fantasising about it is not only arousing but has the spice of being naughtily outrageous. Sex is at once a most serious obsession and a matter from which an immense amount of bawdy glee may be derived. It is wonderful, yet unseemly. The present chapter seeks to provide a context for this approach to sex, and particularly for the Beggars' attitude to masturbation, the most shocking item in their repertoire. It has already emerged that the club was influenced by trends in English pornography, but in the forms their obscenity took they were also responding to much wider social and cultural influences.

The Benison and the Disease of Masturbation

For many centuries past – and indeed for some to come – the 'official' Christian morality of the west had taught that sexual activity and orgasm was only morally acceptable within marriage – and even then, strictly speaking, only if intercourse was undertaken with the conscious intention of bringing about conception. As is the way with ideals, no society ever lived up to these standards of behaviour. Ideals by definition are not reality. But with rare exceptions even those who failed to live up to them accepted the validity of Christian sexual teaching, and thus accepted their own sinfulness. The sixteenth-century Reformation and Counter-Reformation created rival Protestant and Catholic Europes, but the old central orthodoxy concerning sexual activity was not a matter of contention. A few minor exotic sects in the enthusiasm of controversy experimented with novel sexual moralities, but exercised no long-term influence. Indeed in many respects Reformation and reaction against it saw a harshening of attempts to enforce obedience. Protestants were concerned to demonstrate their credentials as the true heirs of the Christian tradition by tightening up on the imposition of 'discipline', and central to the campaign was an assault on illicit sexual activity. Determined not to be left behind, Catholicism sought through the Counter-Reformation to reclaim the moral high-ground. Thus, in the short-term, more rigid insistence on sexual discipline followed the great religious upheavals of the sixteenth century – though in practice discipline was usually concentrated on the commons, there being tacit acceptance by churches that ruling élites were too powerful to discipline, and that to make more than token attempts to impose discipline on them might well be dangerous, alienating their support.

Rival religious camps devoted much energy to cataloguing and publicising the alleged sexual sins of the other. Each gave priority to seeking out and punishing the illicit sexual activities of its own members, though Catholics and Protestants differed in approach. Catholics concentrated on private confession and penance, Protestants on trial through local church courts, involving questioning witnesses and, on conviction, public penance before the godly community that had been sinned against.

In all this lies part of the explanation of the seeming paradox that Michel Foucault drew attention to: that the increasingly repressive attitudes to sex of the sixteenth and seventeenth centuries were accompanied by a vast expansion of the volume and range of discourse about sex.[1] Denouncing illicit sex meant it had to be talked and written and preached about. Men and women had to be taught to make restraint of their sexual behaviour central to their consciousnesses. And if sectarian propaganda was to be made through assertions of the sexual immorality of rival churches, case

studies and shocking details were important to provide credibility
and gain audience attention. Clerics thus led the boom in discourse
on sex. To this expansion of discourse, the Renaissance rediscovery
of classical culture added a very different approach to sex, revealing
both the freedom with which many Roman poets dealt with sex, and
their delight in obscenity. Greek and Roman medical and philosophical treatises disclosed attitudes to sexual behaviour very different
from those of Christian morality. Sculpture and other forms of art
disclosed attitudes to depicting bodies and genitals startlingly varying
from those that had prevailed in the west for a thousand years.

Reformation and Renaissance thus both gave new impetus to
discourse about sex, but confusingly seemed to point in different
directions. Simultaneously, a new media became available which
hugely increased the volume of discourse on all subjects. Printing was
the foundation of the astonishing knowledge-explosion that has
continued ever since. It quickly became a major medium in
Reformation and Counter-Reformation attempts to inculcate sexual
morality and spread scurrilous stories about opponents. Physicians
used printing to spread anatomical knowledge and discuss problems
like impotence and venereal disease in a market wider than that of
fellow-scholars – at first with some caution but over time with
explicit detail. And, of course, there was exploitation of printing on
sex for entertainment – Roman poetry, Medieval bawdy, and new
literature from the mildly romantic-erotic to pornography. For
printers, there was profit to be had from sex, and by the end of the
seventeenth century in Britain there were few tastes not catered for.
Printed sex was booming in all forms, with a market ranging from
guilt-ridden sinners reading denunciations of how disgusting and
ungodly their practices were, to the terrified seeking cure for venereal
disease, to the laid-back seeking entertainment. Moreover, in literature for popular consumption, the genres came to overlap confusingly.
A seemingly moral tract or story might contain descriptive material
that was more likely to arouse than to instil virtue. Sometimes it is
hard to know whether a hypocritical author intending to titillate is
seeking to disguise this by mock-piety – or whether a genuine
moralist is hoping that including a few sexy passages will attract the
interest of the salacious who will then be won round by moral
exhortations.

Until the very end of the seventeenth century there remained some taboo areas, however, and masturbation was among them. Throughout the sixteenth to seventeenth-century boom in religion-inspired sexual repression, the moralists leading the movement had been aware of the potential dangers of the discourse on sex they were encouraging. Sermons or books teaching morality, or the investigation and punishment of illicit sexual activity, might prove arousing and instructive to some consumers rather than edifying. The moral message intended could be consumed as titillation. Therefore there was always a problem about how explicit and detailed exhortation should be. On the one hand there was the need to make it clear what in matters sexual was permitted and what was not. On the other, too much detail might corrupt listeners or readers by introducing them to sins they had never previously heard of. Fornication and adultery were no problem. They were visible in communities and disruptive of them. For social as well as religious reasons they should be publicly denounced and punished. But, beyond that, moralists tended to favour vagueness, denouncing practices in phrases such as 'abominable filthinesses', no doubt hoping that those guilty of them would recognise that it was they who were being denounced. Sodomy and bestiality were occasionally denounced, but generally only when the context demanded it – as when offenders were tried in civil courts. On masturbation silence was almost complete. Partly perhaps this reflected recognition that it would be hard to campaign against it – there were unlikely to be witnesses to the solitary sin. Partly too there may have been tacit acceptance that though masturbation was, technically, a most serious sin (deserving death, according to many theologians), in social terms it was harmless. Better folk masturbate than rape, fornicate or commit adultery. But strongest of all was the fear that being specific in references to masturbation would lead many formerly innocent to experiment. By denouncing the practice you would spread its incidence. Thus, until the end of the seventeenth century the subject was largely taboo among moralists. Sometimes at least it was included in the 'sin of Onan,' though that was also interpreted (from a passage in *Genesis* 38) as *coitus interruptus* (though that too was seldom openly denounced for fear of giving people ideas). There are a few scattered references to self-abuse, but generally the moralists were silent. Similarly, it was not an offence that state courts bothered with – though the Lord Advocate of Scotland pointed out in 1678 that criminal courts should, strictly speaking, punish it by death as a breach of God's law.[2] Medical treatises occasionally mentioned masturbation, but saw little significance in it from the point of view of health, though a moral warning against it might be given. Physicians generally accepted the ancient Greek viewpoint that it was only damaging if excessive – excessive squandering of semen, an essential bodily fluid, could be debilitating.

Moralists dithered about how to deal with masturbation, some physicians mentioned it in passing, even pornographic literature seldom bothered with it. Yet when, from the later seventeenth century, references to it increase, it seems to be regarded as a practice that was extremely widespread, – so common in men that it was hardly worth mentioning, and probably mainly described in women to provide titillation for male readers. Most practitioners would usually have accepted it being categorised as sinful, but probably few felt very much guilt about its. Taboos might have made it a very private sin, not to be spoken of, but this 'unspeakableness' did not indicate it was especially serious. Daily life was full of commonplace sin for fallen man, many of them condoned by acceptance, and masturbation for most lay in this area of things tacitly taken for granted.

In the aftermath of the 1660 Restoration of monarchy in Britain masturbation begins to emerge from silence, as the boundaries of sexual discourse widened rapidly in a cultural-political revolution. The upheavals following Reformation and Counter-Reformation had been political as well as religious from the start, with regimes and factions battling for the moral and theological high ground. In Britain's civil wars (1639–51) the Stuart monarchy was overthrown by Scottish covenanters and English parliamentarians, both committed to puritan culture. Charles I was beheaded, monarchy abolished. The king had, within his own codes, been as strict a moralist in sexual and other matters as the puritans, but in some royalist circles reaction against the ostentatious morality of their enemies lead to reaction in favour of cultivated immorality, designed to defy puritan standards and distinguish loyal royalist culture. Charles II gave a lead to this tendency. Once he was restored to his throne in 1660 the royal court, while officially still upholding religion-based morality, set an example of ostentatious libertine behaviour which many of the social élite hastened to copy. Sexual immorality was fashionable, a sign of loyalty to the king and clear evidence that one did not uphold the standards of the hated puritans. In drama, verse and prose – even private diaries – the standards of what was acceptable widened. By chance it was a Scottish royalist, William Drummond (the son of the famous poet) who seems to have been the first man ever to record masturbation regularly in his diary (1658–9),[3] while Samuel Pepys recorded his sexual activities in unparalleled detail. Though he never recorded masturbation he came near to it: he wrote of achieving spontaneous orgasm, on one occasion by reading a French porno- graphic work, on another by watching and lusting after the king's beautiful mistress, Lady Castlemaine, during a church service. Also in manuscript rather than print, satires on the court for first time made allegations of masturbation about the famous, usually accusing court ladies of addiction to 'Senor Dildo.'[4] John Aubrey now recorded how, many years before, he had discovered the fact that the inattention of his pupil, the duke of Buckingham, was due to the fact that the boy was masturbating.[5]

Thus slowly, masturbation was emerging from the closet of silence. Discussion and writing about all aspects of sex was flourish- ing. Satire against the regime increasingly depicted royal power as phallic power, a sexual absolutism. In this atmosphere of libertinism some moralists, horrified at Restoration excesses, began to question the expediency of keeping silent about masturbation for fear of introducing the ignorant to the practice. It was increasingly hard to believe that such innocents existed to be corrupted. The time had come to speak out. The result was the publication in London in 1676 of a pamphlet, *Letters of advice from two reverend divines to a young gentleman about a weighty case of conscience, and by him recommended to the serious perusal of all those that may fall into the same condition.* This seems to be the earliest known work ever written devoted to masturbation. But the time was not yet ripe, and the work remained obscure. It was reprinted in 1687, but again failed to make any impact.[6] The moral / religious arguments against masturbation had come out of the closet and nobody had noticed.

The creation of the major panic about masturbation that was soon to emerge required an additional ingredient. Medical needed to be added to moral arguments. By this time a few physicians were beginning to suggest that masturbation was responsible for both physical and mental health problems. Not surprisingly in an age in which libertinism had royal sponsorship and discourse on the joys of sex was flourishing, so too did worries about all sorts of sexual-medical problems. It was as if as moral guilt about illicit sexual activity declined, a lingering sense of wrong-doing was transforming itself into fear that it would lead to shameful illness. There was a belief that the incidence of venereal disease, impotence and other disorders were increasing. Part of the reason for this was seen as ignorance and lack of information. Increasingly physicians (and others) felt it was necessary to speak out about – or write about – delicate subjects which had formerly been avoided.[7] If illicit sex brought high risk of illness, it seemed natural to move towards assuming that masturbation must pose health risks.

Some of the increasingly explicit medical writings on sexual ills might be well-intentioned, but it became a field intensely cultivated by the quacks (often hard to distinguish from 'respectable' medical practitioners), who through an endless stream of pamphlets, posters and advertisements offered supposed wonder cures to the public. First the public had to be terrified with horrors of the fates that awaited them if they did not buy. Prominent were cures for venereal disease and other sexual disorders, where quacks could play on shame and need for secrecy as well as fear. Then some unknown moralist had an inspiration. Speak out against masturbation, but in doing so do not just appeal to fears that it is a deadly sin that could lead to eternal damnation (as the *Letters of advice* had done) but bring in medical arguments (or rather assertions) that the practices will cause horrible diseases and disorders. Terror of consequences in this life are much more immediate than ones delayed until the afterlife. This was the origins of *Onania*, published first in 1715. The author's motives were pure – outspokenness in the cause of moral reform, and the book was an immediate success. But a quack surgeon who had previously specialised in venereal disease, John Marten, soon saw the potential of the situation. He and the author combined to offer in succeeding editions of the book near miraculous cures for the consequences of masturbation. Probably the original author's motives were still good – the cures would help sufferers, and he assured readers that he would make no profit from them. But, it turned out, *Onania* had sold its soul. New editions grew greatly in length, with additional material consisting largely of 'readers' letters' – some of which may have been authentic. Many of these were lavish in praise of the wonderful cures *Onania* offered, but others exploited the success of the book in other ways. 'Readers' offered detailed accounts of their sex lives, and other material added more titillating sexual 'facts' and anecdotes. An earnest moralist's message had become a mere introduction to an increasingly pornographic book hyping quack cures.[8]

Once *Onania* had set the masturbation band-wagon rolling others jumped on board, with publications that usually denounced the author of *Onania* in order to sell rival cures. All now agreed that masturbation led to a terrible fate. One of these publications coined the term onanism,[9] which was adopted by the medical profession for centuries as the learned name for masturbation. Up to 1730 new editions of *Onania* averaged one a year. Thereafter its popularity declined, but its influence was long lasting. Physicians in general adopted the new view of masturbation as a major health and social problem with remarkable readiness. The great masturbation panic that was to spread throughout the western world and last until the twentieth century had begun.

This is not the place to discuss why it was that the unscholarly assertions of an obscure moralists, exploited by a quack, should have such a lasting effect. In the context of the Beggar's Benison what is remarkable is the timing of the scare in relation to the club's foundation. Until 1715 masturbation was a low-key matter, generally agreed to be sinful and shameful enough to be generally unmentionable, but commonplace and not controversial. Then it sprang into prominence through *Onania* and the other publications which flooded out up to the 1730s. In the midst of all this the Beggar's Benison is founded, dedicated to the celebration of sex through ritual masturbation.

At first sight this seems crazy. Of all times, this seems the least likely one at which to found such a club. That the provincials of Fife were unaware of the onanism scare is impossible to believe – as already noted, there is plenty of evidence that they were in touch with what London had to offer in literature on sex. Possibly the Benison founding members simply chose to ignore the scare, but it seems much more likely that they were consciously reacting against it. These were men who were malcontents, muttering subversively on politics, on innovations inflicted on them from above – a new dynasty (possibly), union with England (certainly), customs and excise duties (certainly). Now there was another ridiculous innovation from London which affronted them – the idea that masturbation was harmful. What nonsense: it had never done them any harm. It was an attempt to suppress a traditional – and gratifying – pastime, part of their cultural heritage. So, lets mock the whole silly idea. Make fun of it in a ritual which demonstrates that we don't believe a word of *Onania*.

It must be said that there is not any direct evidence at all to confirm this reconstruction of the motives of the inventors of the Benison in concentrating on masturbatory rituals. But the circumstantial evidence is compelling. Masturbation becomes a major public concern, and when publicity on the matter is at its height the Beggars, men bound together by an 'awkward squad' reaction against many features of the world developing around them, found a club with ritual based on masturbation. It is difficult to believe that there is no connection between the two matters, that the chronology is pure coincidence.

The idea of masturbating in each other's company may have seemed the less shocking to the first Benison members because, though members differed greatly in age, they had virtually all attended the burgh schools of the Neuk, and many had grown up together. The post-1715 anti-masturbation literature commonly refers to it as a school boy (and girl) sin, and to boys teaching each other and performing together. Memories of adolescent activity (the Benison seems to have had no members aged under twenty-one or so) may have helped inspire the club's rituals.

There is an allegation that a masturbation club had existed in London earlier in the century, but in some ways the differences between it and the Benison are more striking than similarities. The 'club' was said to have been a peer-group of young, probably very young, men, and their activities seem a continuation of adolescent group experimentation. Their masturbation was repeated and competitive, seeking to prove who had the greatest sexual stamina. The picture is of young males at the peak of their sexual drives – and, therefore, frustrations – relieving the pressure and, typically, making a competition out of it, ranking themselves.[10] This is raw sex. The Benison, by contrast, is more sophisticated (which does not necessarily mean more attractive). Masturbation is an initiation, and a sociable expression of shared sexuality, but it is not an endurance test. And while the ritual celebrates sex, it is about more than just sex. It is symbolic of rejection of convention and the status quo, contradicting in private the members' public images of respectable citizenship.

In rejecting the new consensus about the dangers of masturbation that emerged after the publication of *Onania*, Benison members were not alone. Bernard de Mandeville in his *A modest defence of the public stews*, published anonymously in 1724, concluded that public brothels were the best way to deal with excess male libido, but in the course of his argument he made a strong case for masturbation. As a way of gaining sexual satisfaction it was safe (no fear of venereal disease), private, convenient and cheap.[11] This calm discussion of utility is very different from the horrors portrayed in *Onania*. More light-heartedly, an anonymous mid eighteenth-century Scot debated the relative merits of wives, whores and masturbation. Marriage brought slavery to sexually insatiable wives:

> All the good that they gain by a wife
> Is to be forced to fuck them or have strife.

If men chose to frequent whores instead, they were likely to lose their noses – through syphilis. Therefore masturbation was the best option, coping with need, without risk or undue wifely demands:

> The hand doth take what man can freely spare
> And yet abstaining gives the hand no care.[12]

Even a physician (though admittedly an eccentric one) like John Armstrong could be mild in rebuking masturbators. Their 'unhallow'd pastime' he described as selfish and ungenerous – but not life-threatening. It was wrong

> To disappoint, *increase and multiply*,
> To Shed thy Blossoms thro' the desert air,
> And sow thy perish'd off-spring in the wind.

Therefore

> Banish from thy shades the solitary Joy –
> The vice of Monks, the early Bane
> Of rising manhood. Find some soft nymph
> Whom tender sympathy attracts to thee,
> Sacrifice to her the precious hours ...

and get on with it. If no willing soft nymph was available, then turn to the brothel:

> ... to hie
> To Bagnio lewd or Tavern, nightly where
> Venereal Rites are done ...

Risking infection with venereal disease through prostitutes was a lesser evil than masturbation, though quite why this was so is not made clear.[13] But this was not an alternative available in the East Neuk, sadly lacking in whores and brothels.

In all probability neither the supposed London masturbation club nor the Benison were unique. It quite possible that in other eighteenth-century clubs masturbation took place – but incidentally and informally rather than being central to the club. The phallically decorated Benison punch bowls that seem to have been used after dinner in the private houses of the Wentworths and Curzons (see chapter two) are suggestive of what may have gone on. Given the grossness of manners (by subsequent standards) common in the eighteenth century, when dinner parties might well be accompanied by drinking to the point of falling unconscious or vomiting, and when the claret was accompanied in the sideboard by a chamber pot which was frequently resorted to, it is not inconceivable that, in appropriate company, when conversation and fantasy was sexually arousing, men would wave the organ whose prowess they boasted and masturbate in each other's company as easily as they relieved themselves in the chamber pot.

Masturbation had always been seen as sinful, yet absurdly there were circumstances in which it might be required by law, and this is another possible source of Benison resort to the practice, especially as legally masturbation could be used to provide proof of potency, as in Benison ritual. Procedures sometimes used in cases in which the nullity of a marriage was sought on grounds of impotency involved the husband giving – or failing to give – such proof. Tests were common in the sixteenth to the eighteenth centuries, and though the most detailed study made of them concentrates on impotency trials in France they were also used in other countries. In some instances proceedings included 'trial by congress' in which husband and wife sought to prove before witnesses whether or not they could complete intercourse, but much more common was examination of the male genitals to prove whether erection could be achieved and sustained. Though these were regarded simply as fact-finding exercises, they obviously were processes involving ordeal and humiliation. Already deeply humiliated by the accusation of impotence, many men normally fully capable proved unable to provide the necessary evidence before an audience of doctors. In the case of trial by congress midwives too would be present as men attempted to have sex with wives who often, since they wished for annulment, proved uncooperative and even poured scorn on their efforts. In the 'trials' by erection the accused was obviously obliged to stimulate himself, before an audience demanding the most complete evidence: 'From this point to ordering a "trial by ejaculation" was only a short step which certain experts may well have taken.'[14] Nor were such intimate pryings confined to Roman Catholic countries. Publications of the evidence produced in impotency trials proved in eighteenth-century England, as in France, major sources of semi-pornographic literature feeding a prurient market.[15] In Scotland impotency trials were rare, but courts did sometimes order that allegedly impotent men be examined to establish their abilities, and in the Highlands at least custom allowed that, with the consent of the parties concerned, neighbours might sit in judgement on the effectiveness of a man's genitals, or relatives be appointed to watch an informal 'trial by congress' as he attempted to have intercourse with his wife.[16] Possibly the members of the Benison in establishing their 'trial by ejaculation' had some idea of parodying such extraordinary procedures. To fashionable denouncers of masturbation were they replying not just by elevating the practise to ritual, but by a mocking reference to legal justification for what they were doing? Indeed to religious denunciations of masturbation, were Benison members replying that they were practising it only before witnesses and to demonstrate potency, and that by church law this was allowable?

The final attraction of masturbation as the chosen Benison sexual activity was that it was practical and expedient. Imbued with ideals of licentious pleasures to be gained in defiance of convention, what were the Beggars actually to do in the East Neuk of Fife? The towns of the area were tiny, the countryside outside them sparsely populated. For most the moral discipline of the local church court, the kirk session, was still something to be feared until the last decades of the eighteenth century. So where were partners with whom to practice heterosexual promiscuity to be found? In the 1730s at least girls were found who were ready to be hired to strip off and be lusted after, but that fell far short of fornication. Doubtless there were a few women in the community who, if not full time whores, would provide sex for payment (it is unlikely that kirk discipline was so all-pervasive in the community that sailors were totally denied a port service whose existence was almost universal). But the members of the Benison were outwardly respectable, conventional folk. They were married men with families. In small communities they might get away with jovial private club masturbation, but adultery or orgies could not be kept secret, and would be disastrously disruptive to families and reputations. Semi-libertine behaviour was something to dream of but which could not safely be lived out. It was all very well being promiscuous in a city, in London or even Edinburgh. Numbers of prostitutes increased at least as fast as population grew, demand being fuelled by the breakdown of social restraints and the advocacy of new freedoms. There were outwardly respectable ladies to be found who, in the safety of urban anonymity, might be prepared to venture on affairs. But what on earth were you to do in the East Neuk? Rural fornication was possible for men of very high social status. If they were discreet, the tamed Presbyterian church would turn a blind eye, but very few Benison members of the 1730s approached such status. The Beggars' ideal would have been to implement John Armstrong's advice and find 'sweet nymphs' instead of finding relief in masturbation, but they were not safely available. The male demand side of the equation of unrestrained sexual pleasure was ready and waiting, but the female supply side was tormentingly deficient. If the Beggars were to make their protest against the old sexual conventions based on religion anything more than words, masturbation was all that was left (except for sodomy or bestiality, neither of which were to their tastes and both of which would be hard to conceal – and would incur the death penalty).

Libertinism and Enlightenment

On masturbation the Beggars showed their contempt for new opinions emerging in their own age, and while there may be objection to the distinctly gross ways in which they demonstrated their standpoint, it has to be allowed that from a modern perspective their judgement on the matter seems much more 'enlightened' than that of their contemporaries who conformed to the irrational panic about onanism.

In other sexual matters the Benison was much more in line with the views and practices of contemporaries. In their hailing of sex as pleasure that, in an ideal world, should be freely enjoyed, they harked back to the libertinism of the Restoration, and looked forward to the emerging Enlightenment.

For a significant section of the upper ranks of society the 1660 Restoration had meant there were new sexual freedoms to be enjoyed – or enjoyed more openly than in the past – justified by new moralities, licensed by the crown, displayed explicitly in verse, drama and behaviour at court. It was politically correct, for it represented rejection of Puritanism. Puritanism stood for restraint, its opposite, libertinism, for individual freedom. 'Libertinism embodies a dream of human freedom, recognised from the onset as infinitely desirable and as unattainable.' Above all the libertine dream was of male sexual freedom, rejecting all authority that sought to restrain the use of women. The libertine asserted his right to take his pleasure, with no thought of reciprocity. It was a predatory ideal, where 'taking possession' – and then usually discarding – was central to satisfaction. Colonisation, conquest, invasion, possession of territory were often invoked as metaphors, with 'women as servants to the divine phallus, accessory to the sexual pleasures of the male'. Asserting freedom involved asserting mastery over others.[17] The language clearly recalls the Merryland of the Beggar's Benison – though there it was sexual fantasy rather than a code of behaviour that was acted out in practice. One historian has recently linked aristocratic libertinism in France and England with the consciousness of nobles of 'increasing marginality and powerlessness.'[18] If asserting sexual power and freedom in extreme terms is thus seen as a reaction to perceptions of futility and helplessness, this well fits the early members of the Benison (though most were far from aristocratic), with their mixture of grievances at the *status quo* and use of the club as a channel for their frustrations. The burghs so many members were drawn from were experiencing a long economic decline, blamed partly on union and high customs duties. John McNachtane, sovereign of the club for nearly thirty years, was nominal chief of an ancient Highland aristocratic family reduced to working as a petty official. It was a club of men who may have been of local significance but many of whom may well have felt marginalised and ineffectual, and turned to libertine dreams in reaction.

Libertinism represented a complete break with conventional moralities, a consciously shocking abandonment of theological and other restraints. For most of those who adopted it there was little thought of philosophical justification for their rejection of former conventions of behaviour – beyond the argument that Puritanism having proved pernicious, reaction to the opposite extreme was logical. Nonetheless, libertine ideas concentrating on satisfaction through unrestrained action overlapped with emerging philosophical discussion of individual rights, including that to enjoy pleasure free from the arbitrary and varying pronouncements of theologians. Few went the full way to libertinism, most clinging to skeletons of conventional Christian beliefs. But there was a marked tendency to reassess man's place in the universe in ways which pushed God into the background. His omnipotence might still be recognised, but he was seen not as continually intervening in human affairs but as the creator of the framework within which man lived – the laws of nature. The way to understand God's will was not – or was not only – to agonise over the interpretation of biblical texts, but to study his work as revealed in the natural world. Newton sought to understand the universe through mathematics, and everywhere there seemed an impetus towards collecting and observing and quantifying the things of this world as a way to understand God. Such ideas did not in themselves favour a libertine abandonment of morality and responsibility, but they accepted that new approaches might be made to deciding what was permissible in human behaviour. One conclusion emerging from such re-thinking was that the enjoyment of earthly pleasures was not simply a sadly necessary concession to human weakness and depravity, but valid in its own right. If the universe which God had created made pleasures available, then they were legitimate. A libertine would stop the argument there, but the strands of thought that were to lead to the eighteenth-century Enlightenment saw the inadequacies of such a crude conclusion. Unrestrained individual behaviour was inconsistent with the well being of society, and indeed with individual health. The family unit formed an essential basis for society and reproduction – and for the proper hereditary descent of property rights. Therefore there still had to be strict constraints on behaviour based on rational arguments of expediency. In fact the conclusions most writers reached were fairly conservative. The achieving of the social objectives required, as in the past, that sexual intercourse should be confined to the married. But there was growing, though often unwritten, acceptance that many would not so confine themselves, and that there should not be any punitive authority seeking to punish all those who failed to conform in any way. The old appetite for enforcing constraint through church discipline waned rapidly in Britain, as the will of the governing classes to back up the churches' efforts, nationally or locally, declined. Indeed beneath the veneer of revived morality (supposedly restored by the 1688–9 revolution) there was widespread acceptance that (for men at least) sexual indulgence outside marriage was legitimate pleasure. It was not to be employed with libertine irresponsibility that might damage the social fabric upon which élite privileges rested, but with a degree of discretion – just as kings still had mistresses but no longer flaunted them. Fornication and even sometimes adultery came to be regarded primarily not as serious breaches of divine law but as actions which could be highly inexpedient in their consequences if mishandled. Clerics of all persuasions continued to preach conventional behaviour, and were listened to politely, but their strictures were increasingly ineffectual.

Increasingly the gurus of sexual behaviour were not theologians but philosophers and physicians – the eighteenth century, it has been well said, saw 'the medicalisation of sex'.[19] In Scotland eighteenth-century writers who dealt with sexual behaviour show the influence of libertinism in general acceptance that sexual pleasure could be enjoyed as more than just a necessary concomitant of procreation. It was something that it was legitimate to seek, along with other worldly and sensual pleasures. They were part of God's plan, for He had provided for them in His creation. And yet most writers inevitably, as they were still Christians, had qualms about radical changes in attitude. They might discuss sexual pleasure and its role in life with new freedom, but they tended to be uncomfortable with the idea, finding new arguments to replace religious ones in limiting activity. As threats of hell failed to scare people into moral behaviour, the emphasis on dangers to mental and physical health, and to social structure, grew – paralleling to some extent the changes in attitude to masturbation. Fear of venereal disease provided a strong and medically legitimate argument against promiscuity. The only real arguments against it might be theological, and therefore vanishing from the vocabulary of physicians, but old prejudices against lingered on and were now justified by being dressed up in quasi-medical disguises.

Intercourse within marriage and with procreation in mind contin-ued to be cited as the ideal, but recognition that this old ideal was unlikely to be lived up to in practice was indicated by warnings that sexual activity in marriage should be limited for other reasons. The Greek ideal of 'nothing in excess' and the argument that sex could lead to excessive loss of bodily fluid was emphasised, and there must be suspicion that this was again an unconscious attempt to legitimise lingering Christian suspicion of sex. Philosophers shared physicians' worries about promiscuity in terms of health and social consequences, but added a more abstract worry that enveloped all sex, not just that outside marriage. Enjoyment of sensual pleasure might be legitimate, but somehow sex was not really very nice. True, it was necessary for breeding purposes, but it was not refined and it was not edifying. Men, freed from the excesses of dogmatic religion, should strive for edification, for understanding, for improvement – and things of that nature could not be achieved in bed. Old-style moralists saw sexual pleasure as diverting men from spiritual things. Enlightened moralists feared it as a distraction from high intellectual endeavour.

The philosopher Francis Hutcheson (1747) found it hard to reconcile the acceptance of sexual libido as being natural (so quintessentially natural, indeed, as to lie at the centre of procreation) with the perception that it was not elevating. 'Bodily pleasures have none of that dignity which is the object of praise' he ruled in 1747. However intense the sensations of sex, they were all mean, and many were indeed 'shameful'. Further thought, however, led Hutcheson to climb down a bit from these abstract heights. He conceded that 'a moderate relish for *sensual pleasures* is useful, nay necessary'.[20] Unfortunately Hutcheson did not enlighten his readers as to how it could be possible to limit the sensations of sexual orgasm to 'moderate relish'. Still, 'useful' – a favourite Enlightenment word – was a great consolation, and sex was undoubtedly usefully procreative. Nature in its wisdom had decreed that sexual impulses were 'necessary' to ensure that humans mated. Rationality would perhaps not have been enough: humans fully engaged in elevated thoughts might forget to breed. Hutcheson was conventional in insisting that sex be confined within marriage, but unconventional in arguing for equality of status for man and wife. There was a twist in the tail of this advocacy of equality, for he argued that men and women should be treated equally when it came to promiscuity, and this turns out not to mean less severity towards erring women, but much greater severity towards men.[21]

The lawyer James Burnett, Lord Monboddo, regarded sexual pleasure with a coarser philosophical suspicion than Hutcheson. Sex was a crude physical function, and to make more of it than that would be ignoble. He 'would not allow a philosopher to indulge in women as a pleasure, but only as an evacuation.' Men who fell into the trap of taking pleasure in sexual embraces 'would soon have that enjoyment as a business, than which nothing could make one more despicable'.[22] At the end of the century the physician Robert Couper was much in agreement with Lord Monboddo, for while he applauded the 'animal instincts' that prompted reproduction he also wrote primly of how 'brutal these sensations and ideas may appear to the purified philosopher'. Moreover, though he accepted the 'animal' sexual act for the purpose of breeding, Couper was disgusted by 'human' foreplay, what he called titillation 'during the gross and libidinous commerce of the sexes'. Pleasure in the basic act was sanctioned by nature, but adding to it artificially by sex-play was degradation. Other restrictions are indicated by Couper's warnings that early sexual activity could cause infertility in the male, while too much sex could cause it in the female. However he accepted the belief that many illnesses in women could be cured by sexual intercourse[23] – though this cure should of course only be sought within marriage.

These writers would have had little appeal to the Benison, and it is no surprise that the one physician they quoted in their papers was John Armstrong. For a physician he was unusually relaxed about sex, perhaps because his ambitions were literary as well as medical. In his verse *Oeconomy of Love* (1736) he produced his generation's 'most popular middlebrow how-to-do-it book' in a style which was 'highly idealised, and spoke in flowery periphrasis, without anatomical details.'[24] Armstrong dwelt on the physicality of love-making with a lascivious warmth which was most unscientific. 'A more nauseous piece of work could not easily be found,' the *Dictionary of National Biography* was to declare in a less robust age. Armstrong was however a believer in abstinence from sex for men until the age of twenty or more 'Had steel'd thy Nerves' for 'the soft Embrace Emasculant.' He believed marriage was the proper place for sex, and warned of the dangers of venereal disease from frequenting prostitutes, but has no strict injunctions to morality, relying rather on gentle chiding. In choosing to write in verse Armstrong was aiming to produce a text that was easily accessible and attractive to read rather than dry and dull, and perhaps he saw himself as updating Ovid's famous *Art of love*. The work went through a number of editions between 1736 and 1749, but it may be suspected its popularity rested on it being read for other reasons than the provision of useful information.

Physicians and philosophers with more radical ideas on sex can be found in Scotland, but had to be aware that publication would be fatal to their reputations. It is hardly surprising that the paper written by Robert Wallace 'On venery' (*c.*1760) remained unpublished, for some of the contents would have caused horror and destroyed his position in society. Wallace was a most respectable figure, a leading Church of Scotland minister who had been Moderator of the General Assembly in 1743, and he published a number of books on social and population issues. That he could write his treatise on sex is an astonishing testimony to the change that had come over the ministry of his church in the first half of the eighteenth century. The dominant 'Moderate' ministers had adapted to 'Enlightenment,' and indeed were taking a leading part in it, rejecting with contempt the fanaticisms and narrowness of their predecessors. The idea that a minister of the kirk could write of fornication and flexible marriage arrangements in the cool tones of philosophy would have seemed inconceivable at the beginning of the century.

Wallace had far fewer qualms about sex than Hutcheson, deriving his ideas less from abstract thought than simple observation of humans and how they acted as sexual beings. 'Nature hath rendered the Venereal Act highly Delightfull when it is performed in obedience to nature'. This applied to women as well as men, and he was cynical – or realistic – about ideals of platonic love. A man might claim to respect a woman for mind and conduct, but this concealed 'a secret wish to be familiar with her person'. And as women had sexual lusts, it would not be immodest for a woman to make advances to a man. Still, Wallace had some unease at the though of too much freedom. Nature had given humans 'a strong inclination' to sex to ensure reproduction, and it was basically this that justified it. Fornication should be punished, but for reasons of social expediency rather than sin, and the punishment should be 'gentle'. A misdeed should not ruin a woman's reputation for life. And why should not marriage be by renewable contracts, adding a degree of licensed flexibility to sexual relationships and doing away with much of the temptation that led to fornication? [25] On masturbation Wallace was also radical. The practice was natural, though he had reservations in the case of children. Knowledge of the matter should be kept from them for as long as possible, lest they began the practice too soon and 'became guilty of many dangerous and enervating practices,' though he does not specify what these were. Describing the discovery of masturbation by the young male as 'an agreeable experience,' Wallace does not seem to have expected it to be accompanied by guilt, and had no wish to instil it. [26]

The most eminent of Scottish – indeed British – surgeons of the century, John Hunter, went future than Wallace, boldly publishing his heretical opinions on masturbation in a treatise on venereal diseases in 1786. In discussing impotence he noted that 'This complaint is by many laid to the charge of Onanism'. But 'upon a strict review of this subject, it appears to me to be by far too rare to originate from a practice so general.' In other words, if masturbation caused impotence, the latter would be far more common. In treating patients he had found no connection between the two, and books on masturbation had 'done more harm than good' in Hunter's opinion. Indeed, Hunter came close to actually approving of masturbation, by stating that it was less damaging to the constitution than sexual intercourse, as the emotions were not involved. True, excess could be harmful, but the closest Hunter came to criticism was to call masturbation a 'selfish enjoyment'.[27] This remarkable frankness on masturbation was in many ways typical of Hunter: he was a man lacking in formal education with a strong suspicion of book-learning. But his colleagues preferred not to listen, and he was roundly denounced by his fellow-countrymen, Duncan Gordon, MD, in *A Letter to John Hunter, Esq. ... pointing out the absurdity and immorality of his doctrine in favour of Onanism or masturbation* (London, 1786).

Some Scottish contributions to eighteenth century debate on sex were less serious than the ideas of Wallace and Hunter. Wallace's colleague in the ministry of the Church of Scotland, Daniel Maclauchlan, was either mad or mischievous, probably a mixture of the two. His 1735 *An essay upon improving and adding, to the strength of Great-Britain and Ireland, by fornication* (London 1735) provided a crudely utilitarian vision of sex in the form of a satire on worries about possible population decline. The preface was crammed with coarse double-entendres, but the essay itself was superficially serious, though crude. The great business of men's lives, it is argued, should be to 'Propagate our Kind'. Men had a duty 'to throw our Seed into every fruitful Corner,' to fornicate dutifully, ridding themselves of semen 'by the *Medium* of a pretty Girl'. Women were receptacles that men should make use of indiscriminately to relieve themselves of the torments of lust, just as they would relieve the need to urinate in a chamber pot. The illegitimate children born of these relationships should be brought up by state 'baby convents' so they could be put to work in manufactures or sent to the colonies to fill the world with good British stock through further fornication.[28] Maclauchlan can hardly have been surprised to find himself in a London prison, convicted of writing a 'vile, abominable and obscene pamphlet'.[29]

The greatest of all British eccentrics when it came to teaching about sex was also a Scot, and also paid for his views with imprisonment, but unlike Maclauchlan he was entirely serious. James Graham (1745–94) was a strict moralist but also a flamboyant showman and publicist in the cause of good sex. He descended on England and the American Colonies bursting with zeal to help people. His basic ideas on sex were entirely conventional. Good sex was essential to health, but to be good it had to be within marriage, aimed at procreation, and not an excessive indulgence in 'animal appetites'. It became Graham's mission to help couples having difficulties in achieving conception, partly by spreading advice and knowledge, partly by sensational treatments. He devised an elaborate temple in London containing an extraordinary vibrating magnetic bed. At the head of this Celestial Bed was emblazoned 'BE FRUITFUL, MULTIPLY AND REPLENISH THE EARTH'. Those who hired his bed for copulation would achieve conception. Other equipment for treatment of sexual problems included a cylinder charged with static electricity, and cartoonists seized on this phallic-shaped object with enthusiasm. In one cartoon it is labelled 'Divine Balsam for the Ladies'. In another Graham and a rival sex therapist threaten each other with huge electrically charged model phalluses. Ducks at Graham's feet show that he is a quack – and they quack a thistle to identify him as Scots. The London temple soon closed, but Graham continued to preach his gospel, dreaming of raising the vast sum of £20,000 so he could built a new 'medical-magnetico musical electrical bed'. One would have thought achieving orgasm in such a contraption would have been as daunting a prospect as having to masturbate before the assembled Beggar's Benison. In 1783 Graham found himself imprisoned in Edinburgh Tolbooth for giving obscene public lectures. Soon he turned to trying to found a new church, and vanished into obscurity.[30]

These Scottish contributions to eighteenth-century debate on sex cannot be said to establish any specifically Scottish outlook, but there are a surprising number of them, and it is notable that a high proportion of authorities cited in works on sex in England in the period are in fact Scots. For all the supposed thraldom of the Scots to Calvinism, when it came to sex they seem to have been more loquacious than the English – a point only partly explained by the thriving of medical education and research in Scotland late in the century.

Eighteenth-century Scotland produced two great writers on personal practical, as opposed to theoretical, sex. Robert Burns asserted the right of the common man to sexual freedom, sex without guilt – and at times without responsibility. But James Boswell is in some respects a much more interesting case study, not only because had a varied career of sexual indulgence that far outdid Burns, but because his attitudes to sex were complicated. He was haunted by guilt and naive questioning. Like others, Boswell pondered the question of how God could, through nature, provide men with strong libidos, but then place absurd restrictions on satisfying them. Should not God be reasonable, his actions explicable and not arbitrary? 'Thank heaven for giving me the love of women. To many she gives not the noble passion of lust,' mused Boswell in an optimistic mood, assuming that God was reasonable. But he had doubts: 'think if God really forbids girls'.[31] The thought was appalling – it was almost unthinkable that God would really be so harsh.

Boswell's sex-life began inadvertently. Climbing trees, embracing trunk and limbs and hauling himself along, brought him intense sensations that made him think of heaven, and he would fall to the ground in a swoon. He asked the gardener for an explanation, but 'He, rigid, did not explain it,' the poor man no doubt being unnerved by the young master repeatedly plummeting out of trees with a blissful expression on his face. However Boswell soon learnt the 'fatal practice' of masturbation from a playmate ('fatal' in the sense of inevitable, rather than deadly), regarding it as only a venial sin compared to fornication, but still fearing damnation.[32] He soon graduated to compulsive fornication.

Haunted by the unceasing demands of his libido and worrying that satisfying them was diverting him from great achievements, Boswell was remarkable open, repeatedly asking those whose opinions he respected for advice. He had the sense to avoid asking churchmen or physicians, because what he wanted was reassurance and approval of a libertine lifestyle. But this he never got. His most famous discussion on sex was with Jean Jacques Rousseau in 1764. Rousseau sought to avoid being pestered by the young Scot, but Boswell cornered him, and poured out an extraordinary libertine-feudal-pastoral fantasy of the ideal sex life.

> consider, if I am rich, I can take a number of girls; I get them with child; propagation is thus increased. I give them dowries, and I marry them off to good peasants who are very happy to have them. Thus they become wives at the same age as would have been the case if they had remained

virgins, and I, on my side, have had the benefits of enjoying a great variety of women.

He added Old Testament justification for such promiscuity: 'I should like to follow the example of the old Patriarchs, worthy men whose memory I hold in respect'.[33] It is a fantasy that no doubt appealed to many gentlemen, but only Boswell would have both confided it to a philosopher and then recorded it for posterity. Rousseau tiresomely advised the pursuit of the spiritual. It is a tribute to Boswell's reverence for Rousseau that he actually tried abstinence from women, turning to masturbation as a substitute. However he quickly decided that this was unworthy, or unsatisfactory: 'Swear with drawn sword never pleasure but with woman's aid.'[34] He returned to his old ways – and a brief affair with Rousseau's mistress, though inspired by lust, seems symbolic revenge on the unsympathetic philosopher.[35]

Boswell might dream of willing peasant girls in a rural idyll, but the reality of his sexual activity was a sex-life dominated by endless encounters with cheap prostitutes in squalid urban settings all over Europe, recurring venereal disease. and drunken disillusionment. For him the pursuit of free sex (or, more often, paid-for sex) became a story of personal destruction.

Boswell agonised about sex. The Beggar's Benison worked out sexual frustration through fantasy, laughter and masturbation, not sharing Boswell's distaste for the practice. The club's contribution to the blossoming discourse on sex was highly eccentric and personal, but it showed an interest in the wider debate. It was perverse in its obstinate commitment to traditional relatively relaxed attitudes to masturbation, but could find justification for its attitude in a minority of writers. The physician who lectured in 1813 brought such arguments directly to the club, for he shared Hunter's scepticism about onanism. Three-quarters of both males and females 'have the common trick of using their fingers ... as the most handy way of allaying their craving'. Such onanism 'is denounced as fostering insanity with other ills'. But it was not in fact the sin Onan had been punished for and, the physician concluded, in moderation masturbation could not cause these evils.[36]

Though the masturbatory rituals of the Benison can be seen as reflecting the age and circumstances in which the club was founded – as a reaction against *Onania*, as influenced by libertine ideas, as frustrated defiance of convention – they also share with many ages and cultures a central feature of initiation ceremonies: humiliation and ordeal. As the price of being admitted to a group a would-be member has both to prove himself fit to join and humiliate himself before existing members. Masturbation to orgasm before a critical audience, whether solemn or rowdy, must have been difficult. It proved a candidate's sexual qualifications and at the same time served as ritual humiliation and ordeal before being welcomed as a member. Becoming a member of a group must be difficult if membership is to be worth having.

Notes

1 Foucault, *The history of sexuality* (3 vols., 1976–84; Eng. trans., New York, 1978–86), i, part 2, chapter 1, esp. pp. 34–5.

2 G. Mackenzie, *Works* (2 vols., Edinburgh, 1716–22), ii, 115, reprinted from Mackenzie's *The laws and customs of Scotland in matters criminal* (Edinburgh, 1678).

3 'The diary of Sir William Drummond of Hawthornden, 1657–1659,' ed. H.W. Meikle, *Miscellany of the Scottish History Society*, vii (Edinburgh, 1941), 3–52. D. Stevenson, 'Recording the unspeakable. Masturbation in the diary of William Drummond,' *Journal of the History of Sexuality*, ix (2000), 223–39.

4 Williams, *Dictionary*, i, 18, 555.

5 Williams, *Dictionary*, ii, 862.

6 The only surviving copy of the 1676 edition is in the library of Christ Church College, Oxford. No copies of the 1687 edition exist, but its text was included in some editions of *Eronania* (1724).

7 R. Porter and L. Hall, *The facts of life. The creation of sexual knowledge in England* (New Haven & London, 1995), 92–3.

8 This interpretation of *Onania*'s origins and development will be the subject of a forthcoming article.

9 *Onanism displayed* (London, 1719).

10 *Onanism displayed*, 36–8.

11 Cited in G.J.B. Benfield, *The culture of sensibility. Sex and society in eighteenth-century Britain* (Chicago, 1992), 126.

12 A. Bold (ed.), *The bawdy beautiful. The Sphere book of improper verse* (London, 1979), 90, quoted from NLS, Adv. Ms. 19.3.16 (collection dated *c*.1760).

13 [J. Armstrong], *Oeconomy of Love* (Edinburgh, 1736, 2nd edn 1745); Supplement, 60; DNB.

14 P. Darman, *Trial by impotence. Virility and marriage in pre-Revolutionary France* (London, 1985), 174.

15 P. Wagner, 'Trial reports as a genre of eighteenth-century erotica,' *British Journal for Eighteenth-Century Studies*, v (1982), 117–18.
16 L. Leneman, *Alienated affections. The Scottish experience of divorce and separation, 1684–1830* (Edinburgh, 1982), 252–6.
17 W. Chernaik, *Sexual freedom in Restoration literature* (Cambridge, 1995), 1, 4–6, 22, 25, 26, 214.
18 Chernaik, *Sexual freedom*, 80.
19 Porter & Hall, *Facts of Life*, 65.
20 Smith, 'Sexual mores,' 60, 71 n.94. The discussion in Nora Smith's paper of Scottish ideas about sexuality is an invaluable introduction, and I have drawn on it extensively.
21 Smith, *Sexual Mores*, 62.
22 L. Stone, *The family, sex and marriage in England, 1500–1713* (London, 1975), 597.
23 Smith, 'Sexual mores,' 60, 62, 63, 71 n.95.
24 Porter & Hall, *Facts of life*, 82.
25 Smith, 'Sexual mores,' 60–1, 71; N. Smith, 'Robert Wallace's "Of Venery,"' *Texas Studies in Literature and Language*, 15 (1973), 429–44.
26 Smith, 'Sexual mores,' 60–1; Smith, 'Robert Wallace,' 438; Harvey, *Sex in Georgian Britain*, 118.
27 J. Hunter, *A treatise on venereal disease* (London, 1786), 200–1; Smith, 'Sexual mores,' 63; Harvey, *Sex in Georgian Britain*, 120, 121.
28 [D. Maclauchlan], *Essay*, preface & p.10; Smith, 'Sexual mores,' 61.
29 *Fasti*, iv, 106.
30 Smith, 'Sexual mores,' 63; Porter & Hall, *Facts of life*, 108–19; R. Porter, 'The sexual politics of James Graham,' *British Journal of Eighteenth Century Studies*, v (1982), 199–20; B.B. Schnorrenberg, 'A true revelation of the life and career of James Graham, 1745–1794,' *Eighteenth Century Life*, xv, no. 3 (1991), 58–75.
31 Stone, *Family*, 575.
32 F.A. Pottle (ed.), *Boswell: The earlier years, 1740–69* (London, 1966), 30, 461.
33 F.A. Pottle (ed.), *Boswell on the grand tour: Germany and Switzerland, 1764* (London, 1953), 24; Stone, *Family*, 574.
34 Stone, *Family*, 579.
35 Stone, *Family*, 575.
36 *Supplement*, 34.

CHAPTER FOUR

Politicised Obscenity

Libertines and Jacobites

Spreading stories about the illicit sexual activities of opponents
had long had its place in the weaponry of literary satirists and
political opponents, and Reformation and Counter-Reformation
intensified the process as claiming the moral high ground in matters
sexual became central to sectarian warfare. However, as has been
seen in chapter three, politicisation of sex developed much further
than propaganda mud-slinging in Restoration Britain. Charles II's
example inspired court libertinism in reaction against Puritanism,
and in time those opposed to his politics began to relate them with
his sexual conduct. His inclinations towards absolutism and close
alliance with Catholic France abroad seemed threatening – Catholicism
being seen as naturally absolutist. Moreover, as all good Protestants
knew, Catholics were sexually depraved. The king combined Catholic
immorality with Catholic absolutism, and to some it seemed that
libertinism was leading not to liberty but to tyranny. It became
commonplace among satirists to equate royal power, symbolised by
the sceptre, as the phallic domination of male over female. Instead of
being ruled by the lawful power of the sceptre, the land was ruled by
the unrestrained lust for power of the phallus.

This growing fear of the Catholic-absolutist-phallic ambitions of
the Stuart dynasty helped to bring about its overthrow in the 1688–9

revolution, and the return to a regime superficially at least restoring traditional morality under King William. But the sexualisation of political debate survived among the Jacobites who dreamed of a new restoration of the Stuart dynasty. This is a minority theme within Jacobitism which contradicts the image of Jacobite ideology as wistful and pious aspiration, honest men hanging onto loyalty to a cause that brought many to ruin. It is not a theme that has interested historians of Jacobitism, but it sets the scene for the Beggar's Benison's mock Jacobite beggar-maid myth. Post-1660 Restoration reaction against Puritanism had been libertinism and delighting in obscenity. Superficially at least 1688–9 saw a shift back towards Puritan values, but to some Jacobites it seemed that Restoration libertine themes were still politically relevant. The sexual adventures of Charles II and his successor James VII and II were exploited by their opponents to discredit them, and some Jacobites reacted by proclaiming them as demonstrations of prowess and legitimacy. Their sexual exploits were signs or metaphors of their fitness for kingship, and should be celebrated. And since being mealy-mouthed was back in fashion under King William, this counter-culture loved obscenity.

The outstanding figure in Scottish Jacobite obscenity was Alexander Robertson of Struan. Born in the early 1670s, he was a passionate Catholic, Jacobite, drinker and libertine whose poems lurch uneasily between these obsessions. Excluded by his Jacobitism from public life, Robertson found consolation in the partner-gods of debauchery, Bacchus and Cupid. Sometimes their demands conflicted, and he violently denounces the one and swears allegiance to the other. In his openly libertine celebration of drink and sex he seems a left-over from the Restoration era – and though literary historians have yet to analyse his poetry, it seems clear that he modelled his work partly on the work of the arch-libertine of the Restoration, the earl of Rochester. Robertson suffered from the common libertine rage of frustration that the avid pursuit of pleasure gave no lasting satisfaction. Yet mixed in with the bragging libertine and nihilistic despair is the sincere Catholic and Jacobite. Both as libertine and Jacobite Robertson sought in much of his verse to shock. Bawdy and obscenity were useful as assaults on establishment values, as proclaiming commitment to libertinism through sexual explicitness, and as propaganda weapons to be employed in the Jacobite cause.

A good example is the poem in which he imagines Momus, god of ridicule, giving advice to a 'slighted nymph' who bemoans that her lover is not giving her the conventional sexual satisfaction she requires:

> Since Celadon no more is pleas'd
> With your obsequious Bum,
> To lay the Tickling he has rais'd,
> Ev'n, Chloe, take your Thumb.
>
> Or could you, in that Maner pleasing,
> His long red Nose employ,
> The Swain might get a constant Sneesing,
> And you yourself some Joy.

The ingeniously cheerful obscenity thus recommends masturbation, and nasal sex with sneezing replacing ejaculation.[1] Directly, this bit of smutty fun is nothing to do with Jacobitism, but indirectly, by writing such 'Restoration' type obscenity Robertson is making a political point, and in some poems obscenity does have direct political targets. In attacks on King William, Robertson's main theme is homosexuality. The charge was not new. William's old enemies the French had long accused him of homosexuality as a propaganda smear, building on the fact that he had no children – though in reality William's succession of mistresses testifies to his heterosexual preferences,[2] if not to his fertility. Once he had usurped the thrones of Britain, the accusations were revived by Jacobites and given a new symbolic, ideological content. William was 'unnatural' in having dethroned his father-in-law; King James VII and II, and thus usurped the thrones of a true monarch appointed by God. He was, as it were, a metaphorical homosexual as well as a real one, to be contrasted with the true king whose sexuality was in accordance with nature, the honestly heterosexual James.

Robertson deals with the matter in his 'Ode Inscribed to King William'. The verse seems, until the final lines, to be mistitled. It is a pastoral story of hetero- and homo-sexual intrigue, but it ends with the statement that one of the characters

> To old Jamie's doth prefer,
> A mode brought in by Willy.[3]

The king is a sodomist. Robertson elaborates the sexual attack in another poem. The childless William is presented as not only unnatural but physically incapable of heterosexual intercourse. Some presented the dethroning of James by William as the replacement of the old and weak by the power of youth,

> But since nor Wife nor Daughter ever felt
> Will's manly Parts, but rather thought him gelt,   *castrated*
> James was but ill depos'd, whose fruitful Cods,   *testicles*
> Scatter'd a generous Race of Demi-Gods,
> While t'other unperforming puny Prig
> Could only with his Page retire and fr[ig].[4]

The true power and authority of kingship is demonstrated by healthy genitals and sexual performance, the unnatural usurper characterised by homosexuality. With his irrepressible sense of the ridiculous, Robertson seems here to be caricaturing Jacobite ideology as much as supporting it. Few Jacobites would have been happy with such explicit celebration of even the most legitimate of royal testicles. But the assault on usurping William's genitals was not confined to Robertson. 'And let his genitals be such / As are King William's privities' was a useful curse.[5] But though these lines are found in a Scottish source, they are English in origin, taken from Ralph Gray's satirical 'Coronation Ballad' of 1689.[6] Scottish Jacobites had no monopoly of political obscenity.

Sometimes however Robertson disavows interest in politics. More immediate matters have priority. Venus ever gives delight, and Bacchus never cloys, and obsession with these gods brings indifference to the machinations of politicians and the rivalry of George and James (these are poems written after the '15, with the Hanoverian George I on the British thrones and Prince James Francis, the Old Pretender, the Jacobite claimant).[7] Who cares who is king?

There is a lot in Robertson that recalls the Beggar's Benison. Delight in obscenity, political commitment that faced with the rival attractions of drink and sex collapses into inaction and cynicism, and wit that insists on debunking political mythology with playful obscenity. Masturbation is a theme in several of Robertson's poems. This may simply reflect a striving for shocking topics to mention, but there is a real possibility that masturbation is a metaphor for frustrated failure. After all, masturbation was commonly seen as indicating failure. It was the resort of those isolated and powerless, unable to relieve their sexual tensions except in this sterile, second-best way. Perhaps for Robertson in his more alcoholic moments masturbation stood for the Jacobite dilemma, excluded from the real world of power, denied the social status that was theirs by right, barred from the natural expression of their political-sexual energies? Were their endless plottings and fantasies of success that never led to fulfilment metaphorically masturbatory?[8] Such an interpretation is speculative, but it is especially intriguing in the context of the friendship between Robertson and John McNachtane, the dominant figure in the early decades of that institution of the frustrated, the Beggar's Benison.

Knowledge of the friendship of Robertson and McNachtane comes, appropriately enough, from an obscene verse. Robertson was stung into writing 'St[rua]n's Sentiments of Mitchel's *Highland Fair*, addressed to the Laird of MacNachtane' by the published version of an 'opera' performed at Drury Lane in London in 1731. Joseph Mitchell's work, a play interspersed with songs sung to well known Scottish tunes, bore the full title of *The highland fair, or The union of the clans*. Mitchell was a Scot by birth, eking out a living in London as a poet. He concentrated so much on themes favourable to the government that he became known as 'Walpole's poet', Robert Walpole being the prime minister. *The highland fair* carried a typically obsequious political message, mixed in with mildly bawdy sub-plots. A few years previously the government had raised the Independent Companies as a military force to put down disorder and cattle-raiding in the Highlands, especially among clans with Jacobite inclinations. In Mitchell's opera one of these companies is depicted at work, in terms comic but with serious overtones. Two rival clan chiefs are reconciled by the peace-keepers of the companies. Intervention prevents a cattle raid leading to a feud, resulting in such fervently loyal (if remarkably leaden) lines as

> I wish the *Highlands* had never been without such Companies. Peace and good Order deserve the Government's Care, and we daily see the good Effects of it.

Reconciliation among the clans is seen as a happy parallel to the reconciliation between England and Scotland enshrined in the parliamentary union and the rule of the Hanoverians.[9]

Robertson of Struan was stung to fury by this propaganda celebrating union and the attack on the autonomy of the clans. He complained to John McNachtane

> Sir,
> A Long, long Minute have I spent,
> (Of which I heartily repent)
> Reading that poor pretence to Wit,
> And think it were a great Abuse,
> To destine it for any Use
> But when you go to Shite.

He went on tell his correspondent that if he hesitated about employing the opera as toilet paper, he should at least burn it.

> Yet if you think it too Severe,
> So shamefully the Page to tear
> That strives to sing our Highland Fame,
> Your more indulgent Nature may
> (Tho' much provoked by loos'ning Whey)
> Commit it to the Flame.[10]

Robertson and McNachtane had a good deal in common. The former had been a minor chieftain who had twice had his estates confiscated because of his Jacobitism. The latter too was nominally a chieftain, but his family's fortunes had collapsed through his father's involvement in the 1689 Jacobite rising, and he had had to find employment as a customs officer to support himself. These two representatives of a dying order in the Highlands would have shared a loathing for Mitchell's attempt to present the new dispensation in the north as fairy-tale success. Typically, Robertson still gives McNachtane the title of laird to which birth entitled him but of which events had deprived him.

The Beggar's Benison foundation myth had treated Jacobitism in terms of a satirical sexual allegory about James V. Robertson the Jacobite had in similarly satirical mood almost made a mockery of Stuart claims of hereditary right to the throne by reducing the issue to who had the best testicles. Both have the same message, ideological political struggle is comparable to animalistic sexual competition and copulation. No plotting of rebellion with resolutions to do or die, but tipsy nods and winks and giggles about the Dreel Burn and the sexually available beggar-maid. Toasts to the beggar maid and joy. Celebration of sexual naughtiness mixed with the naughtiness of hinting at the politically subversive. Good old Scotland, the beggar-maid. She was Scotia, and it was she who would bring the true king home – or at least preside over sexual licence in his name.[11]

Anti-Union Obscenity

As a weapon of political opposition, obscenity was not the monopoly of the Jacobites. In 1705 the Knights of the Horn Order appear in Edinburgh, the title immediately giving rise to suspicion of phallic allusion. Members claimed that the name came, innocuously, from a horn spoon used at a meeting and adopted as the club's badge – but 'spoon' as well as 'horn' was a euphemism for penis in the bewilderingly wide sexual vocabulary.[12] An early nineteenth-century antiquarian, Robert Chambers, delicately indicated that 'the common people believe it [the horn] to mean more than met the ear.' Presumably this and his other statements about the organisation are based on local tradition: 'if all accounts be true, it must have been a species of masquerade, in which the sexes were mixed and all ranks confounded;' it was 'a singular kind of fashionable club, or coterie of ladies and gentlemen' who 'caroused for many a day, founded mainly by the Earl of Selkirk'. In a later publication, Chambers was a bit more explicit, attributing 'debauchery in an unusual degree' to the order.[13]

Knights of the Horn are thus added to the tradition of mock-chivalric knights dedicated to the genitals, following the fictitious English Knight of the Burning Pestle (aroused penis) and the Scottish gang known as the Knights of Mortar (vagina) of a century before.[14] A chronologically closer inspiration was possibly an English ballad of the 1660s or 1670s which had introduced the Knight of the Forked Order and told the story of a servant who was paid by his elderly mistress to have sex with her. The theme of the insatiable lust of elderly ladies ends by describing their treatment of their husbands: they 'point them a Beaker, and give them a Horn' – meaning that they induce an erection by offering sexual accommodation for it.[15] If this was indeed a song in the repertoire of the Knights of the Horn, it would give added point to their reference to the horn as a 'spoon:' it complemented the fork of female anatomy in the scheme of sexual cutlery.

The Horn Order is, it seems, the earliest known Scottish club in which interest in sex was significant, and it combined indecency (of an unknown degree) with opposition to the 1707 parliamentary union of Scotland and England. This is indicated, though obscurely, by a satirical broadsheet. Dated February 1707, *The Knights of the Horn Orders address to the fruit maids of Edinburgh*[16] laments the country's decay in sexual terms. By accepting parliamentary union, chaste Scotland has been prostituted, accepting English gold in return for loss of independence.

> The Nations Sins are many fold,
> And Scotland has no name

Scotland had once been honourable, as had been Scots men. Ladies had not been kissed 'at random' and the Horn Order had not existed. But the age of the great patriots was long gone. In the glorious days of Bruce and Wallace

> These Champions did never Fight,
> As Cowards do now in Armour,
> Plain Dealing was the Scots delight,
> When I was a Dame of *Honour*.

On first reading this sounds nonsense. In the Middle Ages men had indeed fought in armour, whereas in 1707 they did not, yet the verse states the opposite. In fact it makes perfect ribald sense. 'Armour' here means condoms. Condoms were called armour as they were seen primarily not as contraceptives but as protections against sexually-transmitted disease[17] (with perhaps a play on the word 'amour' thrown in). So the verse jeers that while champions of old were valiant enough for plain dealing (unprotected sex), modern cowards lurked fearfully in armour, their phallic horns sheathed. Those being satirised are the supposed patriots of the Horn Order, men who had denounced union but failed to act effectively to maintain Scotland's independence, being distracted into libertine activity instead.

John Hamilton, Lord Belhaven, a fierce opponent of the union treaty, also turned to the condom (a novelty in Britain) for metaphorical inspiration, suggesting in 'A Scots Answer to a British Vision' that

there was a need to employ contraceptive devices to prevent the 'union'
or coupling of the two nations giving birth an unwanted new state:

> Then *Sirenge* and *Condom*   *syringe*
> Come both in Request.[18]

Obscure verses denouncing an organisation are not the best evidence
in seeking to determine its true nature. But the linking of sexual
freedom and political freedom for Scotland seems to be the key to
the Horn Order. As in Robertson of Struan's poetry, an anti-
establishment political cause was linked with adherence to attitudes
to sex subversive of establishment values. And, in both cases, the one
had got in the way of other. Robertson wrote about drink and sex as
substitutes for, rather than accompaniments to, political involvement,
and in the satire on the Horn it again seems that sex and socialising
had led to political impotence.

Unlike Robertson, however, the Horn Order was not Jacobite. Its
members disliked the union but they accepted the exclusion of the
Stuarts from the throne. The career of the earl of Selkirk, the only
individual who can be connected with the Horn, supports this interpretation. He was a staunch supporter of the Hanoverian succession,
but he opposed the union treaty. Once it was in place, however, he
was to prove ready to sit in the new British parliament it had created,
and later to accept high political office in the new British state.[19]
There was, it seems, suspicion among some opponents of union that
though Selkirk voted in parliament against the union negotiations,
he had somehow played a double game. He later admitted that he
had not thought that the union's effects on the economy of
Edinburgh would have been so severe as they had turned out to be.
George Lockhart of Carnwath's reaction on hearing of this was
'Impudent or imprudent wretch, thus to acknowledge his own
villainy!' The mischief accomplished by Selkirk and his 'partizans'
had been such that it would be 'a great pity if sooner or later he and
they should not be as high erected on a gibbet as the honour and
interest of the nation are by their means dejected'.[20] Was the wrath of
Lockhart based on belief that instead of making a serious attempt to
organise opposition to the union, Selkirk and his friends had had
their attentions diverted to whatever lascivious pleasures the Order
of the Horn offered?

The only two known references to the Horn Order outside the broadside satire on it are also hostile. Robertson of Struan joined in the denunciation of union. It was a second national betrayal, added to the betrayal of the Stuart dynasty. In 'The wages of sin: Inscribed to Scotia' the Horn Order is listed among lesser evils – but nonetheless described as more deserving of divine destruction than Sodom. Evidently its sin not so much inherent obscenity as the diversion of the attention and energy of those involved from anti-union activism.

> A thousand lesser Sins could I rehearse
> Did they not Stain the Purity of Verse;
> The Secret Lusts of those lascivious Wights,   *people*
> The *Horn Order* and the Crispin Knights;
> Had they appear'd in that more harmless Age,
> When Heav'n on Sodom pour'd its fiery Rage,
> Th' Almighty's Thunder sure had took its Aim
> At them, and Sodom had escap'd the Flame.
> But their Obscenities, not yet disclos'd,
> Are better veil'd with Silence than expos'd;
> Yet these unthinking beardless Boys, of late,
> Preside in Council, and have ruled the State.

As himself an eminent practitioner of the art of staining the purity of verse, Robertson's reluctance to describe the Horn Order's activities may be attributed to rhetoric rather than conviction. But his reference confirms that the members of the Horn Order were seen as betrayers of Scotland over the making of union, a disloyalty exposed by their readiness to accept office in the post-union regime.[21].

From a very different perspective, anti-union but Presbyterian Patrick Walker also denounced the Horn Order (along with the spread of brothels and immoral fashions of dress).

> Some Years ago, we had a profane, obscene Meeting, called *The Horn-order*: and now we have a new Assembly and public Meeting called *Love for Love*, but more truly, *Lust for Lust*; all Nurseries of Profanity and Vanity; so that it is a Shame to speak of these Things that are said and done amongst them.[22]

This is not very informative. All public gatherings of people of both sexes for socialisation and entertainment were anathema to Walker, and likely to be denounced in extreme terms. The new assembly that he denounced as it emerged in Edinburgh in the 1720s was an organisation that provided opportunities, under strict supervision, for dancing and mild romancing, so that Walker's comparison of the horn with the assembly hardly proves the extreme debauchery of the former. What, in matters sexual, the knights of the horn got up to can therefore only be guessed at. It would seem that they held social meetings of both sexes, and that this led to accusations of sexual immorality.

Even more obscure than the knights of the Horn Order are the 'Crispin Knights' that Robertson names alongside them. Only one other reference to the Crispins is known, and it occurs in a variant text of the satire on the knights of the Horn Order.

> The Crispins, and the Crispin pins,
> Were things unknown to us.[23]

Robert Chambers linked the Crispins to the Horn as fraternities 'practising debauchery to an unusual degree'[24] The name Crispin Knights is presumably taken from St Crispin, the patron saint of shoemakers, for the hollowness of the shoe made it a common name for vagina – in which case 'Crispin Pins' must be penises.[25] (At this point doubts may creep in as to interpretation, since it seems that there are few words in the language that have not at some time been used to refer to the genitals. But no other explanation of why the Crispins should so call themselves seems available.)

The most shocking piece of obscenity produced by anti-union fury attacked not politicians but Queen Anne herself. It was written after the union was put into effect, and deals with the supposed fate of the honours of Scotland. The crown, sword and sceptre, central symbols of independent nationhood, remained in Edinburgh, but the writer believed that they had been taken to London – or perhaps used the idea of the honours being moved in the metaphorical sense of the power they represented having moved to London. The crown, it is claimed, had been melted down to make a chamber pot for 'Brandy Nan' (Queen Anne). The sceptre

> 'Tis made a machine to f[ri]g the Queen,
> Lest f[uckin]g much had clapt her.

O What pollution more is?
O What pollution more is?
Than the thing that was,
To touch our laws,
Should now touch her clitoris.

Nor doe they think they ill doe,
Nor doe they think they ill doe,
That the royall Wand
That ruled our land,
Is now become a dildoe.[26]

Thomas Hamilton, 6th earl of Haddington (1680–1735), by contrast, used obscenity with a much lighter satirical touch. He was a good Hanoverian, and a supporter of union in principle, but he mocked aspects of the post-union settlement in Scotland with light-hearted fable. One of his tales satirises the new customs service and government paranoia about Jacobite plots.[27] Government intelligence had picked up reports of a ship being sent to Scotland loaded with armour. Fearing this is a Jacobite arms shipment arrangements are made to intercept the deadly cargo, but it cannot be found. At last, in a farcical conclusion it is realised there has been a misunderstanding Armour, again, meant condoms. The cargo was

To wit, the bladders of some hogs.
A-top with scarlet ribbons tyed,

The authorities

When hoping to find out a plot
Got heaps of cundums to their lot.

There are fascinating overlaps of themes between Haddington's tale and the Beggar's Benison. Sex, smuggling, customs officers, anti-unionism and Jacobitism are mixed together in satire. What this illustrates was not any connection between the earl and the club, but rather the extent to which political grievances were widely shared and could be satirised and frustration defused by introducing bawdy. The Benison, for all its peculiarities, again emerges as very much the product of its age.

Hell-Fire Clubs?

Horn Order and Crispin had, briefly and obscurely, preceded the Benison as Scottish sex clubs. Did Scotland also have hell-fire clubs? The name has become notorious through events in England in the 1750s, when it was applied to the 'Medenham Monks,' led by Sir Francis Dashwood (briefly chancellor of the exchequer), who flaunted sexual promiscuity. Members brought mistresses and prostitutes to cavort at whatever rituals went on in Dashwood's caves at High Wycombe, where open contempt for religion was shown, with parodies of the Mass and devotion to naked Venus replacing Christ on the Cross.[28] This came, in popular parlance to be *the* Hell-Fire Club, and the name is generally taken as referring to the hell to which sexual debauchery would consign its members. In fact what gave the name to this and other clubs was a sin worse than sexual irregularity – blasphemy. Thus when Scottish sources contain references to hell-fire clubs they turn out to be red herrings in the search for sex clubs. To Presbyterians like Patrick Walker and Robert Wodrow in the 1720s the worse nightmare was not clubs devoted to worldly pleasure but earnest discussion clubs, especially among students, which might spread heresy and atheism.[29] Too much thought among divinity students was to be discouraged. There were lurid rumours about the existence of such clubs in London,[30] and in 1726 Wodrow was scandalised by 'sad accounts of some secret Atheisticall Clubs' in and around Edinburgh, meeting in great secrecy. These had originated several years before and were supposedly encouraged by the secretary of the London hell-fire club who had come to Scotland. Divine vengeance had struck, however, for he had gone mad and died.[31] That was the closest that Scotland came to having a blasphemous hell-fire club, but the term was revived in Glasgow in 1793 when a group of drunken radicals, under the influence of atheistical ideas spread by the French Revolution, went to the churchyard of the Laigh Kirk and blew a trumpet in a mock attempt to raise the dead. They then burnt down the church, but that was an accident. They either adopted – or had foisted on them – the name Hell Fire Club.[32]

Yet one later writer in Scotland associated hell-fire clubs with the Beggar's Benison – but with a meaning referring neither to blasphemy nor to sexual excess. Charles Rogers claimed that along the coasts in the dark of night mysterious fires were sometimes seen burning at remote spots, recalling pagan fire rituals and giving rise to superstitious dread. Common belief linked them to the hell-fire clubs which were supposed to exist, taking the fires to mark the meetings of such blasphemous groups. In fact, there was a much more prosaic explanation. They were guiding fires, lit by smugglers to show boats where to land their illegal cargoes. Doubtless smugglers were happy to foster belief that the fires marked un-named iniquities, to discourage locals from investigating. Smugglers' organisations therefore (if Rogers is to be believed) came to be known as hell-fire clubs: 'On the west coast, at every point where prevailed a contra-band trade, a Hell-fire Club obtained scope and footing'. Having lit their guiding fires, they 'leapt through the burning embers, as did the boys through the Beltane fires'[33] – Beltane being a great Celtic fire festival formerly celebrated on 1 May.

Allan Ramsay and Patriotic Bawdy

Alexander Robertson sought to work off his frustration as a Jacobite in a hostile world through drink, poetry and obscenity – and occasional marginal involvement in futile rebellion. He spent a life largely in exile in France or in self-imposed internal exile, turning his back on the regime. Allan Ramsay (1686–1758) expressed his Jacobite sympathies in a different way, through subversion of prevailing cultural standards from within. He knew Robertson, publishing a few of the his poems and contributing to an anthology to celebrate his return from France in the 1720s,[34] but there is no evidence that they were close friends.

The literary culture of Scotland was, in Ramsay's eyes, deficient and in danger of further decline. It was anglicised, and was becoming increasingly so as a result of parliamentary union. Ramsay's reaction was to demonstrate through his own verse that writing in Scots, rather than southern English, could be highly effective, and to republish almost forgotten works by sixteenth century and earlier poets to reveal that a valuable national heritage existed. Scots should take pride in, and build upon, this heritage. Ramsay's programme of building on pre-Reformation culture involved a rejection of the domination of Calvinist cultural influence in Scotland. The country had lost touch with its true past, and its culture had become desperately narrow through generations of bigoted opposition to secular culture and the literature of enjoyment.

The whole-hearted patriotic revival of pre-Reformation poetry, as advocated by Ramsay, included much which to most educated Scots of his day must have seemed daring or even obscene. In his 1724 anthology, *The ever green*, Ramsay printed a wide range of this material which included notable examples of bawdy from sixteenth-century poets. Ancient Greek and Roman obscenity had long been legitimised by antiquity and literary merit, and Ramsay now, on the back of the strength of patriotic anti-union sentiment, sought to raise early Scottish obscenity to the same respectability. Ramsay saw the obscene not only from an antiquarian perspective, as a legitimate part of an old, rich Scottish culture. It also stood for the good old days that culturally impoverished Scotland should revive. The fact that it horrified the pious just showed how effete and untrue to her past Calvinist, anglicised, post-union Scotland had become. In verse that he admitted authorship of, Ramsay never ventured on such open obscenity as in his reprints of older poems. Nonetheless, he staked the claim of bawdy to be a part of the legitimate repertoire of poets of the eighteenth century. It should be something that could be published and acknowledged, and animated by literary talent, not something confined to oral tradition, smutty ballads and crude political satire. Obscenity could be patriotic.

'Lucky Spence's Last Advice' (in the *Poems* of 1721) was Ramsay's most notable venture into the world of bawdy. He explored the underworld of sex, the lives of the whores of Edinburgh, treating prostitutes and associated criminality with a degree of sympathy and understanding. It is shocking, but also attractive. Lucky Spence, a famous whore, explains on her deathbed to her young successors how to conduct business. How, for example, to find a drunk, persuade him that you are a virgin, and let him fall asleep so you can steal his possessions. If he tries to have sex, give him nothing – not even venereal disease:

> When he's asleep, then dive and catch
> His ready Cash, his Rings or Watch;
> And gin he likes to light his Match   *if*
> At your Spunk box,   *tinder-box*

> Ne'r stand to let the fumbling Wretch
> E'en take the Pox.

The lines at the centre of the stanza contain the most explicit references in Ramsay's published verse to the genital basics of sex – though lightly disguised. Rather engagingly, Ramsay was proud of being shocking, and was worried that this might be overlooked by a casual reader. Therefore he resorted to a mock-serious footnote explaining that the phrase 'light his match' needed 'annotation.' Having thus made sure the double-entendre would receive attention, he then failed to provide an explanation on the grounds that 'I do not incline to explain every thing, lest I disoblige future Criticks, by leaving nothing for them to do.' What he really means is 'I hope you've understood my metaphors about "match" and "spunk-box" and have been suitably shocked. Look how naughty I am!'

Lucky Spence gives her benison: not a beggar's, but a whore's:

> My Benison come on good Doers
> Who spend their Cash on Bawds and Whores.[35]

Always on the lookout for pretexts for attacks on Presbyterians and their morality, Ramsay seized gleefully on the Rev. Daniel Maclauchlan's pamphlet which advocated increasing the population by the encouragement of fornication. Ramsay savoured the scandal in ingenious detail in his 'Address of thanks from the Society of Rakes to the pious author of *an Essay upon improving and adding to the strength of Great Britain and Ireland by fornication*',

> Now Lads laugh a,' and take your Wills,
> And scowp around like Tups and Bulls,   *leap; rams*
>   Have at the bony Lasses.
> For Conscience has nae mair to say,
> Our *Clergy-man* has clear'd the Way,
>   And proven our Fathers Asses.[36]

The published poem is restrained compared to a manuscript version which Ramsay thought too explicit to print. In this he envisioned churches with beds replacing pews, mothers bringing along 'their blooming Daughters fair' to fornicate: a paradise for rakes.

Then hast ye Lads and Lasses Braw
Lets serve our Country ane and a
   By fruitful fornication
Thus will we fully man our fleet
And make our armys maist complet
   And clear from debt our Nation.[37]

John McNachtane subscribed to Ramsay's *Poems* of 1721, and
Robert Lumsdaine of Innergellie, who was later to be sovereign of
the Edinburgh branch of the Benison, subscribed to the *Poems* of
1728.[38] Ramsay's subversion of Presbyterian/Hanoverian values
through bawdy was measured, literary and public. Robertson of
Struan preferred extreme but private obscenity (his poems were only
published after his death when, it is said, his valet stole the
manuscripts). The Beggar's Benison's politically-slanted obscenity
was even more extreme, in that it included actions as well as words,
and though secret was expressed sociably within the club. All can be
seen as part of the same tradition, of obscenity which is not just for
obscenity's sake, seeking to shock, but which expresses defiant and
frustrated attitudes to prevailing values. From this wider perspective
it is now time to narrow the focus, and return to Merryland, the East
Neuk of Fife.

Notes

1 A. Robertson, *Poems* (Edinburgh, [*c.*1750]), 81.
2 S.B. Baxter, *William III* (London, 1966), 111–12, 349–52, 359.
3 Robertson, *Poems*, 54–7; T. Crawford (ed.), *Love, labour and liberty. The
eighteenth century Scottish lyric* (Cheadle, 1976), 92–3; partly quoted in A Scott,
Scotch passion. An anthology of Scottish erotic poetry ((London, 1982), 168.
According to T. Crawford, *Society and the lyric* (Edinburgh, 1979), 46, Robertson 'celebrates homosexuality' in the ode. But as the charge of homosexuality is
used to damn King William this is hardly a celebration.
4 Robertson, *Poems*, 83–4.
5 [J. Maidment (ed.)], *A book of Scottish pasquils* (Edinburgh, 1868), 280.
6 P.L. Monod, *Jacobitism and the English people, 1688–1788* (Cambridge, 1989),
55.
7 Robertson, *Poems*, 159–60, 236–7.
8 Crawford, *Society and the lyric*, 47–8, remarks that 'A faintly masturbatory
tendency is to be found in some of the more "refined" Scottish lyrics of the
period,' but unfortunately only cites one reference, to Robertson.

9   J. Mitchell, *The Highland fair* (London, 1731); *DNB*. See T. Tobin, *Plays by Scots, 1660–1800* (Iowa, 1974), 127–31.

10 Robertson, *Poems*, 282.

11 F.P. Lole, 'The Scottish Jacobite clubs,' *The Jacobite. The Journal of the 1745 Association*, no. 81 (1993), 11–16, classifies the Benison as a Jacobite club, but this is obviously misleading – though not quite as misinformed as his calling the Wig Club 'Jacobite.'

12 Williams, *Dictionary*, iii, 1291. However, it is possible that the Horn Order took its name from innocent events a generation earlier involving horn spoons. Late in the eighteenth century an indirect report referred to the Scottish court of James, duke of York, in the early 1680s. 'Lady Janet Bruce, who, being then a young woman, was often at that Court, told Mr Abercromby that the *horn order*, which was held in such abomination, was entirely innocent. The drinking of tea was just beginning at that time, and the Duchess gave her favourites whom she wished to attend her tea-table and balls a small horn spoon twisted at the end. They wore it at their breast as a sort of ticket.' J. Ramsay of Ochtertyre, *Scotland and Scotsmen in the eighteenth century*, ed. A. Allardyce (2 vols., Edinburgh, 1888) i, 62–3n.

13 Chambers, *Traditions*, 156–7; R. Chambers, *Domestic annals of Scotland* (3 vols., 1859–61), iii, 482n. J. Grant, *Old Edinburgh* (3 vols., 1880–3), iii, 122, mentions the Horn Order, but, as in many other instances, he evidently re-works material drawn from Chambers rather than drawing on any additional sources.

14 D. Stevenson, 'What was the quest of the Knights of the Mortar? An indelicate suggestion', *Scottish Historical Review*, lxviii (1989), 182–4.

15 *The Roxburghe ballads* (Ballad Society, 9 vols., 1869–99), iv, 368–70. Unfortunately the editor makes some 'trifling interpolations,' thus bowderlising a text which he found unbearably obscene.

16 Printed in Edinburgh, February 1707, according to a ms. note on the copy at NLS, Ry III. a. 10(19). A variant of the 'Address' appears in J Maidment, *A second book of Scottish pasquils* (Edinburgh, 1828), 73–5. Both these Scottish versions are, in turn, based on Thomas D'Urfey's 'The dame of honour or hospitality, sung by Mrs Willis in the opera call'd the Kingdom of the Birds,' which similarly laments decline from a superior past, though in an English context, T. D'Urfey, *Wit and mirth, or pills to purge melancholy* (6 vols., London, 1719–20, facsimile reprint London, 1872), i, 212–14.

17 The earliest use of armour meaning condom noted is 1707: Williams, *Dictionary*, i, 39.

18 G. de F. Lord (ed.), *Poems on affairs of state. Augustan satirical verse* (7 vols., New Haven, 1660–1714), vii, 25; referred to in Williams, *Dictionary*, i, 39, 291.

19 Charles Hamilton Douglas, 2nd earl of Selkirk, was born in 1663, and thus was in his early forties when the Horn Order was founded. He died, unmarried, in 1739. *SP*, vii, 517–18.

20 D. Szechi (ed.), *'Scotland's ruine,' Lockhart of Carnwath's memoirs of the union* (Aberdeen, 1995), 158, 175.

21 Robertson, *Poems*, 115–16.

22 P. Walker, *Some remarkable passages of the life and death of Mr Alexander Peden* (3rd edn, Edinburgh, 1728), reprinted in Walker, *Biographica Presbyteriana* (2 vols., Edinburgh, 1827), i, 133–5, 138–40. Chambers, *Domestic annals*, iii, 482 cites the passage – but omitting 'Lust for Lust'.

23 Maidment, *Second book of Scottish pasquils*, ii, 75.

24 Chambers, *Domestic annals*, iii, 482n.

25 Williams, *Dictionary*, ii, 1032–4, iii, 1236–8.

26 'The metamorphosis, or the royal honours of Scotland,' in [J. Maidment & C.K. Sharpe (eds.)], *A banquet of dainties for strong stomachs* {Edinburgh, 1828], 15–18. A copy of the verse is glued into a scrapbook of Maidment, NLS, Hall. 169.b.1, and a version with additional stanzas appears in NLS, MS Adv. 23.3.24, f.100r-v. The same manuscript includes a verse commemorating Anne's knighting of David Hamilton, 'the Scots woman['s] doctor' [gynaecologist], containing a repellent description of the medical examination of the ageing and diseased queen culminating in 'Rise up Sir David said the Queen / The first Cunt knight that ever was seen,' f.95r-v.

27 [Thomas, 6th earl of Haddington], *Poems on several occasions* (4th edn., 1765), 33–6. The earl's verses were first published as *Forty select poems, on several occasions, by the Right Honourable the earl of ... Never before published* ([London?], 1753). P. Wagner, *Eros revived. Erotica of the Enlightenment in England and America* (London, 1987), 58, 181–2, 321, 322, 361 erroneously states that Haddington also ran a ribald club known as Crazy Castle. This is a misunderstanding. John Hall Stevenson (1718–85), a Yorkshire gentleman, held bawdy, witty meetings with friends (including Laurence Sterne) under the name of the Demoniacs, at Crazy Castle, the name that Stevenson gave to his residence (formerly Skelton Castle). His poetic effusions for such meetings were published in 1765 as *Crazy tales* (Jones, *Clubs*, 156–63). In 1783 a publisher sought to cash in on the association of Crazy Castle with pornography by producing a reprint of Haddington's verses as *New crazy tales or ludicrous stories...*, claiming that they were printed at 'Crazy Castle', but Haddington had died in 1735, and as Stevenson was then aged only about thirteen it is clearly impossible that the former could have had anything to do with the 'Crazy Castle' created by the latter.

28 Jones, *Clubs*, 116–41.

29 R. Wodrow, *Analecta* (4 vols., Maitland Club, 1842–3), iii, 183.

30 Jones, *Clubs*, 38–47; R.J. Allan, *The clubs of Augustan London* (Hamden, Conn., 1967), 119–23.

31 Wodrow, *Analecta*, iii, 309; Jones *Clubs*, 49–50.

32 'Senex,' *Glasgow, past and present* (3 vols., Glasgow, 1884), i, 249.

33 Rogers, *Social life*, ii, 411.

34 A. Ramsay, *Works* (STS, 6 vols., 1951–74), iii, 191–3, vi, 134–6; A. Robertson, *Mons Struani, in Struani Domini sui reditum* (1732).

35 Ramsay, *Works*, i, 22–6.

36 Ramsay, *Works*, iii, 128–34; A.H. MacLaine, *Ramsay* (Boston, 1985), 53.

37 Ramsay, *Works*, vi, 119–24.

38 Ramsay, *Works*, i, xxxiv; ii, xviii.

CHAPTER FIVE

The East Neuk of Fife

A Provincial Society

What sort of society was it that gave monstrous birth to the Beggar's Benison? The East Neuk of Fife was the name given to the parishes of the south-east corner of Fife which jutted out eastwards into the German Ocean (as the North Sea was then) culminating in the eastern point of the county, Fife Ness. Bounded by the sea on two sides, the Neuk was more vaguely defined on land. To the north lay moorland, not yet brought under the plough, with routes through to St Andrews to the north and Cupar to the north west. The most frequented land communications lay south west, along the Fife coast through a string of small towns, to Kirkcaldy and beyond. Most communication, however, was by sea, seen not as a barrier but an endless and flexible (if capricious and dangerous) highway. Across the Firth of Forth, clearly in sight when summer fogs and winter mists permitted, lay the Lothians and Edinburgh. In the Firth itself floated the Isle of May, south east of Anstruther, and in the distance beyond rose the forbidding hump of the Bass Rock, formerly a state prison. Upstream, the Forth penetrated to Stirling and the heart of Scotland. Venturing out of the firth gave access to coastal trade with north east Scotland and the northern islands of Orkney and Shetland, and southwards to the English coast. Beyond that lay trading contact with France, the Netherlands, Scandinavia and the Baltic.

The people of the East Neuk made their living from the resources that land and sea gave them. They farmed, traded, and fished. There were good times and bad. The weather dictated the harvest and fish stocks fluctuated unpredictably. Politics, national and international, wars and taxes, took their tolls. Geography ensured that trade and settlement concentrated not on one centre but was spread between several, for the generally rocky, inhospitable coastline, interleaved with small sandy beaches, offered only small fissures in which harbours could be contrived. These tiny havens offered shelter to a handful of trading and fishing boats. By the eighteenth century five towns in the East Neuk, based on such harbours, had attained the status of royal burghs, giving them rights of internal government and overseas trading privileges. Accidents of land-ownership split Anstruther into two separate entities, Easter and Wester, facing each other across the Dreel Burn, with the eastern burgh much the larger entity. Tacked on to the other, easterly, side of Anstruther Easter was Cellardyke, the harbour for Kilrenny, which lay a mile inland. A few miles west along the coast from this bundle of three burghs lay Pittenweem, while to the east, out towards Fife Ness, was Crail.

Five small towns, which quickly gave way to surrounding country. The towns were dominate by tiny cliques, largely made up of merchants, who formed the burgh councils, often largely self-perpetuating in membership. Each chose two or three baillies or magistrates, the civil leaders who acted as judges in the burgh court. Larger royal burghs had provosts (mayors), but the eastern Fife burghs were content simply to designate one of their baillies the chief or first magistrate, and he presided in the burgh council. The more success-ful merchants would buy land outside the burgh boundaries, both as an investment and for the social status this gave. A little land and a title (or rather designation) derived from it, and you could flatter yourself that you were gentry – say Johnstone of Rennyhill. But your family might well not be accepted for a generation or two as real gentry by the old landed families of lairds who dominated the countryside and boasted bloodlines stretching back for centuries.

Townsmen branched out into landownership, and there was also movement the other way, as lairds developed commercial interests or sought political control, and their younger sons settled in the burghs to make livings as merchants or craftsmen. Generalisations about rank and hierarchy blur around the edges when communities are put under the microscope. Nonetheless, it was old-established families who dominated the region, though none of the members of this local aristocracy could, in national terms, be regarded as major figures. Sub-division of landownership was a notable feature of Fife, and the men who dominated the East Neuk were therefore of moderate wealth. Most in the mid-eighteenth century largely confined their social and economic activities to the region, but the greatest (above all, the several branches of the prolific Anstruther family) had wider interests, and sought status and power by competing for public offices, seeking appointments as sheriff or sheriff depute of Fife, or lord lieutenant or deputy, or justice of the peace. Or even membership of parliament.

Through parliament the five little royal burghs became significant to landed men of ambition. Since the union of parliaments of 1707 the burghs had formed a single parliamentary constituency, Anstruther Easter Burghs. Legally, the five royal burghs organised their own parliamentary elections. Each burgh council chose a delegate, and the five delegates then met to elect a member of parliament. But in practice the burghs could not withstand the wealth and authority of landowners who intervened in burgh politics. Local landlords with ambitions sought to build up support in the burghs. In day to day business the burgh councils were usually left to their own devices, though the landowners who regarded themselves as having some right to authority over them would keep an eye on their activities, seeking favour for their supporters. Occasionally an Anstruther landowner would himself take a seat on a burgh council – though only attending meetings when annual council elections might need managing in his interests. More often it was easier to ensure that the burgh clerk was one of their men, willing to report to them on local affairs.

On the approach of parliamentary elections, however, the burgh councils often came under concentrated pressure. The attitude of the councillors usually seems to have been not so much resentment as acceptance of the inevitable, and willingness to exploit the situation, manipulating political rivalries to extract maximum advantage. Candidates were often prepared to spend lavishly to secure a seat. As elsewhere in Scotland, the supply of county seats in parliament was greatly outstripped by demand, so landowners took over burgh seats.

Parliamentary elections in the burghs (especially small ones) became disgraceful though entertaining affairs. A few of the councillors involved no doubt had principles or preferences, but for most it was an opportunity for profit. And, even if a man did vote out of conviction, it was only fair that he should receive reward as did the corrupt. With the total electorate at the first stage of the election consisting of only a few dozen councillors, each had to decide how to vote under pressure of threats and promises of favour and financial benefit. Drink flowed freely, and it was often impossible to get those bribed to stay loyal. All sorts of ploys were resorted to by candidates if things weren't going the right way. The burgh clerk could, say, conveniently lose the burgh seal, so he couldn't seal the delegate's commission. Once elected, the five individual burgh delegates faced continuous harassment. They might be persuaded to mislay their commissions. A stubborn delegate could be kidnapped and held until the election was over. Whole groups of councillors could be willingly abducted to be wined and dined for days or even weeks in advance of an election, to keep them in the right frame of mind.

Usually the interests of the Anstruthers prevailed, with a firm base in Anstruther Easter and Wester meaning that they could count on two out of the five delegate votes that decided parliamentary elections. In the aftermath of the '45, when demonstrations of submission to the regime and its representatives were expedient, Sir John Anstruther pulled off a notable coup. Anstruther Easter, Anstruther Wester, Kilrenny and (probably) Pittenweem all accepted his factor, Benjamin Plenderleath, as their burgh clerks.[1] Only Crail, where the clerkship had become hereditary in a local family, escaped the Anstruther net. Anstruther Easter Burghs obtained an outstanding reputation for corruption. In the 1770s it was so blatant that it provoked even a duke to support secret balloting at elections as the only cure. Two thirds of Scottish MPs, raged the duke of Atholl, were men better fitted for the plough than parliament. Sir John Anstruther (the son of the Sir John just mentioned)

> stands foremost on the list. When a man has more money than witt they ought to be parted, that the Debauching and rend'ring Profligate the whole side of the County for one man's folly is a very serious consideration and calls for a Remedy from the Legislature. Election by Ballatt would remove almost all the evils complained of.[2]

Thus the East Neuk burghs exercised their constitutional responsibilities with conspicuous dishonesty, with the eager co-operation of
the gentlemen parliamentary candidates. These landowners might
despise the voters for their corruption, but they and their agents had
to work with them, get to know them, and show concern for their
interests. As for the councillors, which particular gentleman sat in
parliament made little difference to them or their burghs, so getting
the best bargain going made sense. It was also, no doubt, good to see
arrogant gentry fawning for favours from humble burgesses. Giving
them the run-around before deciding how to vote may have been
part of the game. An odd form of social bonding, creating working
relationships between differing groups in society.

As well as occasional parliamentary elections, each of the five East
Neuk burghs had more regular rights to a nominal say in national
affairs. Each sent a commissioner to sit annually in the general
assembly of the Church of Scotland, and a commissioner to sit in the
convention of royal burghs. They might be small provincial towns,
but they took pride in their wider roles.

Anstruther family interests also dominated the Fife county
elections, providing the MPs for most of the century. The Anstruthers,
however, were so powerful that the leading members of the family
tended to be remote from daily life in the East Neuk. They were
actors on a bigger stage, often away in London or elsewhere, and
protecting their electoral interests was one the few things that
concentrated their attention on the East Neuk. Originally the senior
branch of the family had lived in Dreel Castle, standing in East
Anstruther at the mouth of the Dreel Burn, alongside the houses of
the townsfolk. But they had long withdrawn from this intimacy to
estates in the countryside, leaving the castle in ruins, though the
Beggar's Benison, with it habitual imaginative creativity, liked to
claim that the club actually met there. The East Neuk boasted only
one noble family, that of the earls of Kellie, and it was something of
an embarrassment. The title of earl, created for a courtier over a
century before, suggested a status greatly beyond the family's means.
The earl at the time the Benison was founded might tactfully be
described as of very limited intelligence, and his successor was a
jovial spendthrift who eventually had to sell off what family estates
there were. The Neuk was mainly divided into small to moderate

gentry estates, the lairds being often fairly homespun characters. When visiting Edinburgh, it was said that Fife lairds could be identified by their weather-beaten old brown hats. Crossing the Firth of Forth in open boats, they left their best hats at home safe from salt spray and seagulls. They were also regarded as being 'gash' – an obsolete word suggesting 'a shrewd cunning or sagacity combined with self-conscious eccentricity.'[3]

Politics and religion were matters of concern, but not much action. The factional feuding stirred up by parliamentary elections was usually more a matter of individuals than ideology. Many of the gentry were Episcopalian in religious inclinations, and therefore likely to have Jacobite sympathies, but by the 1730s they accepted the Presbyterian establishment set up in 1690 without open protest. Until late in the century Episcopalians had few clergy of their own and were open to persecution, but most Presbyterian parish ministers showed little interest in investigating too closely the beliefs of their betters and paymasters. Many lairds quietly mourned the loss of the old Stuart dynasty, and lamented the coming of the upstart Hanoverians in 1714, but they showed little interest in active Jacobitism. The 1715 rebellion had failed, and the local lairds had no thoughts of being able to change their world, confining themselves to quiet grumbling. At least there was peace. They took a similar attitude to the union of parliaments: it was something they had to live with – with one exception. The high customs and excise duties that union brought with it were widely defied. After all, such matters effected not just principles but wealth.

Over the century of the Benison's existence, however, positive acceptance of dynasty and union grew. In religion removal of persecution allowed Episcopalianism to emerge into the open. In time, the landed classes realised the benefits to themselves brought by being part of a united Britain. Wars, expansion of trade, colonies and government bureaucracy brought opportunities, and by the end of the century there can have been few landed families not plugged into the vast network of patronage, great and petty, which helped provide naval and military commissions and other jobs. Predictably, the Anstruthers were the first and greatest beneficiaries of this expanding world. Sentimental Jacobitism might linger, but by the end of the century it was so clearly a lost cause that even staunch

Hanoverians could feel safe in dabbling in its romantic nostalgia. Lower down in East Neuk society support for the 1688–9 revolution which had overthrown the Stuarts was stronger than among the gentry, based on widespread positive support for Presbyterianism. But though men might be committed to the Hanoverians, resentment at the union and the high customs duties and hard economic conditions that followed it, was widespread, and even the most convinced 'whig' might have a lingering feeling that it was humiliating to have accepted 'the wee German lairdie,' George I, as king. The East Neuk had a settled, fairly harmonious community that basically wanted to be left to get on with its own affairs. Parliamentary elections apart, life was fairly tranquil. But the grievances and nostalgias which loitered underground revealed themselves in bizarre forms in the Beggar's Benison.

Fair Trade: Smuggling and Sex

Lingering Episcopalian or Jacobite sentiments were long-term, low-key causes for discontent for most of the time, though coming dramatically to the fore in 1745–6. Similarly the issue of union in general led to muttering rather than action. But the imposition of the new very high levels of customs and excise duties was seen as a burning, live, day-to-day grievance. Union had been supposedly a necessity for Scotland to rescue her from economic disaster. Instead, according to popular opinion in the decades that followed, it was exacerbating the country's poverty through these iniquitous duties. All over Scotland the duties were the most widespread, concrete causes of discontent with the post-union regime, and of active defiance of the law by men of all ranks.

The parliamentary union of 1707 united the fiscal systems of England and Scotland on an English basis. English customs and excise administrative structures were introduced to Scotland, and payment at English rates. Scottish duties had traditionally been low, collection ramshackle and indirect. The new 'English' duties were sometimes higher than the old ones by several hundred *per cent*; and a new bureaucracy of customs and excise officials – comptrollers, surveyors, clerks, tide waiters – quickly spread across Scotland. These men were the harbingers of new types of centralised government extending to the localities. The customs men were paid from the centre (the Board of Customs in Edinburgh), directly answerable to it, and took their orders from it. Government in the past had nearly always worked through local, traditional agencies – the landowners, or the burgh councils. Now these men, brought up to regard themselves as the natural, legitimate local enforcers of government power, were finding the localities invaded by these new officials over whom they had no control. To make things worse, some of these usurpers were English. This might be sensible until Scots were trained in the arcane mysteries of English fiscal administration, but it added to the resentment. Moreover, the high duties were 'English' in another sense. They were designed for the needs of the English economy, where manufacturing was far more advanced than in Scotland. The emphasis in many cases was on protecting English manufactures from foreign competition, while hindering export of raw materials which might help competitors. The traditional Scottish economy was much more geared towards exporting raw materials in exchange for manufactured goods and luxuries from Europe.[4]

Scottish reactions were predictable. Outrage, and determination to avoid paying customs and excise duties whenever possible. People at all levels of society were united in this. Even firm supporters of the Hanoverian regime did not hesitate to defy the law, while to Jacobites buying smuggled goods became almost a moral obligation, for the duties were illegal levies imposed by usurpers.[5] Support for smuggling was on such a scale that it undermined the regime's credibility as well as its finances. A huge market for smuggled goods emerged, with commodities brought in by both foreign and Scottish ships from all along the western coast of Europe. Customs officials found themselves isolated and in danger of violence. If they caught smugglers and seized goods, they had difficulty in hanging on to them in the face of efforts to release them. Lack of support for prosecutions from those in power locally, from burgh magistrates to landowners serving as justices of the peace, made convictions difficult. Active smugglers might be a minority, but the majority of the population sympathised with them and were ready to buy untaxed goods from them in defiance of the law, and even to protect them from the law and invest money with them in hope of profit. Men and women who regarded themselves as honest, law-abiding, church-going citizens saw smuggling not only as no crime, but as positively virtuous.[6]

A detailed case study (of Dunbar in 1765) led to the judgement that 'It is almost certainly a fair conclusion that a greater value of goods was smuggled into the precinct than was lawfully landed.' A wide variety of goods was concerned in the trade, but the market leaders were brandy, gin and other spirits, wine, tea and tobacco. One public figure of the day who stood out against the trade was Duncan Forbes of Culloden, and in denouncing it he gave a vivid picture of its extent. He explained (in the 1740s) how, after the 1707 union, the Scots 'in place of pursuing *fair* Trade' – which to him meant lawful trade – 'universally, with the exception of *Glasgow, Aberdeen*, one or two places more, took to *smuggling*'. Gain was the main motive, but dislike of the union was also strong. The 'Bulk of the People' came to favour the smugglers, who were guarded by locals so customs officers could not seize their goods. If any of them were arrested, people joined other smugglers to 'rescue' them. Even when cases could be brought to court, '*Juries* seldom failed to find for the defendant'. Officials were helpless.

> When the goods are laid on Land, all Hands are at Work for his [the smuggler's] Service. Cattle and Carriages are ready; every Farm-house, every Cottage is open for their Reception. – Giving the least Information to the Customhouse is, in the Opinion of the People, branded with Infamy.

All this, Forbes stressed, could not happened without the support of the landed gentry, and his main plea was directed to them. In supporting untaxed foreign goods they were destroying attempts to establish industries in Scotland. Moreover, most of the landlords concerned had largely arable estates, and by supporting smuggling they were bringing financial ruin on themselves. Grain prices were falling, pulling rents downwards, and one of the main reasons for this was that smuggled spirits and ale had greatly reduced the use of Scottish grain for distilling and brewing. Ale itself was being replaced by cheap smuggled tea as the staple drink of the common people. Even when it came to reinforcing their tea, people added smuggled rum and brandy instead of Scotch whisky. Tea drinking had been accepted when it had been a luxury confined to the social élite. But now its use had spread, making it 'that *Drug* amongst the *lowest* of the People'.[7] Sir John Clerk, Baron of the Exchequer (and owner of a famed Roman phallus), agreed with Forbes about the scale of the problem: 'at this time there is scarce such a thing as fair tradeing amongst us,' and jurors in the exchequer court 'cut the throat of their countrey' by refusing to convict. 'This madness seems to be countenanced by all ranks and degrees of people and especially those of the richer sort.'[8]

Smuggling was Scotland's biggest and most profitable service industry, but establishing how it was organised and financed is difficult. As an illegal trade those involved obviously kept their profiles as low as possible. At a local level, virtually everyone probably knew something of what was going on (at least who it was that delivered the brandy and tea that they drank), but not who the leaders were. Customs and excise officials might have their suspicions, but the extent of both popular and élite support for this criminal activity usually made attempts at detection of the men behind the smuggling gangs fruitless. The few smugglers who were arrested were almost invariably the little men – sailors landing goods or labourers helping to hide them. They took their punishment and kept quiet as to who, among the merchants and gentry, were the hidden organisers. Only among Scots resident abroad is it easy to identify large-scale smugglers, for they were doing nothing illegal in their adopted lands. Many Scots were employed by the Swedish East Indies Company in Gothenburg, the main source of tea smuggled into Britain, while other Scots in the town established themselves as traders with smuggling adding to their profits. Coutts & Co., the famous banking and merchant company, owed much of its early prosperity to having a partner stationed in the Netherlands supplying goods to be smuggled into Scotland.[9]

In Fife, Lord Elphinstone in the 1730s persistently thwarted the efforts of the customs administration to prosecute smugglers, using his position as a justice of the peace in support of illegality.[10] In Morayshire the provost of Elgin and the justices were similarly obstructive.[11] In Aberdeen the names of the 'most prominent citizens, merchants and manufacturers' were connected with smuggling, but at all levels in both burgh and country the authorities thwarted efforts to suppress it.[12] In Montrose and elsewhere even when troops were sent to back up customs officials the forces of central authority were thwarted by the resistance of those who held power locally.[13] In England Jacobite motivation was often cited as a justification for such lawbreaking. In Scotland patriotism joined Jacobitism and greed in the equation.[14]

One Fife case in 1719 was rare in revealing the sort of alliance that underlay the success of the smugglers. There were three partners in crime. James Grahame, a former baillie of Anstruther Easter (and later a member of the Beggar's Benison), Sir Alexander Anstruther of Newark, and a ship's captain. The three men were arrested and imprisoned in the tollbooth of Edinburgh for trying to smuggle a huge cargo of brandy into the country – 462 casks containing 4700 gallons. But they were released on bail, and immediately acted to sabotage their forthcoming trial. They believed that two sailors from the ship would be damaging prosecution witnesses and, having traced them to Renfrewshire, sent off a gang to seize them and hold them prisoner until the trial was over. The sailors were duly kidnapped and delivered to the houses of two of Anstruther's kinsmen in Fife, his brother Sir Robert Anstruther of Balcaskie and his nephew Sir John Anstruther. Sir Philip Anstruther of Anstrutherfield, another of Sir Robert's brothers, was also involved in this kidnapping of witnesses.

This was a fine haul of leading east Fife gentry, revealing how deeply smuggling penetrated the establishment. Sir Alexander, two of whose sons were to be members of the Benison, was an advocate and as joint clerk of the bills an official of the court of session (though evidently no longer active in either role). In 1725 he was to be forced to assign his office and his estates to his nephew, Sir John, in the aftermath of a scandal involving alleged misuse of government funds. Sir John himself was master of works in Scotland, had formerly served as MP for Anstruther Easter Burghs, and was serving as MP for Fife at the time of the 1719 prosecution.

One of the sailors eventually escaped, and the other was freed after Sir Philip Anstruther of Anstrutherfield was threatened with legal proceedings unless he produced him. Sir Alexander and the captain were then put on trial (Grahame being omitted on a technicality) for *hamesucken* (assaulting men in their own houses) and *plagium* (the stealing of human beings). In spite of the clear evidence a sympathetic jury found the accused not guilty.[15] As for the original issue, the smuggling of brandy, the charges were dropped. What is rare in the case is not that powerful men were patrons of smugglers and sometimes actively involved in their enterprises, but that the matter received publicity. Gentry defying the law over payment of duty was commonplace, but kidnapping attracted attention.

Given the active support for smugglers and the general hatred of the customs and excise duties, it is no surprise that the two most notorious riots of the century in Scotland were related to hatred of the post-union indirect taxes. The Shawfield Riots in Glasgow in 1725 showed popular reactions to a new duty on malt. The Edinburgh Porteous Riots of 1736 stemmed from popular demonstrations in support of a smuggler who was executed. The lynching of John Porteous, captain of the town guard of Edinburgh was an event of national importance, but its origins lay in the East Neuk. James Stark, the collector of excise for Fife, came to Anstruther to supervise a sale of goods seized for non-payment of excise. With the sizeable sum of £200 sterling he set off back to Kirkcaldy where he was based, but he stopped for the night at Pittenweem. Several local smugglers, no doubt furious at their losses, raided the house he was staying in and robbed the collector (who wisely fled through a window). Two of the thieves were subsequently arrested, tried in Edinburgh, and sentenced to death. One escaped, and when the other was brought to the gallows there was much public sympathy for him. The crowd was restive, and the town guard was summoned to maintain order. Captain Porteous lost his head and ordered his men to fire into the crowd. A number of people were killed, but public hatred of Porteous for this was at first appeased when he in turn was sentenced to death for ordering his men to fire. But when a pardon arrived from London, a riot began in Edinburgh. There was a determination to see that 'justice' was done. Porteous was hauled out of prison and lynched by the mob.

Thus smuggling in mid eighteenth-century Scotland was not something peripheral. It was big business, and central to both national and local life. The East Neuk may not have been more prone to smuggling than other parts of the country, but it was deeply involved, and gained notoriety through the Porteous case. It had inherent advantages for smugglers. The string of coastal burghs provided markets for goods, and also man-power – to crew ships and receive and move goods on shore. The towns provided endless hiding-places for newly landed goods. Outside the burgh harbours, the many caves, inlets and small beaches provided secluded landing places. And the East Neuk had an island. Islands made excellent depots for smugglers, to land goods offshore before running them to the mainland, to store them safely, to shelter on till the moment for transferring them to the mainland was right. The Isle of May was ideal. Only a handful of people lived on it, and they doubtless had the sense not to interfere when gangs landed from ships on dubious business. If excise or customs officials landed, then the island was riddled with caves, and the discovery of a timber underground storage chamber constructed by smugglers and covered with shingle to disguise its presence indicates the ingenuity of the law-breakers.[16] The island was a unique natural facility for East Neuk smugglers. The east coast of Scotland from Caithness to the English border had no sizeable islands, unlike the west coast. Moreover, since the Isle of May was a major hazard to shipping, since the 1630s a coal fire in a great iron brazier, Scotland's first lighthouse, had burnt there at night. Not only was the Isle a safe offshore depot, it obligingly provided its own light to guide smugglers to it. Customs' reports are full of references to 'hoverers,' ships that hovered offshore, waiting for a suitable opportunity to make a quick run ashore to land their goods, or, at night, for small boats to creep out to from the shore, to take on board smuggled goods. In the Isle of May smugglers could 'hover' on dry land.

In official terminology, 'fair trade' meant paying customs and excise duties. But in popular opinion true 'fair trade' was free trade, without regulation and duties. Thus entertaining verbal quibbling was possible. One could solemnly declare support for fair trade, seeming to support obedience to government regulations but really meaning the opposite – a bit like drinking a toast to the king, meaning the one over the water. The fair trade quibble was just the sort of thing the Benison enjoyed, and inspired by Mercury, the trickster god of all sorts of commerce, they extended the word-play to embrace their favourite subject, sex. Thus in the institutes and diploma of 1739 sexual innuendo couched in the language of fair trade is added to the topographical language of merryland.[17] Fair trade as legal trade, fair trade as smuggling, and fair trade as free sex jostle together in a welter of deliberate ambiguity.

Not surprisingly, interest in the Beggar's Benison has concentrated on its bizarre sexual activities, and the question of why the club should have been so intent on referring to sex in terms of fair trade has been overlooked. Yet one of the earliest commentators on the club asserts that the Benison emerged from smugglers' organisations.

> The contrabandist clubs of eastern Fifeshire culminated in a society which met at Anstruther under the designation of the Beggar's Benison.[18]

Charles Rogers' account of the Benison is, admittedly, not very enlightening, because in accordance with the sensibilities of his age he only refers to the Benison's sexual pursuits in terms of the greatest obscurity, writing of the activities of 'the monks of Isernia' and fancifully describing the club's rituals as being 'derived from the Druidic rites of Ashtoreth and those of the Roman Lupercaia'.[19] But he was a local man. As indicated in Chapter 2, he had spent his childhood in a parish neighbouring Anstruther, and his autobiographical writings[20] indicate that from an early age he took a close interest in local affairs. What he knew of the Benison must date from after the club disbanded, but it is striking how confident and casual he is in his statement that the Benison was the heir of 'contrabandist clubs', even though, infuriatingly, he says nothing more on the matter, except that certain estates in eastern Fife had been bought with the profits of smuggling by the ancestors of those who owned them in the 1880s.[21] In the East Neuk at least the origins of the Benison in smuggling seems to have been taken for granted.

Another local historian, George Gourlay, confirmed the Benison-smugglers link, though in terms that may puzzle rather than inform:

> The secret of the club was well known in the East of Fife – viz., to provide a kind of platform on which men, elsewhere so likely to meet with drawn swords and cocked pistols, could assemble without fear of espionage for a joyous revel, according to the rough manners of the age.[22]

The men likely to meet with drawn swords and pistols are intended to be identified as smugglers and customs officers. Analysis of the 1739 Benison membership list (see chapter six) confirms that significant numbers of members were either customs officials, or had known interests in smuggling. One of the central roles of the Benison, in its early decades, was to enable smugglers and customs men, professional enemies but personal friends, to socialise together.

Customs officers and smugglers socialising with each other obviously arouses suspicions of corruption, but it seems unlikely that Beggar's Benison meetings were themselves occasions for active conspiracy. Meeting once or twice a year for an occasion dominated by eating, drinking and fantasising about sex hardly provided the right atmosphere for business deals. But it seems entirely plausible to think of Benison meetings as occasions on which those who had interests in smuggling (on one side or the other of the law), regarding themselves as a sort of brotherhood through mutual co-operation, celebrated their relationship. And what more convincing way of diverting suspicion that the club might be linked to conspiracy than to suggest that the shared interest which brought these men together was in fact sex? That would seem entirely plausible, if a bit disreputable. Make a joke of it – admit in diplomas that the club is indeed concerned with fair trade, because everyone will see that is a crudely coded reference to sex. Being known as naughty boys could disguise being criminal boys. And best of all, the sexual antics disguise was not just disguise, but enjoyably enacted reality as well. Seen in this perspective, Benison meetings emerge as the equivalent to a raucous annual business party in a strip club. The Secret Smugglers' Ball?

The Benison may have grown out of smugglers 'clubs,' but its reputed founder and life sovereign was the most senior of local customs officers, John McNachtane. Why should he thus take the lead in associating with smugglers? The most obvious possibility is financial gain – that he was cementing mutually beneficial relations he had built up with smugglers. Less crudely, the Benison might have emerged from the sort of relationship that can emerge among enemies. Like police and criminals, customs men and smugglers might be opponents, but they were fighting in the same war, and this gave them a great deal in common, and this could have developed into mutual respect and understanding. McNachtane and the other customs officers who joined the Benison may have served the Hanoverian regime as employees, but they may well at heart have shared with smugglers anti-union and anti-Hanoverian sentiments.

Moreover, an organisation like the Benison may have helped solve the tricky question of how customs officers, strangers drafted into an area, were to fit into local society. Some might have pretensions to be gentlemen, but they were not gentry in a traditional sense. Nor were they burgesses. And they had a job to do that was likely to make them universally very unpopular. Too much zeal could lead to ostracism and threats. They were isolated, and without proper back-up for strict enforcement of the law. If they were to act at all, and make life bearable for themselves, some compromise with entrenched local interests was necessary. Where does holding back, accepting that limited resources and self-preservation meant the law could not be fully enforced, cease to be a sensible policy decision and become criminal neglect of duty or conspiracy? Life would become a lot easier all round if customs officers could come to some tacit understanding with suspected smugglers that if smugglers acted with some discretion, in return officers would look the other way on occasion. But how far John McNachtane, collector of customs at Anstruther and founder of the Benison, slid down this slippery slope of complicity with those whose illegal activities he was supposed to be suppressing cannot be known.

As time passed, the need for a club linking customs men and smugglers declined. Strangers like McNachtane sent in to police trade became accepted as leading citizens as the years passed. In the last decades of the eighteenth century and the first of the nineteenth, cuts in customs and excise duties and more efficient enforcement of the law undermined the once thriving 'fair trade.' Long before the Benison was dissolved the great days of smuggling as profitable business and patriotic protest were over.

Notes

1 See references in SAUL, B60/6/2, B3/5/2, B3/5/8, B3/5/10, B3/5/17.
2 NRA(S), survey no. 0771, Russell of Ballindalloch, bundle 296, 2 May 1772, 3rd duke of Athol to General Sir James Grant of Ballindalloch.
3 A. Fergusson, *The Honourable Henry Erskine* (Edinburgh, 1882), 131n.
4 For an excellent summary of the specific ways in which the new duties damaged existing areas of the Scottish economy, see B. Lenman, *The Jacobite risings in Britain, 1689–1746* (London, 1980), 99–102.
5 W. Alexander, *Notes and sketches illustrative of northern rural life*, ed. I. Carter (Finzean, Aberdeenshire, 1981. First published 1877), 146.
6 Rogers, *Social Life* i,.404–9 and H.Q. Graham, *The social life of Scotland in the*

eighteenth century (4th edn., London, 1937), 526–30, gather anecdotes on smuggling and its prevalence. F. Wilkins, *The smuggling story of two firths* (Kidderminster, 1993), and D. Fraser, *The smugglers* (Montrose, 1978) presents evidence relating to the firths of Tay and Forth, and to Montrose respectively. For some instances of smuggling in Anstruther see S. Stevenson, *Anstruther. A history* (Edinburgh, 1989), 154–7. Also J.A. Thomson, *The smuggling coast. The customs ports of Dumfries* (Dumfries, 1989).

7 D. Forbes, *Some considerations on the present state of Scotland* (Edinburgh, 1744).
8 T.C. Smout (ed.), 'Sir John Clerk's Observations on the present circumstances of Scotland, 1730.' *Miscellany, x* (SHS, 1965), 206–7.
9 Graham, *Social life*, 528.
10 Wilkins, *Smuggling story*, 101–3.
11 E.D. Dunbar, *Social life in former days* (Edinburgh, 1865), 64–70.
12 T. Donnelly, 'The king's customs administration in Aberdeen, 1750–1815,' *Northern Scotland*, xvi (1996), 187–98.
13 Lenman, *Jacobite risings*, 216–17.
14 For links between Jacobitism and smuggling in England see P.K. Monod, *Jacobitism and the English people, 1688–1788* (Cambridge, 1989), 111–18 and P.K. Monod, 'Dangerous merchandise: smuggling, Jacobitism and commercial culture in Southeast England, 1690–1760.' *Journal of British Studies*, 30 (1991), 150–82.
15 W. Roughead, 'Plagium: a footnote to Guy Mannering.' *Juridical Review*, xxxiii, 23–35, cited in A.W. Anstruther, *History of the family of Anstruther* (Edinburgh, 1923), 54–6.
16 W.J. Eggeling, *The Isle of May. A Scottish nature reserve* (Edinburgh, 1960), 26–7. Wilkins, *Smuggling story*, introduction, notes the significance of the east coast's lack of islands – but fails to see the glaring exception of the Isle of May.
17 While it is dangerous to pursue what may be chance verbal similarities too far, there is an outside possibility that the Benison got the idea of its 'fair trade' sexual vocabulary from John Cleland. Describing sex in a suitably aquatic context he writes 'we were well under way with a fair wind up channel, and full-freighted, nor indeed were we long before we finished our trip … and unloaded in the old haven.' *Fanny Hill*, ed. Wagner, 207. Orgasm thus becomes unloading cargo.
18 Rogers, *Social life*, ii, 411.
19 Rogers, *Social life*, ii, 412.
20 C. Rogers, *Leaves from my autobiography* (Grampian Club, 1876).
21 Rogers, *Social life*, i, 408.
22 Gourlay, *Anstruther* (1888), 165–6.

CHAPTER SIX

The Benison Class of '39

Thirty-two men signed the Benison code of institutes in 1739, and may be regarded as the founder members of the club in its reorganised form. The *Records* includes short notes on most of them, and research in other sources shows that, with one or two exceptions, the information given in the *Records* is accurate.

Members of the Beggar's Benison, 1739

Information is tabulated in eight columns:

1 Burgesses (**Anstruther Easter, Anstruther Wester, Crail, Kilrenny, Pittenweem**)
2 Service in burgh as a baillie
3 Commissioner to the convention of royal burghs
4 Office in the Church of Scotland as elder on parish kirk session, or commissioner to the general assembly
5 Service as customs officers
6 Known involvement in or connivance at smuggling
7 Politics: involvement in Jacobite activities specifically mentioned as **Whigs** or **Hanoverians**
8 Dates of birth

	1 Burg.	2 Baillie	3 CRB.	4 Kirk	5 Cust.	6 Smug.	7 Polit.	8 Birth
Aitkenhead, David	AE	X	X	X	X?			
Anstruther, David								
Anstruther, David								
Anstruther, William								1703
Applin, Richard								
Aytoun, William								1698
Blair, Alexander				X				
Cleland, Robert	C	X	X		X?		J	
Couper, John	K	X				X	W	
Erskine, Sir Charles						X		1687
Erskine, John								
Erskine, Thomas	K?					X		
Grahame, James	AE	X	X					c1680?
Grahame, Mungo	AE?							
Hamilton, Robert						X	J	c1710?
Hunter, Robert	AW	X	X	X				
Johnstone, Andrew	AE	X	X					
Leslie, David	A?							1680
Lumsdaine, James								
Lumsdaine, Robert								
McNachtane, John				X	X			c1689
Melville, Alexander	P						W	
Moncrieff, James	C		X?					1714?
Myles, Alexander	K					X	W	
Nairne, Thomas	AE	X	X	X				1693
Oliphant, Thomas	AW	X	X	X			J	
Paton, Philip	AE	X	X		X?			
Pringle, Robert								c1684?
Rolland, William	AW							
Row, David					X	X	J	
Waddell, Robert	K	X	X	X			W	pre 1700
Wightman, Charles	AE					X	J	
(AE 7; AW 3; C 2; K 4; P 1)	10	10	6	6	7		(J 5; W 4)	

All these men lived within a radius of a few miles of Anstruther, and all except the customs officers were natives of the East Neuk, but it was one of these of these incomers, John McNachtane, who dominated the Benison as the club's sovereign for nearly thirty years.

John McNachtane

McNachtane made a modest career for himself as a customs officer, a servant of the Hanoverian regime, but he had another, suppressed identity, as the nominal chief of a dispersed Highland clan whose downfall was at least in part the result of support for the Jacobite cause. One way of interpreting his passion for the Beggar's Benison is to see it as the expression of the tension between these two identities. He served the establishment, but showed his underlying attitude to it through the rejection of its official values in his club.

The McNachtanes had once been a powerful clan in the West Highlands. From their castle at Dundarave their chiefs had held lands and the allegiance of men from Loch Awe to Loch Fyne. But, like many other clans in the region, in time they found themselves being swamped by the rising tide of Campbell power, and in the political struggles of the seventeenth century their support for the Stuart cause proved fatal. At Killiecrankie in 1689 the chief, John McNachtane (father of the Benison member) fought for the exiled James VII, and forfeiture of his lands was ordered. Reprieve came and the order was not enforced, but by this time the chief was deeply in debt to the Campbells of Ardkinglas. In 1710 he was forced to resign all his lands to the Campbells. He was still alive in December 1711, when he signed 'bands of provision' promising to pay his younger son John and his daughter £30 each for their maintenance, and he probably died soon afterwards. His eldest son (who had sought a career in the British army) had died in 1702, so the right to the empty title of chief passed to his younger son, John.[1]

John McNachtane, who was probably born in the year of Killiecrankie, first appears in records as a third-year student at Glasgow University in 1706. Like many students from the gentry, he did not graduate.[2] But whereas those looking forward to the life of landed gentlemen had no need of a degree, in his difficult family circumstances McNachtane needed to make a career for himself, and a paper qualification might have been useful, so perhaps financial hardship cut short his studies. Birth gave him some status in his native Argyll. In 1711 he was made a burgess of Inveraray and he can be traced serving on a jury in the justiciary court of Argyll and the Isles.[3] However he needed income as well as status, and there were complications in his private life, for also in 1711 he appeared before the kirk session on charges about his relations with Isabel Campbell, daughter of an indweller in Inveraray.[4] In Gaelic tradition, moreover, a disastrous first marriage is related. John McNachtane was in love with a younger daughter of Campbell of Ardkinglas, but was tricked into marrying the eldest. He had a son by her, but then eloped with his true love. Both his sister-in-law-lover and the son died, and John became known as 'the cheated bridegroom.'[5] The romantic story finds no support in the cold evidence of genealogy, however, and it should perhaps be interpreted metaphorically. What Ardkinglas 'cheated' McNachtane of was not his bride but his clan's lands. He may in fact have married Isabel Campbell, but if so she did not live long, for McNachtane married Jean McArthur in 1721 as his second wife.[6]

In seeking a career McNachtane sought help from his uncle, the earl of Breadalbane (his mother's step-brother),[7] head of one of the most powerful Campbell dynasties. In 1709 he wrote desperately to the earl, begging him to use his influence to hasten 'an appointment' that he was awaiting, as his fortunes were at a very low ebb.[8] When he did find a post, it was a humiliatingly humble one for a man of his birth. He became boatman in the customs service at Montrose in 1714. In the same year he was promoted to tidewaiter at Bo'ness, then transferred back to Montrose with the same rank. He was dismissed for reasons unknown in 1717, but then appointed landwaiter at Anstruther in 1725. It was to be his home for thirty-five years. In 1728 he was promoted to collector, the head of the local customs precinct, but it was still a badly paid, ignominious job for a would-be chieftain. 1761 brought a move to Edinburgh as one of the two customs inspectors general of outports, and he retired five years later.[9]

From resented government-appointed lackey in Anstruther, McNachtane over the years turned himself into a respected local citizen – with the help no doubt of the bonds formed through the most un-respectable Beggar's Benison. He can be found serving as an elder on the kirk session of Anstruther Easter between 1753 and 1761, and sat for the burgh as an elder in the presbytery of St Andrews in 1760. After he moved to Edinburgh he was useful to local church courts in that he was a man with local connections who could attend the annual general assembly of the Church of Scotland as their commissioner without much expense – he served for Anstruther Easter in 1763 and 1767, but declined to act in 1769 as he had already been elected to sit for the presbytery of St Andrews.[10] But he is also to be found as a witness at an Episcopalian christening (1737),[11] indicating an outward Presbyterianism which was not bigoted. Another side of his character is revealed by the fact that he was a keen freemason.[12]

McNachtane also involved himself to some extent in the politics of parliamentary elections, his contacts with the wider political scene being through 'John Campbell of the Bank'. This was an illegitimate grandson of the 1st earl of Breadalbane, who made his career as business agent of the 2nd earl and as cashier of the Royal Bank of Scotland: 'of the Bank' ambiguously awarded him what sounded like a territorial designation, but at the same time stressed that he (being illegitimate) lacked lands of his own. Thus McNachtane maintained his link to the family that had probably brought him his first position in the customs – and which may have brought him promotion as well, for John Campbell had been a member of the customs board in Edinburgh in the 1720s and 1730s. To McNachtane, John Campbell and the 2nd earl of Breadalbane (his first cousin) were kinsmen, but superior ones to be cultivated – 'Please make my complements to the Good old Earle, and to all friends;' 'Best wishes to Mrs Campbell and the children;' 'I begin now to long for an account of your welfare, and families, with that of our friends at Taymouth and Restalrig.'[13] He might be a provincial customs officer, but he had links to the powerful and noble, and was proud to the end of his ancient blood. In 1753 he had the text of a 1267 charter to one of his ancestors printed, with a note in Latin proudly recording that

> John M'Nauchtan Customs Officer at Anstruther descended in an unbroken male line from the aforesaid Gillecrist had this copy printed A.D. 1753.[14]

Two hints at McNachtane's literary interests have already been noted – his subscription to a work by Allan Ramsay, and his acquaintance with Alexander Robertson of Struan. A third is a poem addressed to him by one 'W. Douglas' in 1740:

> ... M'Nachtane, in whose gen'rous breast
> Reigns each humane and ev'ry social virtue?
> Who, in a selfish and deceitful age,
> Shows Truth and Friendship have not left the world?
> Friend to the Nine, O lend a patient ear...[15]

The 'nine' are the muses. This is routine high-flown flattery, but such literary connections add another dimension to McNachtane. He emerges as a man with four faces. A man of ancient blood, hanging on to memories of a might have-been-life as a Highland chief; a man with literary pretensions; a respected minor government official and local worthy; and the leader of the Beggar's Benison where he revelled in obscenity, caroused with smugglers, and dabbled with Jacobitism. He died in 1773, and an obituary notice referred to him as 'John Macnachtane Esq., of Macnachtane.' He had not in life used the designation of chieftancy, but would have been well satisfied that in death it was recognised.[16]

That McNachtane, a newcomer to the East Neuk, actually founded the Benison seems unlikely. A plausible scenario would depict him as establishing contacts with local men through his work, including working relationships with local smugglers, cementing them through joining their club – and then coming to dominate it and influence its development.

Customs Officers

David Row succeeded his father as comptrollor of customs at Anstruther in the early 1720s,[17] and was thus second to McNachtane in the local customs hierarchy. In 1742 his career came to an abrupt end. He was sitting in Cambo House drinking smuggled brandy with his fellow-member of the Benison, Sir Charles Erskine of Cambo, and the laird's brothers, when the house was raided by excise men (always in rivalry with customs men) from Kirkcaldy, backed up by soldiers. The consignment of brandy was seized, to the fury of Row, who aggravated his offence by shaking his cane at the raiders, using 'opprobrious and abusive Language', and trying to incite Cambo's servants and others to rescue the brandy. However, it was carried off by the triumphant excise men, and locked in the king's warehouse in Anstruther until it could be disposed of. It then disappeared. Investigation proved that David Row, who lived next door to the warehouse, had at some time dug a passage from his cellar to the warehouse cellar. The presumption was that he had stolen the brandy, and he had doubtless used the passage before for similar criminal activities. Row was dismissed from office but not prosecuted.[18] He stayed on in Anstruther, seeking a living as a 'broker',[19] but through the Jacobite rising of 1745 the failed Hanoverian official hoped for a chance to restore his fortunes. He joined Glengarry's Jacobite regiment and saw victory at the battle of Prestonpans, but during the Jacobite army's retreat from England he was captured at Carlisle, tried, and hanged in York.[20] When a parish minister tried to make his widow see the hand of God in her husband's well-deserved fate, she replied defiantly 'Na, na, there was nae hand in't but the Deil's and the Duke of Cumberland's'.[21]

The other customs officials who were members of the Benison had less lurid fates, and had no known links with smugglers except through their membership of the club. Robert Hunter became collector's clerk in 1737, and was so impressed by his boss that he called his son McNaughton Hunter. Subsequently Hunter became surveyor of customs at Kirkcaldy, then served in the same position at Anstruther before moving on again to Montrose in 1767 as collector. He served as a baillie of Anstruther Wester a number of times, and on nine occasions represented the burgh in the convention of royal burghs. He was active in local politics, opposing General Philip Anstruther, but in the '60s swung round to take a lead in getting Anstruther's nominee as burgh clerk restored after a local coup had deposed him. It is tempting to link his political change of heart to his promotion to collector, which followed soon afterwards.[22]

The links of other 1739 members of the Benison to the customs service pre- or post-date that year. David Aitkenhead had been surveyor at Crail from the 1720s until 1737[23] and Robert Cleland was probably tide surveyor there in the 1710s and 1720s.[24] Philip Paton, an Anstruther Easter councillor in 1739, was later collector of customs at Kirkcaldy – or perhaps that was his son.[25]

Smugglers

Identifying customs officials is fairly simple: they were the servants of a bureaucracy which kept excellent records. The smugglers aimed to leave no trace of their activities. Only in the rare event of their being discovered were their activities recorded. This sort of evidence immediately supplies four Benison names. James Grahame had been involved in the notorious case involving kidnapping in 1719, and the involvement of David Row, Sir Charles Erskine of Cambo and his brother Thomas Erskine has been noted above.

Tradition produces other names – tradition which, where they mention detail which can be checked, usually proves accurate. Alexander Myles, a well off inhabitant of Cellardyke, was regarded as a dour Presbyterian, but willing to take part in landing smuggled tea and gin, working with his friend and fellow Beggar John Couper, who was also a Whig – a supporter of the regime. Both men farmed land in Kilrenny parish.[26] Robert Hamilton younger of Kilbrackmont had been involved with other students of St Andrews University in 1727 in 'deforcing' customs officers – forcibly preventing them from carrying out their duties, though that was a rather marginal case of active involvement in smuggling.[27] Andrew Johnstone can be counted merely as a consumer, being recorded in 1755 acting as a magistrate in the burgh court of Anstruther Easter while under the influence of smuggled gin.[28] But the leading merchant of the day in the same burgh, Charles Wightman, was notorious for his smuggling activities. His house stood next to the site of Dreel Castle, and smuggled goods could be brought ashore through a back entrance leading onto the beach. It was said his house was haunted by a 'Black Lady' a tale perhaps intended to deter anyone inquisitive about what went on in his premises at night.[29]

Jacobites and Whigs

David Row here takes his third bow, as the only Jacobite to die for the cause among members of the Benison. Charles Wightman surprisingly escaped punishment, even though it was reported after the '45 that he 'has alwayes been known for a disaffected person.' Further, it was said he had gone with his wife and waited on Prince

Charles Edward ('Bonnie Prince Charlie'), and that he paid a soldier to serve in the Jacobite army. He acted as factor for the 5th earl of Kellie, who joined the rebellion, and collected excise duties imposed by the Jacobites. Finally, tradition relates that after Culloden he hid fugitives, including French soldiers, in the places in which he normally concealed smuggled goods, until smugglers' ships could carry them to safety on the Continent.[30] The fact that in spite of his wealth Wightman never held office in Anstruther Easter may be an indication that he was a committed long-term Jacobite who was unwilling to take oaths of loyalty to the regime abjuring the Stuarts.

Wightman's sympathies had been well known. Others only revealed themselves after the '45 rebellion had started. Robert Cleland, one-time baillie of Crail, is said to have been 'the life and soul of the Jacobite party,' and incriminated himself by persuading traders not to pay customs and excise duties.[31] Thomas Oliphant, though an elder of the kirk, showed Jacobite sympathies by helping to carry a barrel of gunpowder to the rebels and drinking a toast to the Pretender.[32]

Robert Hamilton younger of Kilbrackmont went much further, assisting rebels in seizing arms from Lieutenant General Philip Anstruther's house of Airdrie, and joining the Jacobite army. But he left it after the battle of Prestonpans, and it was subsequently argued that he had been at the time 'greatlie disordered in his judgement.' He 'long lay in great distress at his father's house ... as his physician and surgeon will assess.'[33]

Five Jacobites out of thirty-two members, with evidence of long-term commitment only in the case of Wightman, hardly qualifies the Benison as a Jacobite organisation. But there is strong suspicion that others had Jacobite sympathies even though they did not act in the cause when the '45 crisis came. Erskine of Cambo, for example, was of a family generally considered Jacobite but never openly committed. Several times in the 1730s he acted as godfather at baptisms in the little Episcopalian congregation at St Andrews,[34] a strong indication of where his political sympathies lay.

When the Benison had been founded in 1732 Jacobitism had no longer seemed a credible political cause, and for those with lingering Jacobite sentiments playing with irreverent variations of the 'king over the water' myth in the James V and the beggar maid story seemed harmless fun in which they could join with Hanoverian (if discontented) friends. The coming of the '45 probably saw a rapid sobering-up of many members of the Benison. They had been fiddling with something that had seemed safe as token defiance of an unpopular government, and it had turned out to be potentially dangerous.

Of the four men noted in the *Records* as 'Whigs,' indicating positive support for the regime, two, Robert Couper and Alexander Myles, are also identified as smugglers, indicating the limits to their loyalty. Alexander Melville is said to have been 'one of the Whig Councillors' in Pittenweem,[35] but this must have been before 1727 as the council minutes, which survive from that date, contain no mention of him. Robert Waddell, shipbuilder in Anstruther, became a burgess of Kilrenny in 1717, was elected a baillie, and served frequently as a baillie there up to 1752. He sat in the convention 17 times in 1719–52, and twice in the assembly, 1735 and 1746.[36] 'A zealous Whig' and supporter of the Anstruther family interest,[37] he was kidnapped during the 1722 election campaign (when he was the Kilrenny delegate for the final vote) and held prisoner in Cambo House by Sir Alexander Erskine (the Lord Lyon – Chief Herald of Scotland – and father of Waddell's later Benison colleague Sir Charles). When released on election day, however, he showed he had not succumbed to pressure, and cast his vote for the Anstruthers.[38] When in 1756 the Fife and Anstruther Whale-Fishing Company was established Baillie Waddell was one of its two ordinary managers – and the main promoter of the scheme was Sir John Anstruther, which confirms his close connection with that family.[39]

Gentry

In social terms, the Beggar's Benison of 1739 was led by members of the local gentry, but the families involved, except for the Erskines of Cambo, were very minor ones. The Cambo family was a junior branch of the Erskines of Kellie, and it participated in national life mainly through its connections with the court of the Lord Lyon. Sir Charles, the 3rd baronet, had served successively as Bute Pursuivant and Lyon Clerk, both his father and his grandfather having been Lords Lyon. But Sir Charles had resigned office in 1727, and lived thereafter as a country laird. John and Thomas Erskine were probably his younger brothers, the former holding office as Albany Herald.[40] The idea that the solemn state rituals presided over by the Lyon Court contributed something to the Benison's obscene ceremonies is entertaining but not provable.

The Lumsdaine family contributed two representatives to the original Benison. Robert Lumsdaine of Innergellie, though a member of a family long established in the area, had only bought the estate of Innergellie in 1730. He married the daughter and heiress of James Lumsdaine of Stravithie, advocate and fellow Benison member, who died in 1749.[41] Robert Lumsdaine, his house at Innergellie presided over by the mischievously ambiguous Mercury, was to be sovereign of the Edinburgh Benison from 1752 until his death in 1761.

The greatest family of the East Neuk, the Anstruthers, was only marginally represented in the 1739 Benison. William Leslie Anstruther was the eldest son of Sir Alexander Anstruther of Newark, the laird involved in smuggling and kidnapping in 1719. Sir Alexander had married the heiress of the 2nd Lord Newark, and the family claimed that the terms of her father's peerage meant that the title should descend through her. Therefore after her death in 1740 William Anstruther as her son took the title Lord Newark. This was accepted (locally, at least) in his lifetime, but in the 1790s the House of Lords ruled that the title had become extinct on the death of his grandfather, the 2nd Lord. Thus William Anstruther's right to be seen as the Benison's first noble member is dubious. His life is exceptionally obscure. All that is known of him is that he served as a captain of a formation known as 'Jordan's Marines' until they were disbanded in 1749, and in that in 1755 he was appointed to command a 'Company of Invalids'. He died unmarried in 1773.[42] The 1739 list includes two David Anstruthers. One was Lord Newark's younger brother, about whom nothing at all is known except that he also died unmarried and that an obscene toast he gave to the Benison survives. No second David appears in the Anstruther family tree at any suitable point, and the name may simply have got duplicated in error.

Robert Hamilton of Kilbrackmont was of a very minor gentry family. The only times when official notice was taken of him was when he helped smugglers as a St Andrews student, and as a confused Jacobite in 1745. He was another bachelor member of the Benison.

1. Beggar's Benison: Medal. Sex sacred and profane. The legend of the obverse, 'Be fruitfull and multiply', repeats the divine order to man to have sex, and Adam gestures Eve off to the left to obey. On the reverse the Beggar's motto 'May prick & purse never fail you', a female figure, legs obscenely spread, holds a bag of gold, the payment for sex, gesturing towards the genitals of the male figure beside her. British Museum (Appendix 3, no. 1.2).

2. Beggar's Benison: Medal, 1826. Sex Sacred and Classical. The theme of the 'Christian' side of the medal (top), remains unchanged, but the 'Classical' is rather more seemly. A sleeping Venus (accompanied by Cupid) reclines in the foreground while Adonis the hunter creeps up to her with a cartoon-style thinks-bubble reading 'lose no opportunity'. National Museums of Scotland (Appendix 3, no. 1.4).

3. Beggar's Benison: Seals. One seal (top left) refers (indistinctly) to 'love's cave', the other (top right) reveals what this means by depicting vulva within a heart with the inscription 'sight improves delight'. National Museums of Scotland (Appendix 3, nos. 3.1, 3.3).

Bottom: The 'Anstruther' and 'Edinburgh' seals. The Benison 'phallus and bag' badge dominates both, the former bearing also the anchor of Anstruther, the latter the castle badge of Edinburgh in a subordinate position, below the anchor. National Museums of Scotland (Appendix 3, nos. 3.4, 3.5).

4. Beggar's Benison and the Wig Club: Seals. Top left: A Benison seal, perhaps abandoned after it was noticed that the enthusiastic engraver had included three testicles. British Museum (Appendix 3, no. 3.3.1). Top right: The building of a lighthouse on the Isle of May is celebrated with a phallic lighthouse with vulva in its side, evidently drawing on Hindu symbolism. National Museums of Scotland (Appendix 3, no. 3.6). Bottom: This seal with the classical motif of cock and hen with heads replaced by human genitals occurs on a Wig Club minute signed by Lord Doune in 1805, so it may have been a personal seal rather than the club's. St Andrews University Library (Appendix 3, no. 15.1).

5. Beggar's Benison: Test Platter. Made in the 1780s or later, the platter was used during ritual initiations – as an obscene inscription on the bottom indicates. St Andrews University Collections (Appendix 3, no. 4.1).

6. Beggar's Benison: the Breath Horn. Blown to accompany initiation rituals. St Andrews University Collections (Appendix 3, no. 5.1).

7. Beggar's Benison: Wine Glass. Several glasses, made in the 1770s, survive.
Private Collection, London (Appendix 3, no. 7.2).

8. Beggar's Benison: Bible and Snuff Box. The brass hasp of the lock on the Bible has an obscenely allusive keyhole, and the inscription refers to the 'tree of knowledge of good and evil' in the Garden of Eden. National Museums of Scotland (Appendix 3, no. 8.1).

The snuff box contains, according to the note kept in it, pubic hair of one of George IV's mistresses, presented to the Beggar's Benison by the king when he visited Edinburgh in 1822. St Andrews University Collections (Appendix 3, no. 9.1).

9. Wig Club: Wig Box and Stand. The stand and its base slide out of the box on the left, while on the right there is room for 'objects appertaining to the wig', such as comb and purse, with felt pockets to house some of them. St Andrews University Collections (Appendix 3, nos. 13.2 – 13.4).

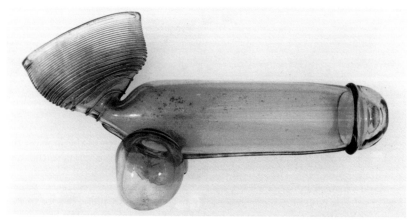

10. Wig Club: Prick Glass. Two prick glasses survive, from which toasts were drunk to the wig. St Andrews University Collections (Appendix 3, no. 6.1).

11. Anstruther. View from the north (1841), looking down the Dreel Burn towards the bridge linking the two Anstruthers. The tower of the kirk of Easter Anstruther is on the left, that of Wester Anstruther on the right. The mill to the left of the burn is mentioned in a poem supposedly recited by John McNachtane: '....... The Meal Mill-wheel / Clucks round and round in dashing rote'. Hidden behind the mill is the site of Dreel Castle: 'In former times it had its day,/ At present its joys are but a dream' (Supplement, 65), Charles Gray, *Lays and Lyrics*, Edinburgh, 1841. St Andrews University Library.

12. Vincenzo Lunardi. The 'bold adventurer' was enrolled as a member of the Beggar's Benison in 1785 after his balloon landed in Fife at the end of the first-ever long-distance flight in Scotland. J. Kay, *A series of original portraits and caricature etchings*, 2 vols., Edinburgh, 1837-8. St Andrews University Library.

13. The Whig Club. A cartoonist satirises the 'Whig Club', an organisation of English Whig politicians, in 1784, using a pun on the words 'wig' and 'whig' by showing members all wearing huge wigs. Though this was published after the Wig Club was founded in Edinburgh, some such play on words may underlie the Tory club's appropriation of the punning name of their political rivals for their club. British Museum.

14. The Quacks. An English cartoonist (1783) depicts the rivalry between James Graham (whose duck 'quacks' a thistle to identify him as a Scot) and another sex therapist. Each brandishes the rods charged with static electricity that they employed in therapy, their phallic shapes being a gift to satirists. British Museum

15. Beggar's Benison: Diploma. Engraved diploma produced for the earl of Kellie, who became sovereign of the Benison in 1820. Clearly he had no qualms about balancing his own coat of arms (top left) with the phallic coat of the Benison (top right). St Andrews University Library.

...monly Benificent
...ly Benevolent
...as Earl of Kellie
...TTENWEEM, A BARONET.
...of Gustavus Vasa
...ent and Most Puissant
...enson and Merryland
...is Guardianship and in

...Happiness and Prosperity of our Well beloved
...Merryland and the encouragement of Trade
...ing And Whereas We are fully satisfied that
...nce Esquire

...AS SUFFICIENT ABILITIES, and other
...d Laudable Purposes, and Willing that such
...ouragement, We do hereby CREATE, ADMIT,
...st Ancient and Most Puissant Order of the
...the Name Stile and Title of Sir Thomas
...him in all time coming with Our full Powers
...from and to and to and from all the Har
...hilets upon the Coasts of our Said E ...
...yment of Sell Custom or any other Taxes &c

...on Chambers at Anstruther, upon the
...the vulgar by the name of November 1820
...der ...

16. The Innergellis Mercury. Dating from c.1740, the statue standing above the main entrance shows Mercury in his most respectable guise – fig leaf well in place, with winged hat and sandals, holding a caduceus. Only Robert Lumsdaine of Innergellie and his Benison friends appreciated that beneath the surface lay Mercury the god who facilitated sexual encounters, his huge phallus and purse symbolising the inextricable link of sex and commerce. And, beneath that, the god who taught masturbation to mankind.

Though a wastrel, he was amiable, with a wry sense of humour often directed at himself. Thus, when increasing poverty forced him to sell even the trees around his house, and the bidders who had come to attend the auction indicated that it was customary to provide brandy to encourage bidding, he responded that if he could have afforded brandy he wouldn't have been so stupid as to sell the trees.[43] He died in poverty in 1769, having 'run through his estate'.

Several other Benison members owned land, and took territorial designations from them, but were so intimately associated with burgh life that they can hardly be counted as landed gentry. Andrew Johnstone, baillie of East Anstruther, was to be known successively as 'of Pitkierie' and 'of Rennyhill' as he prospered. William Aytoun of Kinaldy, and James Moncrieff of Sauchope both inherited their lands after 1739, and seem to have lived the lives of townsmen. In numerical terms they and the true townsmen dominated the Benison.

Merchants and Craftsmen

The majority of the members of the Benison in 1739 lived in one or other of the five royal burghs of the East Neuk. Eighteen can be identified as active in the leading employments of townsmen, making their livings as merchants or craftsmen. Several others lived in the burghs but their occupations are not known, or farmed land just outside the burghs. The largest of the burghs, Anstruther Easter, contributed seven members, the smallest, Pittenweem, only one.

Of the eighteen burgesses identified, at least ten acted at one time or another as baillies of their burghs, some for only a year or two, others sitting (with intervals) over many years. Ten represented their towns in the convention of royal burghs, again sometimes on many occasions. David Aitkenhead and Robert Waddell sat together for their burghs in eleven consecutive conventions in 1740–50. Fewer, perhaps not surprisingly, sat in church courts, but at least four did serve as elders in their kirk sessions or as commissioners to the general assembly. Most of the Benison burgesses were merchants, and none of the few craftsmen were practitioners of the more lowly crafts like weaver or soutar (shoemaker). Thomas Nairne was a surgeon, the son of a successful ship's captain who had bought the little estate of Claremont near St Andrews, and the brother of the parish minister of Anstruther Easter, on whose kirk session he served as an elder in 1735–40.[44] Mungo Grahame was a surgeon and apothecary, Thomas Oliphant a wright (builder), Robert Waddell a shipbuilder, and William Rolland a shipmaster.

The impression given is that the burgess members of the Benison were generally leading members of their communities, though this is not to say that Benison members dominated their burghs: there were many other burgesses who served as baillies who are not known members of the club. But in 1740 four of the five burghs were represented in the convention of royal burghs by Benison members: Andrew Johnstone (Anstruther Easter), David Aitkenhead (Anstruther Wester), Robert Cleland (Crail), and Robert Waddell (Kilrenny). Perhaps, on their official visits to the capital, they found opportunities to put their dreams of promiscuity, frustrated in the East Neuk, into practice. Overall, 1739 membership of the Benison was a cross section of middle to upper-ranking East Neuk society. In common with many clubs, there was an intermixing of men of differing statuses, but only to a limited degree – richer townsmen and middling to lesser gentry. On the one hand it did not include poorer townsmen, on the other the most important members of major families like the Anstruthers remained aloof. The thirty-two members of 1739 came together through a mixture of the forces that formed all clubs, personal friendship and common interests (not necessarily either legal or respectable) and prejudices. The mixture of interests in this case, beyond sociability and drink, were unusually diverse, but they were linked by disgruntlement with the *status quo* expressed through obscenity.

One final point to emerge from investigating the thirty-two 1739 members is some indication of the age-profile of the Beggars. Birth dates of only a few members can be established, and they reveal the following approximate ages at the time of the signing of the 1739 institutes:

William Leslie Anstruther	36
Sir Charles Erskine	52
David Leslie	59
John McNachtane	50
James Moncrieff	25

In other cases careers show that other members were far from the first flush of youth. James Grahame had first been elected a baillie in 1704, and Robert Waddell had become a burgess in 1717, for example. Thus the – admittedly very defective – evidence suggests that while there was a fairly wide range of ages among members, the Benison contained far more middle aged family men (and middle aged bachelors) than wild young rakes. Even if it is assumed that the older of the 1739 members of club had first joined when it was founded in 1732, such founder-members had not been very youthful. The Benison was not a club of the most strongly libido-driven of the male community, and it is likely that in the club's obsessions with sex there was a strong element of nostalgia. Club members were ageing men recalling the good old days when they had been (or liked to think of themselves as having been) young studs, fantasising as about how it still might be, masturbating in frustration for the lack of the varied willing partners their libertine ideas led them to believe they were entitled to. Nostalgia for Scottish independence, for unfettered trade, for the Stuart dynasty as a symbol of lost independence, and for sexual opportunities? Golden ages always lie in the past.

Notes

1 A. Macnaughtan, 'The chiefs of Clan MacNachtan,' *Scottish Genealogist*, ii, no. 1 (Jan. 1955), 13); D. McNaughton, 'John MacNaughton and the "Beggar's Benison,"' *Scottish Genealogist*. xiv, no.3 (1967), 55–6; NAS, RD3/125, pp. 230–2.

2 C. Innes (ed.), *Munimenta alme Universitatis Glasguensis* (4 vols., Maitland Club, 1854), iii, 186.

3 E.A. Beaton & S.W. MacIntyre, *The burgesses of Inveraray, 1665–1963* (SRS, 1990), 187; J. Cameron & J. Imrie (eds.), *The justiciary records of Argyll and the Isles, 1664–1742* (2 vols., Stair Society, 1949–69), ii, 266.

4 McNaughton, 'John MacNaughton,' 56.

5 Lord Archibald Campbell, *The records of Argyll* Edinburgh, 1890), 46–7. The story calls Ardkinglas 'Sir James,' but the baronet at the time was Sir John, died 1752, *CB*, iv, 307.

6 McNaughton, 'John MacNaughton,' 56.

7 *SP*, ii, 202.

8 NAS, GD112/39/230/19: see also GD112/39/251/1,13.

9 NAS, CE3/1–11; Scottish customs establishment books; *Calendar of treasury books, 1714–15*, xxix (ii), (London, 1957), 89, and *1717*, xxxi (iii), (London, 1957), 626.

10 SAUL, CH2/625/3, 306, 307, 316, 359, 363, etc., and SAUL, B3/5/10.

11 Stevenson, *Anstruther*, 184.

12 The evidence for this is a letter from T.D. Murray, of Anstruther, to Sir Duncan Campbell of Balcardine, 18 December 1913. Murray had in his possession letters of McNachtane addressed in 1764 to the lodge of which Murray was master. Scarsdale papers, Kedleston Hall, Derby.

13 Letters of 1746 and 1754, NLS MS. 5075, Erskine-Murray Papers, ff.136–7 & 5078, ff.103–4.

14 A.I. Macnaghten, *The chiefs of Clan Macnachtan and their descendants* (Windsor, 1951), 53.

15 *Scots Magazine*, iv (1742), 414–16.

16 *Scots Magazine*, xxxv (1773), 223. D. McNaughton, 'John MacNaughton and the "Beggar's Benison,"' 57, states that this obituary expressed surprise that McNachtane could live so well on his meagre emoluments. In fact it says nothing at all about his living standards.

17 NAS, GD18/2837, Clerk of Pennicuik Muniments; *The criminal process... against Sir Alexander Anstruther of Newark...* (Edinburgh, 1720), 11–12; NAS, CE3/4; *Records*, 26.

18 H.D. Watson, *Kilrenny* (Edinburgh, 1986), 61–2, citing NAS CE1/6, 10 Feb 1742.

19 NLS, MS.17522, 46r.

20 B.G. & J.G. Arnot (eds.), *Prisoners of the '45* (3 vols., SHS, 1928–9), iii, 291; W. Macleod (ed.), *List of persons concerned in the rebellion* (SHS, 1890), 68–9.

21 M.F. Conolly, *A biographical sketch of the Right Rev. David Low* (Edinburgh, 1859), 130.

22 Stevenson, *Anstruther*, 66–9, 184; *Records*, 25; SAUL, B3/5/17; NAS, CE3/3/12/1.

23 NAS, CE3/4, 7, 8.

24 NAS, CE3/1,3,4.

25 NAS, CE3/11; Adam, *Political state*, 124.

26 *Records*, 22;. Stevenson, *Anstruther*, 187

27 F. Wilkins, *The smuggling story of two firths. Montrose to Dunbar* (Kidderminster, 1993), 77, 79.

28 G. Gourlay, *Fisher life; or the memorials of Cellardyke and the Fife coast* (Cupar, 1879), 17.

29 A. Thirkell, *Auld Anster* (Anstruther, 1977), 24, 67–8).

30 Macleod, *List of persons*, 68–9; Thirkell, *Auld Anster*, 24, 67–8.

31 *Records*, 5, 23; MacLeod, *List of persons*, 64–5.

32 Macleod, *List of persons*, 66–7.

33 NLS, Ms. 17522, f.45v.

34 E.G.A. Winter (ed.), *Register of baptisms and marriages for the Episcopalian congregation of St Andrews, 1722–1787* (SRS, 1910), 9, 10.

35 *Records*, 24.

36 SAUL, B3/5/2,3; *RCRB*; SAUL, CH2/515/1, p. 310 and B3/5/2.

37 *Records.* 24–5.

38 SAUL, B3/5/2, 6, 9, 13 April 1722; Watson, *Kilrenny*, 68–90.

39 NLS, RB. S. 1995, *Contract of copartnery of the Fife and Anstruther Whale-Fishing Company* (1756); NAS, GD26/13/648/1–3.

40 *CB*, iv, 256; Wood, *East Neuk*, 462; F.J. Grant (ed.), *Court of the lord lyon* (SRS, 1946), 2, 3, 5, 6, 16, 17.

41 Grant, *St Andrews*, 213.

42 [F.J. Grant (ed.)], *Register of the burials in the chapel royal or abbey of Holyrood* (SRS, 1900), 17; A.W. Anstruther, *Family of Anstruther*, 95, 102; *CP*, ix, 507.

43 Conolly, *Biographical sketch of the Right Rev. David Low*, 125–7; Wood, *East Neuk*, 208–9, 297; G. Hamilton, *A history of the house of Hamilton* (Edinburgh, 1933), 568.

44 *Fasti*, v, 180; *Records*, 24; SAUL, CH2/625/3, pp. 105,155, 162, 168, 177, 182.

CHAPTER SEVEN

The Beggar's Benison, 1739–1836

For the Beggar's Benison of 1732 to 1738 there are brief notes of meetings – though questions about the authenticity are a complication. From this murk appears a flash of light in 1739, with the text of the diploma, the code of institutes, and the list of members who signed the latter. Then, for the remaining century of the club's existence, its history had to be constructed out of a scattering of fragments and later traditions. Passing references to the club come from a wide range of sources, but it is the surviving membership diplomas which allow the skeleton of club history to be reconstructed, for they reveal not only the identity of some members but the names of officials.[1]

Aftermath of the '45. The Benison and the Duke of Cumberland

Diploma evidence reveals that John McNachtane became sovereign in 1745 or 1746, and was re-elected several times subsequently. It may be coincidence that his 'reign' began at the time of the '45 rebellion, but considering the shock that the brief civil war must have been to the Benison it seems likely that it had a part in McNachtane gaining what was to be lifelong control of the club. With one member executed for treason, and several others involved to a greater or lesser extent in aiding rebellion, membership of a body that had dabbled in Jacobitism, however irreverently, was potentially dangerous. McNachtane's election as sovereign may have been intended to provide proof, if necessary, of respectability – at least in political terms – in time of crisis. His heart may have toyed with Jacobitism, but outwardly he was a servant of the regime, and indeed one who was made responsible, as a collector of customs, for reporting the names of suspected rebels in his area. McNachtane's status in Anstruther Easter was such that when the baillies of the burgh submitted their own list of suspects, as ordered, they also got him to add his signature. In these lists McNachtane includes the names of his Benison colleagues whose rebellious activities were so well know that it was impossible to overlook them – though he carefully neglected to mention that David Row had been his second-in-command until a few years before.[2]

In the aftermath of rebellion, fulsome declarations of loyalty and gestures of gratitude to the regime were expected – especially from those whose allegiance might have been in doubt. John McNachtane obliged on behalf of the Beggar's Benison. What better way of showing that the club had nothing to hide than for him to invite the victor of Culloden, the duke of Cumberland, to become a member, just six weeks after the battle? Even better, offer to elect him sovereign at the next annual meeting.

Unto His Royal Highness
Prince William Duke of Cumberland

The Humble Address of the Honourable Society of the Most Ancient and Puissant Order of the BEGGAR'S BENNISON and MERRYLAND

Your Royal Highness is humbly entreated to Accept of an Admission into this Most Ancient Order under the Sun, which is hereby offered to your Highness, free of all exterior ornaments, or pompous embellishments, Things greatly despised by our celebrated Society, as that of puris naturalibus is the peculiar characteristick of the Order.

And as it would add a shining lustre to our Society, that the first Hero of our age, would deign to accept of the Sovereign Guardianship of the Order, we beg leave in the most submissive manner, to entreat your Royal Highness would accept thereof, at our ensuing Annual Election, which falls upon St Andrews day next to come: On which gracious condescension, the Titles and Seal of Office shall be suitably altered and properly amended, that for the future all Diplomas, Charters and Patents, may be issued from our Office under your Royal Highness's illustrious and auspicious name.

We further humbly beg leave to add our most sincere and chearful congratulations on the Glorious Victory obtained by your Royal Highness, over His Majesty's Rebellious Subjects at the battle of Colloden, and on the Total Suppression thereby, of the Very Wicked and Unnatural Rebellion.

Given at our Office at Anstruther this second day of June 1746 at the desire of the Society and signed in their presence by

Jo. McNachtane, Guardian.[3]

Such extreme flattery and cringing wording was entirely in accordance with the conventions of the time, the sort of hyperbole that can be found in many loyal addresses. 'Wicked and unnatural' was the stock phrase used to describe the rebels and their actions. Yet the invitation was never presented to the duke, and it seems likely that it was never intended to be, for the satiric undertones are so strong that even the duke would surely have detected them as he lapped up the flattery. In thus pretending to cringe to the establishment, the Benison was playing with fire. The standard image of the victorious duke portrayed him in full military uniform, embellished with medals, badges of rank and sashes. Honours were heaped upon him. All this display is mocked by the Benison's invitation's urging that membership was free of external ornaments and pompous embellishments. The club declares that it greatly despises such things, and stands instead for unadorned nature.

Even if the invitation was only intended to be a satire for private enjoyment, it was dangerous to compose it in the immediate aftermath of Hanoverian victory, when any hint of mockery might be seen as treasonous. Having fun at the expense of the Jacobite concept of the king over the water was one thing. Hinting that the hero of the hour was a pompous fool was another. Presumably the invitation reflected McNachtane's inner conflict. He was acting the loyal official, and did his duty punctiliously in reporting the names of rebels. But he then relieved his feelings on paper, in the sort of concealed and subversive satire that was a hall-mark of the early Benison.

The Benison, 1739–1790

Known recruits to the Beggar's Benison, 1755–90

Roman type indicates that the member's diploma survives, or that he signed one or more diplomas as an official of the club. Italic type indicates that membership has been determined from other sources. Dates are generally those of joining the club, but those in square brackets indicate earliest dates at which men are known to have been members, or periods of active membership.

[1730s?]	*Nathaniel Murray (clerk of the Customs, Anstruther)*
1746?	George Paton (bookseller, Edinburgh)
[1750s?]	*Lieutenant Colonel Alexander Monypenny of Pitmilly (officer; gentry)*
[1750s]	*Sir John Malcolm of Lochore, Bt. (gentry)*
[1750s]	*Thomas Dishington (clerk, Crail)*
[1750s]	*William Don (schoolmaster, Crail)*
[1753]	*James Lumsdaine 'of Stratharthie' (gentry)*
[1755]	Chambre Lewis (clerk, Customs House, Edinburgh)
1755	Thomas Brown of Braid (gentry)
1755	Walter Ferguson (clerk, Customs House, Edinburgh; recorder, Edinburgh BB))
1758	William Gibson, of Edinburgh (merchant?)
[1761]	*William Bruce*
[1760s?]	*Thomas Erskine, 6th earl of Kellie (noble; sovereign, Edinburgh BB?)*
[1760s]	*Sir Thomas Wentworth, 5th Baronet (gentry; English)*
1763	David Steuart Erskine, Lord Cardross (noble, antiquarian)
1763	Lieutenant John Duddingston younger of Sandford (gentry, officer)
1764	Mr Thomas Mathie (merchant, Cockenzie)
1764	John Bruce Stewart of Symbister (gentry, merchant)
1764	Ensign Colin Campbell
1765	Sir John Whitefoord, Bt. (gentry)
1765	Andrew Ramsay (merchant, Glasgow)
1766	Duncan MacDougall (writer, Lorne)
1770	James Stewart, Esq. (gentry or merchant?)
[1770]	Shadrach Moyse (clerk, Customs House, Edinburgh; recorder, BB)
[1770]	*James Cummyn (lyon clerk depute)*
[1770]	*Neil MacBrayne (Glasgow)*
[1771]	*Robert Douglas*

1771	Mr James Nairne of Claremont (parish minister, gentry)
[1773]	James Lumsdaine of Innergellie (gentry; sovereign, Edinburgh BB. Possibly identical with the JL listed under 1753)
1773	Mr Thomas Rennie (writer, Edinburgh)
1773	Sir William Nairne of Dunsinane, Bt. (gentry, lawyer)
[1773]	James Durham (recorder, BB)
1775	Hon. Nathaniel Curzon, later 2nd Lord Scarsdale (gentry; English)
[1775]	Philip Anstruther
[1778]	*Captain Robert Lumsdaine (gentry, officer)*
[1778]	*Lieutenant Henry Wilson (officer)*
1778	Patrick Plenderleath (clerk; deputy recorder, BB)
[1780s?]	*Andrew Duncan (physician)*
1781	Captain William Douglas Clephame (gentry, officer)
1783	George, Prince of Wales
1784	Alexander Strachan of Tarrie (merchant, Montrose)
1785	Sir Thomas Dundas, Bt. (gentry, MP)
1785	Vincenzo Lunardi (officer, ballonist)
1786	Captain William Robertson of Lude (gentry, officer)
1788	Professor Hugh Cleghorn (academic, diplomat)
1788	Lieutenant Sir William James Cockburn, Bt. (gentry, officer)
1790	Lieutenant David Parkhill (officer)

The 1739 list of the Benison's members had revealed a club catering exclusively for the local élite of the East Neuk of Fife. The list of members who are known to have joined in the following half century shows a very different pattern. Members are drawn from all over Scotland, and a few from England, but very few are from the East Neuk A first reaction on examining these new members is that, as 1739 members died off, there can hardly have been a club left to meet at Anstruther, for many, if not most, of the scattered later recruits probably never visited the burgh. The club has become a periphery without a centre. But this impression is almost certainly misleading. What has happened is that two types of member have emerged. Most of the evidence identifying recruits comes from diplomas, and diplomas were probably not normally issued to local members, the men who actually meet in Anstruther annually. Instead, diplomas are used by sovereigns to bestow honorary membership, on a pretty random basis, to friends, acquaintances and visitors (like army officers stationed in Fife) who were amused by the idea of belonging to a club which was becoming widely known for its celebration of sex. They would be amused by the diploma's sexual innuendoes, and by the motto, 'may prick nor purse n'er fail you,' and by the themes on the club medals. As to the club's masturbatory rituals, that was a wonderfully shocking 'secret,' but something which the 'honorary' members granted diplomas had no wish to take part in – and perhaps some did not even know of them.

Local members are very hard to detect because they did not receive diplomas. Nathaniel Murray, customs clerk in Anstruther (and thus serving under John McNachtane), was rumoured to have been the author of the diploma and of an obscene piece of prose full of double entendres, but is not listed as a member in 1739.[4] The earliest surviving diploma admitted George Paton, an Edinburgh bookseller. It is dated December 1745 and authorised by John McNachtane as sovereign. But whereas the dating on all other diplomas indicate that McNachtane became sovereign in 1745 or 1746, Paton's diploma refers to his being in the eighth year of his guardianship in 1746. Moreover, written on the same sheet and at the same time as the diploma is a notice appointing Paton 'Agent for the affairs of our order and stationer in ordinary' – and this is dated 1750, in the 10th year of McNachtane's guardianship, and signed by Robert Hunter as recorder, who is otherwise only known signing diplomas in the 1760s. Adding to the irregularities, the seal attached to the diploma is not found on any other diplomas, and was probably suppressed because of an error by the engraver: he had over-enthusiastically endowed the usual Benison horizontal phallus with three testicles. Thus the diploma seems to be an incompetent attempt to rewrite Benison history, suggesting that McNachtane was sovereign long before he took up office, and it may be that it also seeks to indicate Paton entered the club earlier than was the case. He was an Edinburgh bookseller who went bankrupt in about 1760, after which his friends found him a job as a clerk in the Customs House in Edinburgh, and he can be found acting as McNachtane's Benison recorder in 1765. It was probably then that Paton became a Benison member. In later years he became a distinguished bibliographer and antiquarian.[5]

The identity of the James Lumsdaine who delivered the talk on the act of generation to the club in 1753 is uncertain,[6] but he was from the East Neuk, and a whole group of such early members can be identified from the reminiscences of Andrew Duncan (1744–1828), a most distinguished medical professor at Edinburgh university. The son of a merchant and shipmaster in Crail, Duncan was a highly sociable man, playing a leading part in a number of medical clubs. In 1818, in nostalgic old age, he recalled the Benison 'an order of which I have had the honour of being one of the knights companions for many years'. Duncan recorded the names of four fellow members of the Benison, who had become almost legendary figures in the revels of the club, and whose names appear also in late nineteenth century accounts.[7] The names of three of them are, in addition, enshrined by the fourth, Colonel Alexander Monypenny, in a re-writing of an old song as 'Was you e'er at Crail town'. Monypenny died at a great age in 1801, and his verse, which was published in 1778 celebrated heroes of the Benison past days – though without mentioning the club.[8] Sir John Malcolm of Lochore, Bt., had died in 1753. A humble writer in Kirkcaldy, accidents of hereditary descent had brought him his baronecy unexpectedly, and his manners evidently did not accord with his new social status. He had a small estate at Grange, near Anstruther, and on joining the Benison seems to have been regarded as an amiable buffoon.[9] 'If he's a wise man I mistak him,' according to Monypenny, who then added that as for 'Sandie Don' 'He's ten times dafter than Sir John' – the joke being that William Don was the schoolmaster in Crail, and thus supposedly of some intelligence. Andrew Duncan recalled having been taught by him. Finally, Monypenny poked fun at Thomas Dishington, the burgh clerk of Crail, who died in 1755.[10]

> Was ye e'er in Crail town?
> Did ye see Clark DISHINGTOUN?
> His wig was like a drouket hen,   *wet*
> And the tail o't hang doun,
> Like a meikle maan lang draket gray goose pen. *big; sodden*

Nonsense Latin tags interspersed the song, no doubt in mockery of the ignorance of supposedly educated butts of the joke.[11] But it may be suspected that Duncan is relating club folklore as much as hard fact, for the identification of individuals is hazy. Is it the right baronet of Lochore – or Dishington (there was a whole dynasty of

Dishington clerks of Crail). 'Sandy' usually means Alexander, so why is William Don so called? Perhaps it doesn't matter, the amiable insults of the poem being transferred from man to man over the years.

Only one local member in 1739–90 is known to have had a diploma: John Nairne (1771), minister of Anstruther Easter. Both he and his father (with whom he long served as joint parish minister) designated themselves as 'of Claremont' (a small estate near St Andrews), indicating that they maintained pretensions to be gentry, not mere ministers. Nairne was aged about sixty when he received his Benison diploma in 1771, and that it was signed within two weeks of his father's death suggests that readiness to join had previously been inhibited by parental disapproval.[12] Nairne may actually have attended Benison meetings – but perhaps the 'honorary' status bestowed on him by the diploma excused him. However that a minister of the kirk was interested in membership of a club that made no secret of the fact that it stood for free sex is an indication of how much the Church of Scotland had changed in the generations since the Benison had been founded. The 'Moderate' clergy who now dominated the kirk had adapted to cultural and social change. Conviviality and the cultivation of secular interests and pleasures was now acceptable, the harshness and narrowness of the past seen as barbarism. Nonetheless, a minister's membership of the Benison is startling. The boisterous culture of Nairne's lesser-gentry status here perhaps outweighed the restraints of his ministerial one, and it may that by this time the Benison had watered down its rituals. After all, the Benison was no shocking innovation. It had existed for all Nairne's adult life, and become an accepted, almost traditional, element of the local cultural scene. Ribald, but distinctive, part of Anstruther's heritage.

The Edinburgh branch of the Benison was evidently founded in 1752, with Robert Lumsdaine of Innergellie as sovereign.[13] Going beyond the Anstruther Benison, the Edinburgh branch appointed a grand master, in imitation of the freemasons. The holder of the office, Chambre Lewis, was a former customs officer, thus renewing in Edinburgh the Benison's link with such officials. Lewis had served as assistant comptroller general of the customs in Scotland in 1736–46, then collector of customs at Leith until 1770.[14]

Robert Lumsdaine died in 1761, and coincidentally John McNach-tane moved to Edinburgh in the same year. The separate sovereignty of the Edinburgh branch was evidently soon abandoned, and no other diplomas are known that claim to be issued from Edinburgh. But though all diplomas are now dated from the Benison chambers in Anstruther, it seems the 'Anstruther' was often as fictitious as the club's supposed 'chambers' there always were. Now established in Edinburgh, McNachtane sometimes used Robert Hunter (customs clerk in Anstruther) to act as recorder in issuing diplomas, but often it was more convenient to use clerks in Edinburgh who worked under him in the Customs House: George Paton, or Shadrach Moyse, who was later promoted to became 'secretary of the Customs.'[15]

In the years immediately after McNachtane's arrival in Edinburgh the branch there flourished, and it became well enough known for an item on its activities to appear in the press. In 1765 the *Edinburgh Advertiser* carried a report on a meeting held on 26 January:

> We are informed, that there was a very numerous meeting of the Knights Companion of the ancient order of the BEGGARS BENISON, with their Sovereign, on Friday last at Mr Walker's Tavern, agreeable to appointment, when the band of music belonging to the Edinburgh Regiment attended. Everything was conducted with the greatest harmony and cheerfulness, and all the Knights appeared with the medal of the order.[16]

A meeting attended by a regimental band was clearly not performing the more indecent of Benison rituals. The Edinburgh branch had no wish for secrecy about its existence, and perhaps enjoyed drawing attention to itself so its members could enjoy themselves by intriguing outsiders about the meaning of their medals. This high profile and the fact that the band was made available also indicates that the Edinburgh Benison recruited men of considerable social status. A passing reference in the Benison *Records* to the Edinburgh branch as an 'aristocratic Guild' supports this impression: 'Tradition indicates the manners and customs' of the Edinburgh guild 'the chief arcana having been burnt'[17] but these traditions, still known in 1892, have now been lost.

Similarly when Glasgow members of the Benison began to hold meetings they had no qualms about publicity. An advertisement in the *Glasgow Journal* on 16 May 1765 indicated that the Benison was well established in the city. 'The knights companions of the Beggar's Bennison, in or about Glasgow' were desired to attend a meeting of the order at the Black Bull Inn on Wednesday 22 May at 5pm.[18] The Black Bull had been built just a few years before in Argyll Street, and its status in the hierarchy of hostelries was indicated by the fact that in 1761 it had been thought an appropriate resting place for the body of the duke of Argyll, formerly Scotland's most powerful political manager, before his burial.[19] That Glasgow members could hire a room indicated that there were a considerable number of them, and the location shows that they were men of some means. But none of their names are known.

John McNachtane retired from the customs service in 1766, and died in 1773 aged eighty-four. His links with Anstruther remained strong, for in retirement he lived on an annuity he had bought from a fellow member of the Benison, Andrew Johnstone of Pitkierie.[20] His enthusiasm for the Benison remained undiminished to the end, for in his final months he solemnly deputed authority over Russia to a branch of the Benison in St Petersburg (see Chapter 8 below). He had failed to snare the duke of Cumberland at the beginning of his sovereignty, but must have relished this grandiosely absurd Russian coup to round off his career. McNachtane was succeeded in office by James Lumsdaine of Innergellie, son of the former Edinburgh branch sovereign. He was to beat McNachtane's record of nearly thirty years as sovereign, holding office for over forty-five years until his death in 1820.

Briefly, during the American War of Independence, the Benison took an interest in national affairs, seeking to encourage recruitment to the British army. As time had passed and membership extended geographically and socially, the strong currents of frustrated subversiveness in the club had clearly weakened. However, patriotic zeal was limited to helping army officers who were members of the club. In January 1778 the Anstruther 'chapter' offered one guinea to recruits joining Captain Robert Lumsdaine's company in the Earl of Seaforth's regiment. As payment was to be made at Anstruther the advertisement, though placed in an Edinburgh newspaper, must have been designed to attract Fife recruits.[21] The captain was the sovereign's brother, who also had the support of the masonic lodge at

Crail which organised a procession for him 'for the favour they have and regard to' Innergellie, marching through the town with a 'proper band of music' and flags hoisted on the ships in the harbour, before repairing to 'a most elegant entertainment' in the town hall.[22] The Anstruther Benison didn't run to such extravagance, but it was perhaps its example that inspired the Glasgow Benison 'chapter' to issue an advertisement from their 'Hall' the following month, offering five guineas to recruits who enlisted in the Glasgow Volunteers under one of their members, Lieutenant Henry Wilson.[23]

The Glasgow and Anstruther Benisons advertised for recruits in 1778. The Edinburgh branch evidently did not, and this may be significant, for after its meeting accompanied by a regimental band in 1765 no further reference to its existence appears. Surviving wine glasses enamelled with its badge probably date from some years later – perhaps the early 1770s,[24] but the branch may have collapsed soon after that. Its disappearance may reflect a dispute with Anstruther. At first the Anstruther and Edinburgh Benisons had co-operated amicably, agreeing on separate badges and seals in the 1750s and on sharing the club bible (as is indicated by the initials of Parent and Branch – P.B.B.A. and B.B.B.A – appearing on the book's lock), but the strains between the provincial parent, catering for middling sorts of folk, and the metropolitan branch dominated by aristocrats, may lie behind the formation of the Wig Club in 1775.

Assuming that there was a dispute, its timing suggests it was linked with the death of John McNachtane in 1773. His 'sovereignty' over both Edinburgh and Anstruther may have been accepted through respect for his long service, but resented by those who wanted the club to be more under the control of branch members, less the fiefdom of a life sovereign issuing diplomas as he pleased. Edinburgh members may have been reluctant to see James Lumsdaine take over the club almost by hereditary right, with the assumption that East Neuk men would always run the club. McNachtane had lived, latterly, in Edinburgh, but Lumsdaine based himself in Fife, using a local clerk to issue diplomas – Patrick Plenderleath, deputy clerk of Anstruther Easter since 1767 under his father, Benjamin, and clerk in 1776.[25]

The Edinburgh Benison vanished. The Glasgow branch still existed in 1792 when a press advertisement was issued grandiloquently from 'Beggar's Benison Hall' summoning members to a chapter meeting and dinner on 11 July 1792.[26] Thereafter it too disappears.

Many of the names on the 1739–90 list of members are those of obscure men, but a few made some impact on national life. David Erskine, Lord Cardross (1763) was to succeed as 2nd earl of Buchan in 1767 and bring about the foundation of the Society of Antiquaries of Scotland in 1780. Buchan devoted much of his time to his literary and antiquarian interests but was regarded as distinctly tiresome: fussy, meddlesome and vain, fond of grandiose schemes. His Benison membership seems out of character, but he may have come across the club when he attended classes at St Andrews University in 1755–9.[27] Sir John Whitefoord (1765) almost caricatured enthusiasm for sociable clubs. An Ayrshire laird who inherited his baronecy in 1763, he was a master of the St James's Lodge of freemasons at Tarbolton, through which he became acquainted with Robert Burns and became one of his early patrons.[28] He served as senior grand warden of the Grand Lodge of Scotland (1765–6), was a member of the Poker Club and the Pandemonium Club (1776–7), and a leading stalwart of the Wig Club from 1775 until his death in 1803.[29] William Cummying [1770] was Lyon Clerk depute and in 1780 became the first secretary of the Society of Antiquaries of Scotland (the president being his Benison colleague, the earl of Buchan).[30] William Nairne of Dunsinane (1773) subsequently became a lord of session and a lord of justiciary. It is tempting to connect his becoming a member of the Benison with the visit of Samuel Johnson and James Boswell to St Andrews in 1773, as he accompanied them on their journey to east Fife.[31] Hugh Cleghorn (1788) had a much stronger St Andrews connection, being Professor of civil history at the University of St Andrews. But he had left Fife shortly before being granted his Benison diploma, and did not return for twelve years – in the interim having played a leading part in bringing Ceylon under British control.[32]

William Bruce is intriguing though obscure. His membership is only known through a 1761 document appointing him 'Knight Conservator of all the Liberties, Privileges and Immunities' appertaining to the Benison all over the world – a sphere limited later to Africa and Asia. Bruce, it is related, had served in these continents as a lieutenant in the regiment of the Hon Colonel Stuart, making the

Benison known among Christians, Turks, pagans and infidels. At the end of the text of Bruce's appointment is a reminder of what the Benison's cause which he was agenting was – a reference to *Genesis*, chapter 38, which dealt with the sin of Onan. The club thus sponsored the international cause of masturbation.[33]

While the club undertook this missionary activity round the world (in theory at least) it also spread its influence in England. Only one diploma survives, that for the Hon. Nathaniel Curzon (1775), and though he may never have visited Scotland, let alone Anstruther, he was interested enough in the Benison to procure a punch-bowl from China carrying the Benison badge – and Sir Thomas Wentworth did the same, suggesting that he too was a member of the club. Both men came from extremely wealthy landed families, but what Scottish connections brought them in touch with the Benison is unknown.

Judging by numbers of surviving diplomas and other signs of activity, the mid 1750s to the 1780s were the decades in which the Benison was most thriving. On at least one occasion, in 1768, its annual dinner in Anstruther was regarded as newsworthy enough to be noted in the Edinburgh press – just after an item recording the freemasons' annual St Andrew's Day dinner in Edinburgh and the election of the grand master. Perhaps a joke at the expense of the freemasons is present, an implication that the choice of a grand master of freemasons and a sovereign of the Benison were events of comparable importance.

> We learn from Anstruther, that same day, the 30th ult [November], being the Collar-day of the most *Puisant* and Honourable Order of the BEGGARS BENNISON; the *Knights Companion* being met there for the choice of SOVEREIGN for the ensuing year, unanimously re-elected SIR JOHN M'NACHTANE, Sovereign of that Order: being the twenty-fourth year of his Guardianship.[34]

Vincenzo Lunardi and the Prince of Wales

Having honoured water transport in its foundation myth, it is appropriate that the Benison should also have honoured the first successful pioneer of aerial transport in Scotland. French balloonists had proved the viability of both hot air and hydrogen balloons in

1783, and James Tytler made a short flight in Scotland in 1784. But this was soon eclipsed by the exploits of Vincenzo Lunardi, secretary to the Neapolitan embassy in London. After several flights in England in 1784, he brought his hydrogen balloon and gas-making apparatus to Scotland in 1785.

His made his first ascent on 5 October, from the grounds of Heriot's Hospital in Edinburgh, and south westerly winds wafted him over the Firth of Forth to eastern Fife, where the incredible sight of a large object floating in the sky with an incoherent voice shouting from it caused consternation. The balloon landed at Ceres, near Cupar, and Lunardi (dressed in the uniform of a Neapolitan army officer) became an instant celebrity, to be paraded around and fêted. In St Andrews he was made a member of the golf club and a burgess, and was shown around 'that noble institution'. the university. He was also greeted by James Lumsdaine, sovereign of the Benison.

Lunardi is one of only two members of the Benison to leave a record of how he was recruited, and he was the first to print the text of the club's diploma. On 11 October, having returned to Edinburgh, he wrote

> I am just now favoured with a Letter and Diploma from Sir James Lumsdaine, constituting me a member of a very respectable Society, called *Knights Companion of the Beggar's Bennison*: and I am the more elated with this new honour as I understand that my Patron the Prince of Wales had the same conferred on him a few months ago. I cannot now explain to you the enigmatical meaning of the Beggar's Bennison, but shall endeavour to do it *ad aures*: the following transcripts must gratify your curiosity for the present.

Thus Lunardi knew enough about the nature of the body he had joined to judge that it was only fit to be communicated verbally, it being too indecent to be committed to paper. Lumsdaine' letter accompanying the diploma read

> To Lunardi, Walker's Hotel, Edinburgh.
> 'Sir,
> As it seems to be set for fine weather, I hope to see you in Fife to-morrow: But in case I should not again have that pleasure, I have admitted you a Knight Companion of the most ancient and puissant

order of the Beggar's Bennison, and with this have sent you a diploma.

Captaine Erskine and my brother, Major Lumsdaine, make offer of best compliments to you.

That the Beggar's Bennison may ever attend such bold adventurers, is the sincere wish of

Sir,

Your most humble servant

Jas. Lumsdaine

Innergellie near Anstruther,

10th October 1785

P.S.   I shall be glad to hear you have received this. J.L.

Thus Lunardi's membership was justified as he was a 'bold adventurer.' a term used in the diploma – though his demonstrated skills were not within the Benison's usual range of interests. The balloonist never returned to Fife, and though further honours followed – burgess-ship of Edinburgh, membership of the Royal Company of Archers, and initiation to masonic lodge in Kelso when he happened to land there – Lunardi soon returned to obscurity.[35] But a fashion for balloon hats among ladies commemorated his exploits for a few years.[36]

Vincenzo Lunardi's reference to George, Prince of Wales (later George IV, having received a Benison diploma confirms the strong tradition that he was a member. If John McNachtane had sought to recruit the duke of Cumberland (George's grand-uncle) and had commissioned a Benison branch in Russia, why should not James Lumsdaine recruit the king's son in a similarly grandiose gesture? Nathaniel Curzon had joined the Benison in 1775, and as he was a close friend of the prince it is possible he had suggested that he might be invited to join. George was an ideal candidate – sexually speaking, a worthy successor in the traditions of royal sensual indulgence established by James V and Charles II. Prince Charles Edward, latterly 'King Charles III' to Jacobites, had died some years before, leaving no children. His heir as Stuart pretender to the throne was his younger brother 'King Henry IX.' and as he had become a cardinal there was no hope of a legitimate heir. By this time there were few in Britain who could feel a Stuart restoration in Britain was possible, or even desirable. Even among those with sentimental attachment to the lost cause, practical allegiance had switched to the Hanoverians. And, to the aberrant loyalists of the Beggar's Benison who valued delight in sexual pleasure in a king above all else, who could now better represent true, rampant royalty than the young Prince George? His sexual wanderings were already notorious, as was his liking for boisterous, drunken sociability. In spite of the unfortunate breaches of the principles of hereditary descent represented by his family, this was a prince the Beggar's could relate to.

Prince George had been issued with a diploma two years before Lunardi, on 2 August 1783.[37] It is probably significant that this was just ten days before the prince's twenty-first birthday. What better a coming of age present? That Lumsdaine told Lunardi about the royal recruit indicates that the prince had no qualms about his membership being publicised, but he has only one further known – or alleged – connection with the Benison. Nearly forty years later as George IV he visited Scotland (1822). When he landed at Leith, it is said, he was greeted by the sovereign (then the 9th earl of Kellie) and presented him with a sample of pubic hair from one of his mistresses.[38] That the surviving hair is indeed a grizzly memento of some distant sexual encounter may be true – though the royal connection may be an invention of the trickster knights of the Benison. However, a 'tradition' noted in the early twentieth century gives an explanation of the royal gift. A famed wig composed of pubic hair from Charles II's mistresses had once had a part in Benison rituals (presumably in the Edinburgh branch), but its owner had withdrawn it and presented it to the Wig Club in 1775. As compensation, George bestowed on the Benison a similar token of royal sexual prowess, harvested from his own labours.[39] It almost sounds like an obscene allegory of allegiance changing from Stuart to Hanoverian, of recognition of George as the true virile successor of James V and Charles II. It might also be seen as satire on Jacobites who treasured locks from the head of Bonnie Prince Charlie. As on other occasions, the Beggars are playing games with concepts of loyalty, masters of confusion. It is even possible that the story is true.

In the case of Sir Thomas Dundas's recruitment to the Benison, as in that of Lunardi, evidence survives of how James Lumsdaine went about bestowing membership. Again, it seems the new member was presented with a *fait accompli*. Lumsdaine wrote to Dundas inviting him to join the club of 8 May 1785, but had already signed his diploma on 28 April, and it may well have been enclosed in the letter.[40] There may, however, have been previous contact between the two men, for Dundas (MP for Stirlingshire, 1768–94; Lord Dundas of Aske 1794) was a friend of the Prince of Wales, who may have suggested he was a suitable candidate.[41]

The Earls of Kellie and the Benison

That the earls of Kellie were leading figures in the Benison is an infuriatingly vague statement that has often been repeated. There were six earls during the existence of the club, and only two can be assigned membership with any conviction.

Alexander Erskine, the 5th earl, is not one of them, but it is tempting to believe that he ought to have been a member. He was made for the part. An amiable, sociable drunk of extremely limited intelligence, he eagerly joined the '45 rebellion, and was noticed in Edinburgh decked out in full Highland gear. As one of the few nobles to join the Jacobite army he might have been expected to gain a high place in rebel affairs, but his obvious limitations outweighed social status, and his only appointment was to the position of governor of Lochleven, someone having devised a post for him in which he could do no harm. He did not march into England with Prince Charles Edward's army, but is recorded in Perth roaming the streets drunk, making a nuisance of himself by trying to persuade people to play backgammon with him. He was present at Culloden, and after the battle fled home and, traditions claims, hid up a beech tree, lowering a rope to a trusted servant who supplied food. Perhaps, in his dim way, he recalled Charles II having hidden in a oak tree after the battle of Worcester.

As suspects were hunted down, Kellie was reported to be 'Lurking in or about his own house', and a threat was circulated that he would be harshly treated unless he gave himself up. He did so, and was whisked off to fairly comfortable imprisonment in Edinburgh Castle until 1753. No attempt was made to bring him to trial. Testimonies by witnesses such as 'I never heard that he was an idiot' and 'I couldn't say how far he was disordered by drink – but heard that he was given to it' did not suggest he had been any real threat to the Hanoverian state. His captors concluded that he had 'lived obscure and little regarded by any Body, his Fortune small, and his Understanding of an inferior Size, not many removes from the very lowest.'[42]

The Jacobite earl was succeeded by his son Thomas Erskine, 6th earl of Kellie (1756–81). A much later note on the title page of the Benison Bible reads 'Beggar's Benison, Castle of Dreel, Anstruther. Given for use by Thomas Earl of Kellie, at the Initiation of Standing Members', while a note on the back of the page proclaims of the 6th earl that 'Thomas was the Sovereign'. This is the only evidence that he was ever 'sovereign', and there is no room for him among the 'Anstruther' sovereigns, but he may have been sovereign of the obscure (historically if not socially) Edinburgh Benison, for some years after 1761, in succession to Robert Lumsdaine

The 6th earl would certainly have been appropriate as a sovereign. Thomas Erskine was a man with two distinct faces. On the one hand he was a talented and assiduous musician and composer. He had trained in Germany, and became a leading figure in Edinburgh musical circles, organising and conducting St Cecilia's Day concerts. But he was also noted for the coarseness of his wit and his drunken carousing even in an age when such things usually aroused little comment. His insatiable appetite for puns was wearisome and his love of contriving toasts designed to annoy others made his company tiresome. The man who did much to spread interest in classical music to the cultured of Edinburgh would switch after concerts to enjoyment of more homely entertainment. He might be the maestro, but he was also 'fiddler Tam' with a patriotic taste for traditional plain Scots foods. The English visitor Edward Topham was horrified at a dinner he attended at Fortune's Tavern in 1776. It met with the highest approbation, being 'applauded to the skies by Lord Kelly, and other celebrated knights of the trencher'. But haggis, 'Cocky-leaky' soup, sheep's head, and solon goose (gannet) proved too much for Topham's tastes, and he could only console himself that there had been plenty of good claret.[43] Anne, countess of Balcarres, recounted that Kellie proclaimed that his dinners were for the *Eaterati*, thus mocking the famed intellectuals of the age, the *Literati*. He would then laugh at his own puns until he went purple.[44] He seems to have been the leader of the notorious craze for 'saving the ladies'. At his fashionable St Cecilia's Day concerts, most of the 'celebrated beauties' were present. Afterwards, their admirers would retire to a tavern and argue their relative merits. He 'that can drink the largest quantity' to honour his choice was declared to have thus 'saved' her. She became the object of public toasts for the following year, and all the other entrants in the beauty contest were declared to be damned. It is to be assumed that this drunken choosing of the saved and the toasting of her thereafter were not matters of much delicacy.[45] The 6th earl of Kellie had in common with his fellow Beggar, Robert Hamilton of Kilbrackan, a feckless lack of concern about the future, spending far beyond his means. Eventually he had to sell off the family estates, leaving only Kellie Castle and its grounds to his brother and heir.[46]

The 7th and 8th earls appear to have had no connection with the Benison, but the 9th earl (another Thomas) became sovereign in 1820, in succession to James Lumsdaine. Though this is his earliest documented connection with the Benison, he was then an old man and had probably been a member for several decades. By birth he was a nephew of Sir Charles Erskine of Cambo, and it was only the extinction of the main line of the Erskines of Kellie and the death of a nephew without heirs that eventually brought him the title, in 1799. In youth he had needed to make a career for himself, and in 1759, at the age of thirteen, he had been sent to Gothenburg to work in commerce. In time he amassed a fortune as a merchant, his business interests including involvement in the profitable smuggling trade with Scotland. His family evidently had Jacobite sympathies, and these would have found echoes in the Scottish merchant community in Gothenburg, for a number of Jacobite exiles had settled there and thrived in trade – Erskine's first employer had served in Prince Charles's life guard at Culloden. Thomas Erskine founded the Bachelors' Club in Gothenburg in 1769 'for billiards and pleasant, undisturbed fellowship', it being illegal to play billiards in public in Sweden at the time. Whether the club, catering for young clerks and accountants like himself, was really so bland may be questionable, but it was respectable enough to gain the name Royal Bachelors' Club in 1787 – and it survives to the present day.[47]

On visits home Erskine's lingering Jacobite sentiments were shown by his becoming one of a small circle of friends of James Steuart, a writer in Edinburgh, who held a dinner annually to celebrate the birthday of Prince Charles Edward. At one of these dinners, probably between 1770 and 1775, Thomas Erskine presented Steuart with half a dozen wine glasses, decorated with enamelled portraits of the prince.[48] In exactly the same period, the Beggar's Benison acquired enamelled wine glasses bearing the Edinburgh version of its badge. It seems more than possible that the rich Gothenburg merchant had favoured the Benison as well as Steuart with a gift.

By this time expression of Jacobite sentiments of the sort that inspired James Steuart's dinner parties no longer indicated opposition to the existing British regime, and in 1776 Thomas Erskine was appointed British consul in Gothenburg, to gather intelligence on arms shipments to the American rebels.[49] By the time accidents of blood brought him his earldom in 1799 he was a rich man and a respected figure: at last there was an earl of Kellie who had the resources to live up to his social status – even if the money had been made in trade. He returned permanently to Scotland, buying up land in Fife to compensate for that sold by his predecessors. When he became sovereign of the Benison he was aged about seventy-four, and regarded as the grand old man of the East Neuk.

From Blessing to Toast

Even if at first the existence of the Beggar's Benison was kept secret by members, by 1765, when the first advertisement was placed in the press mentioning the club, any such policy had been abandoned. This being the case, the lack of contemporary references to the club seems surprising, given its obscene activities. Probably it indicates both a wide tolerance of what men got up to when socialising in private, and that knowledge of quite what went on at Benison meetings (in Anstruther at least) was not widespread. To contemporaries, in a world where bizarrely named clubs with odd, often boisterous and bawdy, activities abounded, the Benison did not seem particularly startling. Yet the meaning of the club's title, the blessing on prick and purse, was known, and for a time it became a fashionable, if risqué, toast. It emerged in Chapter 1 that what was to become the Beggar's Benison motto and toast – to prick and purse – was known in England before the club was founded, and it appears in English collections of toasts – in 1756, for example, as 'May our p—k and purse never fail us.'[50] But using the toast in a disguised form by drinking simply to 'The Beggar's Benison' seems to be Scottish inspiration.

It is a Scot who first mentions the toast, and he used it in a Scottish context. In his novel *Humphrey Clinker* (1771), Tobias Smollett depicted Edinburgh life in a letter written by an English visitor.[51] This early tourist, Mr Melford, described a ball held during Leith races by the caddies of Edinburgh – the errand boys or messengers of the town. The caddies were a conspicuous part of the Edinburgh scene, remarked on by many visitors, useful for running errands of all sorts. Not least, they were notorious for carrying confidential messages promoting sexual liaisons; and sometimes acted as pimps.[52] As Mr Melford put it, 'They are particularly famous for their dexterity in executing one of the functions of Mercury'. The caddies had a society, and had organised a ball during the Leith Races, which were the social event of the year, crowding the city with nobles and gentry. Some of the caddies were well known local characters, and could be on informal terms ('rudely familiar,' Mr Melford thought) with those of status for whom they carried messages. In the novel, the caddies boldly invite all the young nobles and gentlemen in town for the races to attend their ball – encouraging a positive response by assuring them that 'all the celebrated ladies of pleasure would grace the entertainment with their company'. Mr Melford accepted the invitation, and found himself at dinner with about eighty lords, lairds, courtesans and caddies mixed together, presided over by 'a veteran pimp'. As the evening progressed endless toasts were drunk. Pint glasses were issued so the claret could be consumed faster. Among the toasts were three which were incomprehensible to Melford, 'The Best in Christendom', 'Gibb's contract' and 'The beggar's benison'. The first of these is an allusion to female genitals,[53] the second has been rather obscurely explained as a toast to 'stark love and kindness'.[54] Smollett is, though a supposedly innocent character, citing in a mainstream novel obscene toasts which were fashionable, getting away with this by the fact that the obscenity was veiled. Those in the know would laugh, those who didn't would be simply puzzled.

Two other references to the Benison toast being used outside the club itself are factual rather than fictional. The toast appears in England, in aristocratic circles, being recorded by a Scot proud at this advance of Scottish cultural influence. James Boswell notes that in 1775 he and other Scots dined one day with Lord Mountstuart (later 1ˢᵗ marquis of Bute) – a Scot but highly anglicised. The two men were old friends, having shared a prostitute – and consequent bouts of gonorrhoea – in Venice ten years before.[55] Boswell was pleased to have his anglicised friend recognise his Scottishness, by his choice of a toast:

> My Lord showed me tonight how he could adept himself to a Scotch company. He made bumpers of claret circulate quickly, and drank 'the beggar's benison' and a number of such toasts.[56]

Boswell recognised Scottish identity in fast drinking and obscenity. In 1781 Boswell again drank the toast in noble company, this time at Somerset House with the duke of Hamilton, Lord Townshend and others:

> By and by a general toast 'The Beggar's Benison.' 'You are obliged to us [the Scots] for that said I, and told the story of Queen Mary's father.

Thus Boswell eagerly proclaimed the Scottish royal derivation of the toast – Mary Queen of Scots's father having been James V – and thereby provides what is, by over a century, the earliest reference to the Beggars' foundation myth. On this 1781 occasion the company's phallic pride in drinking a toast to each other's genitalia must have been undermined by the dispirited Lord Townshend. The distinguished soldier and former lord lieutenant of Ireland, then in his late fifties, confided gloomily: 'poor as my purse is, my p[ric]k is worse.'[57]

The ownership of punch bowls decorated with the Benison by landed gentlemen (assuming the two that survive were not unique) suggests that 'The Beggar's Benison' toast was drunk in country houses as well as in London, and that it was common in England among the lower as well as the upper ranks of society is indicated by its inclusion in a dictionary 'of the vulgar tongue' a few years later, being defined as a blessing or popular toast consisting of the words 'May prick nor purse never fail you.' 'The Beggar's Bennison or Thannie na beuchᵗ horo' even appeared as a supposedly old Scottish dance.[58]

In time, however, sensibilities changed, and dirty toasts went out of fashion – or went underground. No further examples of usage of the Benison toast (outside the club itself) are known. One thing that is noticeable about this group of references is that the toast was often drunk by men who were not only not members of the Benison, but who probably knew nothing of the club. 'The Beggar's Benison' was simply an amusing bawdy toast, not a reference to an institution. The same is probably true of a trans-Atlantic reference. In 1760 the sloop *The Beggar's Bennison*, owned by three New York merchants, was seized by the navy in the West Indies for trading with a French colony in time of war, echoing the theme of 'fair trade'.[59] The popularity of the genial genital toast originating in Anstruther stretched from Russia in the east to America in the west.

The Benison, 1790s–1836

Known recruits to the Beggar's Benison, 1755–90

Roman type indicates that the member's diploma survives, or that he signed one or more diplomas as an official of the club. Italic type indicates that membership has been determined from other sources. Dates are generally those of joining the club, but those in square brackets indicate earliest dates at which men are known to have been members, or periods of active membership.

[1792]	William Elliot (recorder Glasgow BB)
17995	Hon. William Maule (gentry)
[1795]	M. Hunter (hereditary recorder, BB)
[1790s]	*David Wilson* (presbyterian minister, Pittenweem)
[1790s?]	*David Low* (bishop, Pittenweem)
1812	David, Lord Ogilvie (noble, officer)
1813	Andrew MacVicar (Edinburgh)
[1813]	John Grahame
[1815]	*[James?] Dow*
1816	William Arnot (merchant, St Petersburg)
[1820]	Thomas Erskine, 9th earl of Kellie
1820	Thomas Marshall Gardner of Hillcairnie (gentry, Kilmany)
1820	Lieutenant Colonel William Wemyss (gentry, officer)
[1820]	Archibald Johnstone (recorder BB)
1825	Lieutenant general James Durham of Largo (gentry, officer)
1825	John Cleghorn (officer)
1825	Peter Cleghorn
[1834]	David John Rodger
1834	James Rodger (merchant, Anstruther)
1834	Captain James Black (naval officer, sovereign)

[*1836*]   *Matthew Forster Conolly* (clerk, interim recorder BB)
[*1836*]   *John, Lord Arbuthnot* (noble, lord lieutenant of Kincardineshire)

Inflated claims as to membership haunt the history of the Benison. 'From Cambo to Largo, without one exception, all the Lairds were Knights ... With few exceptions the Parish Ministers of the Four Eastern Burghs were duly installed Knights,' boasts the *Records*,[60] but nothing specific is cited to support such claims. 'Judging from the records of the Club that have been preserved, it is difficult to say who, of any prominence in literature or society, at that time, was not a member of the Beggar's Benison', trilled Alexander Ferguson, on the basis of no evidence.[61] Within a year of the establishment of the Edinburgh Branch Benison it 'included the first wits of the city. A Scottish peer opened another with no less *éclat* in London', and the Prince Regent became sovereign. Gossip, rumour – but no evidence.[62]

Such exaggerations are implausible if they are supposed to refer to the decades before 1790. After that date they become even more incredible. The Benison received a shock from the French Revolution from which it never fully recovered. The pattern of survival of diplomas clearly indicates the decline. Only one survives for the years 1791 to 1811. Thereafter a trickle appears, with a brief revival in the 1820s after the 9th earl of Kellie became sovereign.

The French Revolution had a profound influence on the hedonistic upper and middle ranks of British society in the years after 1789. For generations the hierarchy of society had seemed stable, something that could be taken for granted. Men of wealth and status had become increasingly open in their enjoyment of pleasure in defiance of conventional morality: Prince George not only had mistresses and gorged and drank, but flaunted his promiscuity, in spite of increasing press criticism. The pretence that the post 1688–9 Revolution regimes stood for a restoration of morality had been abandoned once it had proved that pandering to the conventionally moral was not necessary to preserve stability. What those without the wealth or taste thought of the behaviour of their social betters did not seem to matter. Deference from the lower orders could be taken for granted and life was not to be taken too seriously. With the revolution across the channel fear swept this élite paradise. In the most elaborate of aristocratic nations, where royal power exercised on behalf of the privileged classes had been thought to be absolute, monarchy and aristocracy had been overthrown by the masses. Execution of the king and the Terror followed, sending waves of dispossessed nobility into exile in Britain.

Nervousness grew about displaying swaggering immorality and extravagance in the faces of the poor, for perhaps after all the privileged did not hold their positions absolutely. They were conditional on their behaving in ways considered acceptable by those below them, on their performing certain functions in the running of society, and on setting (at least outwardly) a good example. Life was serious after all, and to retain wealth and power one needed to at least pay attention to threats from within as well as prepare for the feared French invasion. Traditional hierarchical values might be re-asserted with new reactionary zeal in response to revolution in France, but this was coupled with the recognition that changes in behaviour were necessary. The upper orders experienced a new sense (genuine if self-interested) of mission and responsibility. Suddenly, upholding traditional moral values seemed not a quaint and senseless restriction on pleasure but a necessary line of defence against revolutionary subversion.

Excessive drinking, gambling wildly and sexual license were increasingly hard to enjoy without pangs of conscience or fear. One had to try to behave respectably. Some clubs closed altogether, for the brief emergence of radical political societies aroused old fears that men meeting together in groups which were secretive about quite what they got up to (part of the fun for many clubs) meant conspiracy. Others toned down their activities, but nonetheless found that in a new atmosphere of sobriety and dread fewer members were ready to 'waste' many of their evenings in talking and drinking as good fellows. The very words brotherhood, fraternity and club now had sinister undertones. In time confidence returned. Even before the generation of war with France finally ended in 1815, fear of revolution had waned, and the restoration of the Bourbons and aristocracy in France led to further relaxation, while the antics of Prince George as regent and then King George IV (1820–30), as an ageing playboy, set the tone. But the Beggar's Benison was never the same again.

Lack of known diplomas for 1791–1811 does not necessarily mean no recruitment, and it was probably in the 1790s that two members joined whose names are recorded in the Benison *Records* because they were churchmen, their membership being therefore regarded as particularly scandalous. David Low (1768–1855) was a well known and respected local figure for many years. Born in 1768, he became minister of a little Episcopalian congregation in Pittenweem in 1790, benefiting from the gradual relaxation in persecution. He also held services in Crail, and tramped around indefatigably ministering to the scattering of Episcopalian lairds in the East Neuk. In 1819 he became nominal bishop of Ross, Moray, Argyll and the Isles, though he continued to live in Pittenweem. He resigned his bishoprics in 1850 and died five years later. His life was commemorated by his fellow Beggar, Matthew Conolly, in a biographical sketch which a reviewer denounced for giving the impression that Low 'was simply a comic Bishop and master of broad grins'.[63] The trouble was that, though Conolly revered Low and never mentioned his Benison membership, he took Low's piety for granted and concentrated on the man he had known as a friend – an informally sociable man, a left over from a past age of boisterous good humour: 'As a private individual, the Bishop was one of the most amiable of men – he was also one of the most interesting relics of the older days of Scottish character and manners'. Conolly celebrates David Low's hearty laugh, great sense of the ludicrous and gifts as a conversationalist, but notes that in mixed company his 'manner bordered on reserve'. The love of the lack of restraint that came with exclusively male company made him a born clubman. He was, in manner, a man of the late eighteenth-century, with a heartiness – or grossness – that Conolly, looking back with nostalgia, loved.[64] But by the time that Conolly was writing, in 1859, it was thought shocking to present a bishop in such a light. High piety and seriousness were expected.

Another writer recalling Low described him as 'A tall, lang figure with an old-fashioned shovel hat, with slender gaiter-clad legs … a familiar figure on all the roads of the East Neuk, striding out to Cambo or Innergellie' to visit members of his flock. He was the 'very last representative of the old Scottish Episcopalian Jacobite'.[65] Anecdote recounts that in his later years, aware of changing sensibilities, he asked that his name be erased from all the Benison's records. The secretary obliged – but then maliciously minuted his action, noting that forty references to the bishop attending annual meetings had had to be deleted. A good story, perhaps with a basis of truth behind it. Certainly the one recorded joke that Low contributed to Benison humour would have caused horror if attributed to a cleric in the Victorian age he lived into: a girl caught unexpectedly in a hen-house tries to explain her presence by saying she is looking for a hen. Reply: 'Ah! ye het bitch, ye're no seeking a *Hen* – ye're seekin' a *Cock!*'

The other churchman who probably joined the Benison in the 1790s was David Wilson, minister of the Relief Church in Pittenweem from 1794. None of the other East Neuk burghs had significant numbers of such seceeders from the Church of Scotland, but the Pittenweem congregation had emerged out of a patronage dispute in the 1770s when some parishioners had refused to accept the imposition of James Nairne (son of John Nairne, the Anstruther minister who was a Benison member) on the parish as its minister. The Records describe Wilson as 'a prime knight', '"the Cock" of all assemblies, latterly nicknamed "Cap-oot" from his Bacchanal armours' – presumably caput, head or leader, is meant. Here, as with David Low, it may be suspected that there is a tendency to exaggerate involvement with the Benison because Wilson was a minister.[66]

The trickle of Benison diplomas restarts in 1812, with the admission of Lord Ogilvie, a captain in the 42nd Highlanders who was accepted by many as being earl of Airlie though the title, forfeited by an ancestor after the 1715 rising, was not restored until 1826. The pattern of diplomas (so far as pattern can be safely detected in so tiny a sample) continues to be much as before 1790, dominated by gentry, soldiers and merchants. The club's seal dated 1816 based on the Isle of May lighthouse and a new issue of the club's medal in 1826 suggest attempts at revival, and when the 9th earl of Kellie became sovereign in 1820 he designed an impressive new diploma, elaborately engraved and boldly bearing his own coat of arms as well as that of the former Edinburgh Benison, which suggests he may have hoped to revive the branch.

Advertising the annual St Andrews Day dinners in the local press was also tried, in the hope of encouraging members to attend, but this was probably a sign of weakness rather than strength.[67] How random recruitment could be, and how little a membership diploma may reveal about the character of new members, is revealed by the experience of Hugh Cleghorn. After his years of service abroad he had settled at Srathvithie in Dunino parish. He evidently took no interest in the affairs of the Benison, of which he had been a nominal member since 1788, and was surprised to receive in 1825 membership diplomas for his sons John and Peter from Lieutenant General James Durham of Largo, who had proposed them to the club 'unknown to me'. Hugh Cleghorn forwarded the diplomas, with the caution 'keep them out of female sight'. Evidently his sons knew already of the Benison and of his membership of it, and he felt enough for the old club to pay his sons' admission fees of six guineas. After all, it was part of the local establishment, nearly a century old.

Recruitment unseen failed to restore the Benison's fortunes. The times were against it. There might be a scandalous king on the throne in the person of George IV, but increasingly the days of crude drunken conviviality and vulgar humour – let alone rampant phallicism – were looked on as the shocking aberrations of previous generations, out of place in a new world which was increasingly adopting what would soon be labelled Victorian values. The earl of Kellie died in 1828, and in 1833 or 1834 Captain James Black became sovereign. Born in Anstruther in 1777, 'Daring Jimmie' had had a distinguished career in the navy, including service at the Battle of Trafalgar (in which he was wounded) on *HMS Mars*. Retiring to his birthplace he became a rather eccentric figure. He built a fine house (now the clubhouse of the Golf Club), named it Marsfield, and set up the figurehead of his old ship to glare out across the Forth. 'Darling Jimmie.' as he was known, was remembered many years later with 'a white hat surmounting a yellow mottled face, his blue coat and nankeen continuations.'[68] It was a sign of changed suscep-tibilities that a euphemism had had to be found for breeches or trousers. He issued the last known Benison diploma in 1834 (using one of the blank diplomas printed by the earl of Kellie, pasting his own arms over the earl's), to James Rodger, an Anstruther merchant, the recorder being David John Rodger, who had been described some years earlier as one of the 'resident gentry' of Anstruther.[69] The club was returning to its roots, representing East Neuk merchants and gentry. But it was dying, and was laid to rest two years later.

On 27 October 1836 a notice appeared in the *Fifeshire Journal*:

BEGGARS BENISON
NOTICE is hereby given that a Meeting of the Order is to be held within Laing's Inn, at Anstruther, on Saturday, the 5th of November next at 2

o'clock afternoon, for the purpose of considering the propriety of Dissolving the Club, and of distributing, or otherwise applying, the funds thereto belonging.[70]

M.F. Conolly
Anstruther *Interim Recorder*

A follow-up appeared on 24 November, indicating that to the very end the club was undecided on how to spell 'Benison':

BEGGAR'S BENNISON
AN ADJOURNED MEETING of the KNIGHT'S COMPANIONS of the ORDER is to be held in LAING'S INN, ANSTRUTHER, on Wednesday the 30th instant (being Collar day), at 3 o'Clock afternoon, for the purpose of arranging and settling the pecuniary affairs of the Order, and of deciding upon the proposition for its Dissolution.

After disposing of the business of the Meeting, the Members, and such of their friends as choose to join them, are to Dine together at the Inn.

Dinner on the Table at half-past 3 o'Clock.

Those Gentlemen who mean to attend are requested to leave their names at the Inn on or before the 28th instant.

B.B. Chambers of Anstruther,
21st November, 1836.[71]

That only half an hour had been set aside for business suggests that dissolution was regarded as a foregone conclusion. The meeting was held as a last annual formal St Andrew's Day meeting – collar day, on which the members wore their medals hung on sashes or collars round their necks. The dinner that followed was no doubt a sentimental occasion, with recollections of the good fellowship of the past, with the vulgarity of a past age remembered with a nostalgia sometimes tinged with embarrassment. Great times, but such things just wouldn't do in the modern world. Only one member, it is said, Lord Arbuthnot, opposed the dissolution.

The dissolving of the Benison in Laing's tavern ended a century of meetings in Anstruther taverns. The club had always hired a room or rooms for meetings, but liked to keep up the fiction of having its own accommodation, and indeed of having met originally in Dreel Castle. The *Records* assert that the meetings were at first 'in a Chamber or Chambers, designated "the Temple"' in the castle. But this was a myth, not reality. Shortly after Charles II's 1651 visit the castle was wrecked by the troops of Oliver Cromwell's invading army,[72] and the Anstruthers of that Ilk abandoned the ruined castle in the 1660s, building a new house, the Manor House or Anstruther Place, on higher ground inland of the castle site, using the old castle as a quarry for stones. A ruined castle would hardly have been a suitable place for convivial meeting – let alone viewing naked girls – in winter. The Benison therefore met in a tavern near the castle ruins. In about 1812 Andrew Johnstone of Pittowie, who was treasurer of the club, bought the inn – or at least an inn adjacent to the site of the castle, and they met (or continued to meet) there. After Johnstone sold it, the building became Robertson's Commercial Inn or Hotel, and the Benison went on meeting in this respectable-sounding institution. In modern times it has been transformed into the Smugglers' Inn, a name perhaps having some historical justification as it backs on to the Dreel Burn, so convenient for clandestinely landing goods – it is next to the site of the house of Charles Wightman, the Jacobite smuggler.[73]

In tavern rooms new members – 'real' local members, not the honorary diploma-bearers – were initiated. In later years at least new members (or perhaps only those who had diplomas) paid three guineas. Another guinea bought a silver-gilt medal, and one guinea was the annual subscription.[74] Issuing honorary diplomas had the advantage of helping to pay for food and drink and girls for meetings.

Did the scenes of ritual masturbation described in the 1730s continue to take place until the 1830s? It is impossible to know. Perhaps over the decades, just as the anti-government edge to the Benison faded, so too did the gross obscenity which had been partly a gesture of defiance. Orgasm giving way to drunken talk, reminiscence and recitation on sexual themes, with the obscene relics looked at with a degree of detachment by nineteenth-century members, awed by how gross the ways of their fathers and grandfathers had been. Already by the time the club was dissolved their value may have been coming to be seen as antiquarian rather than as symbols of sexual freedom.

Notes

1 For details of diplomas see Appendix 2

2 NLS, MS 16613, ff.134–7, and MS 17522, ff.45–6.

3 NAS, GD26/11/84, Leven and Melville Muniments. It is notable that McNachtane, addressing a genuine 'royal' does not himself use the title sovereign, being content with 'guardian.' However, for the president of a club to be called the sovereign was not unique. The Cape Club, for example, had a sovereign.

4 Gourlay, *Anstruther*, 166; *Records*, 7–8; *Supplement*, 54–5.

5 *DNB*; H. Hecht, *Songs from David Herd's manuscripts* (Edinburgh, 1904), 3–8;

6 *Supplement*, 45 describes Lumsdaine as 'of Stratharthie, Parish of Dekins.' There is no such parish, and the estate has not been traced. One possibility is that 'of Stravithie, parish of Dunino' is meant. James Lumsdaine of Stravithie was cousin and father-in-law of Robert Lumsdaine of Innergellie, to whom Stravithie passed on James's death, and this James may have been the 1753 lecturer. But another possibility is that the lecturer was Robert's son James (the later Benison sovereign), using the Stravithie designation during his father's lifetime. See A.H. Millar, *Fife, pictorial and descriptive* (2 vols., Cupar, 1895), i, 334.

7 A. Duncan (ed.), *Miscellaneous poems, extracted from the records of the Circulation Club at Edinburgh* (Edinburgh, 1818), 15n; *DNB*.

8 Duncan, *Miscellaneous poems*, 13–14, 14–15n; 83. Duncan gives Monypenny's first name as 'James' in error. Rogers, *Social life*, ii, 413–15, copies Duncan in taking the song to apply to the Benison, but without acknowledgement. D. Herd, *Ancient and modern Scottish songs, heroic ballads, etc.* (2 vols., Edinburgh, 1776, reprinted Edinburgh, 1973), ii, 99. F. Collison, 'The oyster dredging songs of the Firth of Forth,' *Scottish Studies*, v (1961), 15–16, asks whether it is not 'too fanciful' to regard the song as a seventeenth century dredging song. It is indeed too fanciful: the evidence cited is highly implausible, and the Crail connection is ignored. Nonetheless, scholars of Burns (interested as Burns copied the poem's style in his 'On Captain Grose') have adopted this peculiar suggestion: Kinsley, *The poems and songs*, iii, 1365; J.A. Mackay, *The complete works of Robert Burns* (Alloway, 1986), 415,

9 Millar, *Fife*, i, 383; Wood, *East Neuk*, 191; *CB*, iv, 246.

10 SAUL, B10/10/2, 3 Feb., 6 Mar. 1755

11 J. Marshall, *A winter with Robert Burns, being annals of his patrons and associates in Edinburgh* (Edinburgh, 1846), 88, says Lunardi was received in Anstruther by Mr Claud Dishington and other 'wags' – by implication members of the Beggar's Benison (which Marshall refers to simply as a 'club'). This may have been another member from this family of Crail clerks.

12 *Fasti*, v, 180–1; Conolly, *Eminent men*, 347.

13 The *Records*, 12, erroneously date the founding of an Edinburgh branch to 1766.

14 *Calendar of treasury books and papers, 1735–8* (1900), 282; NAS, CE3/7, CE3/8, CE3/12/2.

15 Grant, *Edin. marriages*, 647.

16 *Edinburgh Advertiser*, 25–29 January 1765, p. 69. Cited in Grant, *Edinburgh*, iii, 123. Grant identifies the regiment as the 25th Foot.

17 *Records*, 12–13.

18 'Senex,' *Glasgow past and present* (3 vols., 1884), ii, 303. Mentioned in Jones, *Clubs*, 182.

19 'Senex,' *Glasgow*, i, 81–3, 349, 511, ii, 307, 385, 389.

20 NAS, CC8/8/222/2, Edinburgh Register of Testaments, f.196r.

21 *Edinburgh Advertiser*, 3 Feb 1778, p.77. Transcripts in Jones, *Clubs*, 188–9 and Stevenson, *Anstruther*, 189. from a typed copy in BBWCC.

22 D. Brown and J.E. Elder, The lodge of St Andrews at Crail, 1761–1961. The Story of Two Hundred Years (typescript, copy in SAUL B10/14/659, p.2.

23 *Edinburgh Advertiser* 4 Mar 1778; Transcript in Stevenson, *Anstruther*, 189–90, from a typed copy in BBWCC.

24 Wine Glasses, Appendix 3 nos. 7.1–7.3.

25 SAUL, B60/6/2, B3/5/2, B3/5/8, B3/5/10, B3/5/17.

26 *Glasgow Courier* 7 July 1792. Typed copy in BBWCC.

27 R.G. Cant, 'David Stuart Erskine, 11th Earl of Buchan: founder of the Society of Antiquaries of Scotland,' in A.S. Bell (ed.), *The Scottish antiquarian tradition* (Edinburgh, 1981), 1–30; *DNB*.

28 R. Burns, *Letters*, ed. J. de L. Ferguson & G.R. Roy (2 vols., Oxford, 1985), i, 15–16, 67–9; ii, 116, 486–7.

29 Information from Robert Cooper, Grand Lodge of Scotland; *BOEC*, iii, 148; NLS, MS Acc. 9653, Minutes of the Pandemonium Club.

30 The evidence of Cummying's membership of the Benison is notes sent by John McNachtane to him calling him 'Sir James'. As he was not a knight or baronet in the world at large it must be assumed that they were knights of the Benison (members are thus addressed as 'Sir' in membership diplomas). The same notes call Neil MacBrayne and Robert Douglas 'Sir,' indicating their membership. EUL, Ms LaII, 82/4, 434 &435.

31 *DNB*; *CB*, iv, 426; J. Fergusson, '"Worthy Nairne:" Lord Dunsinnan,' in *Lowland Lairds* (London, 1959), 120–34.

32 A. Clark, *An Enlightened Scot. Hugh Cleghorn, 1752–1837* (Duns, 1992), 23.

33 British Museum, Department of Medieval and Later Antiquities, M.566.

34 *The Weekly Mercury, or Edinburgh Amusement*, 8 Dec 1768, p.319. Gourlay, *Anstruther*, 166 mentions this notice, but with a garbled explanation of its source as *Ruddiman's Magazine* and the year of McNachtane's guardianship cited as the 4th.

35 V. Lunardi *Five aerial voyages in Scotland* (London, 1876. Reprint Edinburgh 1976 with introduction by A. Law – omitting the original illustrations), 30, 41, 52–4, 62.

36 W. Creech, *Fugitive pieces* (Edinburgh, 1791), 175. In 'To a Louse' Burns refers to a louse daring venture onto 'Miss's fine Lunardi,' R. Burns, *Poems and songs*, ed. J. Kinsley 3 vols., Oxford, 1968), i, 194.

37 *Records*, 13 states that George was made a member during a visit to Edinburgh when was Prince Regent, and was also presented with several glasses and insignia of the order. But George was not regent in the 1780s, and did not visit Edinburgh until he was king, in 1822.

38 See Appendix 3, no. 9.3. For an 1783. advertisement summoning the Anstruther chapter of the Benison to meet in its chamber for dinner at half past two see J. Grant, *Old and new Edinburgh* (3 vols., 1880–3), iii, 124.

39 Canch Kavanagh in BBWCC.

40 North Yorkshire County Record Office, ZNK X2/1/558, ZNK X2/22/87. I am most grateful to David Brown of the National Archives of Scotland for providing me with these references.

41 L. Namier and J. Brooke, *History of parliament, 1764–94* (London, 1968), ii, 364–8.

42 D. Wemyss, Lord Elcho, *A short account of the affairs of Scotland in the years 1744, 1745, 1746* (Edinburgh, 1907), 284; W. Macleod (ed.), *A list of persons concerned in the Rebellion* (SHS, 1890), 64–5, 373; R. Forbes, *The lyon in mourning* (3 vols., SHS, 1895–6), iii, 144; R.F. Bell (ed.), *Memorials of John Murray of Broughton* (SHS, 1898), 419; B.G. Seton & J.G. Arnot (eds.), *Prisoners of the '45* (3 vols., SHS, 1928–9), ii, 310–11; J. Allardyce (ed.), *Historical papers relating to the Jacobite period, 1699–1746* (2 vols., New Spalding Club, 1895–6), i, 339–40.

43 E. Topham. *Letters from Edinburgh* (London, 1776), 156–61.

44 A.W.C. Lindsay, Earl of Lindsay, *Lives of the Lindsays* (3 vols., London, 1849), ii, 322n.

45 W. Alexander, *The history of women* (3rd edn, 2 vols., London, 1782: 1st edn 1779), i, 225.

46 D. Johnson, *Music and society in Lowland Scotland in the eighteenth century* (London, 1972), 68–84.

47 J.G. Duncan, 'Scottish trading links with Sweden,' *Scottish Local History*, no. 23 (March 1991), 10–13; J. Berg & B. Lagercrantz, *Scots in Sweden* (Stockholm, 1962), 63–5; L.H. Ulvenstam, *The Royal Bachelors' Club, 1769–1944* (Göteborg, 1947), 94–7; *The Royal Bachelors' Club, 1769–1994. Jubileumsskrift* (Uddevalla, 1994).

48 The story of Thomas Erskine's presentation of the glasses rests on strong family tradition, which is detailed in J.M. Bacon, [*Bulletin* or *Transactions of*] *The Circle of Glass Collectors*, no. 30 (Sept 1942), 1–3. See also J. Steuart, 'At the back of St James's Square.' *BOEC*, ii (1909), 172–4; G.B. Seddon, *The Jacobites and their drinking glasses* (Woodbridge, 1996), 123, 132–3; F.P. Lole, 'The Scottish Jacobite clubs.' *The Jacobite. The Journal of the 1745 Association*, no.81 (1993), 14. Anon., 'The portrait glasses of Prince Charles Edward in enamel

colours'. *Glass notes. collected and compiled by Arthur Churchill Ltd*, no. 16 (December, 1956), 21–6. One of the glasses survived in the Steuart family until presented to the National Museums of Scotland. Some modern writers (like Lole and Seddon) have taken these dinners to indicate the existence of a body called 'the Steuart Club.' But there is no evidence for the existence of such an organisation. Admittedly the definition of 'club' is very flexible, but these dinners were private affairs, held in Steuart's own house. There is no sign of the rules, offices, paying of subscriptions or sharing of expenses of entertainment that are characteristic of a club. Robert Burns accepted Steuart's invitation to attend the last of these dinners, in 1787, and his acceptance gives no indication that he was to dine with a club rather than a private party, R. Burns, *Complete letters*, ed. J.A. Mackay (Ayr, 1987), 416. Steuart's dinner party was evidently the occasion that Burns referred to in 1796, calling it a meeting of Jacobite gentlemen in Edinburgh at which he had been made poet laureate, H. Cook, 'When Burns was in Burns country,' *Scots Magazine*, Jan. 1993, p.13, citing the ms diary of James Macdonald in SAUL.

49 J.F. Chance (ed.), *British diplomatic instructions, 1689–1789*, v, *Sweden*, 1727–1789 (Camden Society, 1928), 232, 233.

50 *The frisky songster* (1756), 149.

51 T. Smollett, *Humphrey Clinker* (London 1954 edn.), 229–31.

52 In 1763, according to William Creech, members of the Society of Caddies had been 'useful and intelligent,' but by 1783 his view confirmed Smollett's: they were 'generally pimps.' Creech, *Edinburgh fugitive pieces* (1st edn, Edinburgh, 1791), 72

53 For 'the best in Christendom' see E. Partridge, *Dictionary of historical slang* (London, 1973), 66. Rochester had referred to the toast a century before; 'Mine host drinks to the best in Christendom, / And decently my lady quits the room, *The works of the earl of Rochester*, ed. D.M. Vieth (Yale, 1968), 69. The toast occurs also in *The free mason: an hudibrastick poem* (London, 1723) referring to a noted prositute of the time.

  Another favourite risqué toast of the time, 'both ends of the busk' (103), may have been avoided by Smollett as its meaning was too easy to guess -the busk was the whalebone stay down the front of women's corsets, the ends pointing to genitals and breasts.

54 'Rab Gibb's contract,' in A Cheviot, *Proverbs, proverbial expressions and popular rhymes in Scotland* (Paisley, 1896), 282.

55 L. Stone, *The family, sex and marriage in England, 1500–1800* (London, 1977), 580.

56 C. Ryskamp and F.A. Pottle, (eds.), *Boswell. The ominous years, 1774–1776* (London, 1963), 130.

57 J.W. Reed and F.A. Pottle (eds.), *Boswell. Laird of Auchinleck, 1778–1782* (London, 1977), 332–3.

58 F. Grose, *Classical dictionary of the vulgar tongue* (1st edn 1785), under 'Benison.'

Angus Cumming, *A collection of strathspey, or old Highland reels* (Edinburgh, 1780), 14. Dr Domhnall Uilleam Stiubhart interprets the Gaelic as a very garbled version of the English title.

59 *Lords commissioners of appeals for prizes: The Beggar's Bennison* ([London, 1765], in British Library, L20el, 1765 (82, 83). In 1777 and 1778 the sloop *Beggar's Benison* was armed and commissioned by Maryland to act against British shipping in the American War of Independence, *Archives of Maryland* (Maryland Historical Society), xvi (1897), 309; xxi (1901), 144.

60 *Records*, 11–12.

61 Fergusson, *Henry Erskine*, 148.

62 Gourlay, *Anstruther*, 168. The fictitious London Branch is again mentioned in *Scottish Notes and Queries*, vi (1892–3), 44. Other exaggerations about membership can be found in, for example, R.H. Bruce Lockhart, *My Scottish youth* (London, 1937), 11–12

63 *Athenaeum* (July-Dec 1859), 557–8.

64 M.F. Conolly, *A biographical sketch of the Right Rev. David Low* (Edinburgh, 1859), 32–3, 64–70; Conolly, *Eminent men*, 300–1.

65 NLS MS 170, ff.8–9.

66 The unfortunate double-entendre of 'Relief Church' in the context of the Benison may be compared with the intentional reference to an 'Idol, call'd Masturpro, with this Inscription over it, *a chapel of ease*,' Williams, ii, 862.

67 *Fife Herald*, 25 Nov 1824, 24 Nov 1825, 25 Nov 1830.

68 Stevenson, *Anstruther*, 96–7; Conolly, *Eminent men*, 62–4; M. Barbieri, *A description and historical gazetteer of the counties of Fife …* (Edinburgh, 1857), 85.

69 *Pigot & Co's. new commercial directory of Scotland for 1825–6*, 341.

70 *Fifeshire Journal*, 27 Oct 1836, p.1. I am most grateful to Mr A.J. Campbell for drawing my attention to this notice, which also appeared in the *Fife Herald*, 27 Oct 1836, p.139.

71 *Fifeshire Journal*, 24 Nov 1836, p.1; *Fife Herald*, 24 Nov 1836, p.153.

72 Millar, *Fife*, i, 407.

73 *Records*, 14–15; Stevenson, *Anstruther*, 153. The account in the *Records* assigns a different site to Johnstone's inn from that of the Commercial Hotel. The ruins of Dreel Castle were demolished in the first decade of the nineteenth century – as was Anstruther Place. The latter had become largely redundant in the early eighteenth century when the Anstruthers had settled on Elie House as their main residence.

74 *Records*, 8–9.

CHAPTER EIGHT
To Russia with Lust

At first membership of the Beggar's Benison had been confined to the East Neuk of Fife, but the obscure local club had then, under the sovereignty of John McNachtane, proceeded to spawn branches in Edinburgh and Glasgow, and recruit members scattered throughout Scotland. The initiative in this expansion policy came from McNachtane himself, and the culmination of his imperial ambitions came shortly before his death. Russia became a province of Merryland.

Evidence of this remarkable development was only discovered in the 1980s, when Professor A.G. Cross was examining the papers of a British diplomat, Allen Fitzherbert, later Lord St Helens, who had served at the court of the Tsarina Catherine the Great as envoy extraordinary in 1783–7, and at the court of to Tsar Alexander II as ambassador in 1801–2. All knowledge of a Russian Benison has been lost in Scotland, but Fitzherbert acquired notes recording the foundation and rituals of the Beggar's Benison of St Petersburg.[1] The spread of western ideas and institutions to Russia in the eighteenth century is a major theme in Russian history, but finding the Beggar's Benison contributing to this 'civilising' process is something of a surprise.

However, obscene clubs were no novelty imposed on an innocent Russia by the west. At the end of the previous century Peter the Great had established the 'Most Drunken Synod' as a defiant attack on the religious and social conservatism that was thwarting his plans for westernisation, and the idea of institutionalising debauchery in a religious guise was taken up with enthusiasm by the small British community in Russia. Allied to the Most Drunken Synod there emerged the 'British Monastery.' No fewer than fifty-five offices in the club were fancifully named, ranging from metropolitan through orator, professors and solicitor general down to bagpiper, keeper of the seraglio, cooks, prick farrier and cunt-peeper. Another indication of the revelling in obscenity central to the monastery is one of the imaginative punishments laid down for wrongdoers: smearing the penis with egg yolk and oats and setting two hungry ducks to work. The monastery's alternative name, Bung [Drunken] College, confirms what could already have been taken for granted, that drink and obscenity were combined. The membership of the monastery is unknown, though Scottish influence may have inspired the bagpiper, and Welsh influence probably combined with phallic shape to make the leek the badge of the society, to be worn on the hats of members when they attended the proceedings of the Most Drunken Synod.[2]

Synod and monastery died with Tsar Peter in 1725, and in the decades that followed the British community devised rather more seemly social clubs and masonic lodges, but in the 1770s the atmosphere was certainly not one in which there was likely to be much moral objection to the revival of obscene entertainments. Catherine the Great's sexual voracity was notorious. Her lover (until 1772) Gregory Orlov had helped in the murder of her husband, Tsar Peter III, and had built a great palace near St Petersburg which contained the most remarkably explicit pornographic furniture decorated with carved and gilded male and female genitals and entwined figures, while frescoes depicted a girl and a satyr in numerous sexual positions.[3] In this cultural context, the phallic rituals of the St Petersburg Benison are not out of place.

The initiative in founding the Russian branch of the Beggar's Benison came, predictably, from a Scotsman, William Porter. Born in about 1741, he had found employment as a schoolmaster before, in 1764, travelling to Russia with Daniel Dumaresq, the former chaplain to the English Factory in St Petersburg. Dumaresq had left Russia in 1762, but in 1764 Catherine the Great had invited him back to sit on a commission to investigate educational reform. Porter went with him, his experience as a teacher making him a suitable assistant in such work. The commission reported in 1766 and Dumaresq returned to Britain, but Porter stayed on in St Petersburg as a teacher of languages.[4] Later he was 'induced to enter into commercial life' – or, as Jeremy Bentham put it, he 'crept by degrees into a commercial house'.[5] He joined the organisation of British merchants, the Russian Company, in 1770, and can be traced dealing in the products of such leading British manufacturers as the Boulton foundry and Wedgwood potteries.[6] Porter's abilities aroused the enthusiasm of Samuel Bentham, who met him in 1780. His brother Jeremy had asked him to find someone who could give him information about some aspects of Russia, and Samuel recommended Porter, who was about to visit England. Porter would be able to instruct the philosopher on Russian jurisprudence, something none of the other British merchants knew anything about, as they despised everything Russian. Porter was also well versed in physics, a good metaphysician and a lover of clear ideas, but his main delight was political knowledge. 'He is master of a great flow of language, so as at a kind of private spouting club there is here to be able to attract the attention and astonishment of the company for 2 to 3 hours together on any subject.'[7]

William Porter was clearly a man of energy and ability, and when *A comparative estimate of the advantages Great Britain would derive from a commercial alliance with the Ottoman, in preference to the Russian Empire* (London, 1791) was published it was at first thought that he was the author, though it later emerged that his contribution to the work had been the furnishing of information to the real author, Joseph Ewart – who thanked his anonymous 'commercial friend' for his help.[8] Porter had a flattering view of the worth of himself and his merchant colleagues.

> Liberal sentiments, enlarged views & a considerable portion of general information, together with strict integrity and a high sense of character are leading features in the portrait of a British Merchant

he pontificated. This was especially so in the case of merchants residing abroad, and the members of the Russian Company were no exceptions.[9] For a time he prospered in Russia, but eventually he suffered losses and hardship. By 1794 he was in Britain, serving on the Russia Company's court of assistants, but he was evidently back in Russia in 1807.[10] Later he was made a commissioner of revenues in

Scotland, perhaps a sinecure designed to provide him with an income in old age. He died in London in 1815. His obituary states that even in hard times his honour and integrity remained unblemished. He was a man fruitful and ardent in friendship, in conversation and society 'peculiarly interesting,' excellent in principles and morals, with a virtuous and patriotic heart.[11]

The sort of interests that led Porter to found the Beggar's Benison in Russia were not those that get mentioned in obituaries. Little is known of his contacts with the land of his birth after he left for Russia, but they were sufficient for him to join the Society of Antiquaries of Scotland as a corresponding member in 1782 – and to adopt the regimental march of the Black Watch as an anthem for the Russian Benison.[12] It may be surmised that he knew of the Beggar's Benison before going to Russia, and indeed that he was a member of the club.

The notes (probably compiled by Porter) which are the only source of information about the Beggar's Benison in St Petersburg reveal a club far more ambitious in ritual than its Scottish parent. What is recorded is partly the ceremonial installation of the prince – Sovereign McNachtane's Russian deputy – in 1773, and partly the initiation and other rituals of the club. There is much the same mixture in these notes as is found in the records of the Beggar's Benison back in Anstruther: phallic bawdy, double-entendres, mock-solemnity in ritual and ceremonial, and conspicuous revelling in obscenity.

At the installation the Prince sat on his throne, wearing his robes of state. The chancellor, William Porter, entered preceded by the usher and the benison king at arms, the latter bearing McNachtane's letter of deputation on a cushion. Behind followed the knights of the 'consistory,' walking two by two. The chancellor's speech explained that they came to present the prince with 'the confirmation of your dignity as Viceroy of the Province of Merryland, sent from Scotland by our superlatively benevolent and supereminently beneficent Sovereign Sir John McNauchton.' The officers of state and other knights, it is related, had already seen the order flourish under the prince's 'sceptre' and the 'uprightness' of his government, and hoped that he would live long to demonstrate his 'prowess' in the cause of his empire. The social distinction of knighthood was intended to reward members for their merits and spur them on to the cultivation of our natural faculties and the vigorous exertion of our Powers for the pleasure or benefit of our fellow creatures. An *upright* conduct and a manly strait forward dealing are at all times rewarded by the internal rapture they produce.

Loss of 'antidiluvian records ... washed away by the Flood' had destroyed evidence of the foundation of the Benison, but its antiquity was asserted.

After Porter's speech the deputation was elaborately delivered to the prince:

Letter supposed to have been received from the sovereign along with the deputation as follows

Truly and well beloved Cousin we greet you well

It is with the greatest satisfaction that we learned from our valorous knight Sir William Porter that there was opened an agreeable prospect of extending the interests of our Empire, and the beneficent purpose of our Guardianship over the province of Russia, and our benevolent intentions on behalf of the sound hearts and true Bottoms there found were sufficiently declared in our Patent of Deputation issued forth of our Court of Anstruther the – day of —.

Our personal knowledge as well as the fair report we have received of your *parts*, *Talents* and zeal for the interests of our Order and happy Country, have prompted us to give way to our personal prepossessions in your favor, and to nominate you as our vicarious guardian in that province. From the same causes we are concerned that our Royal Favor will be an additional Motive to your assiduous exertions to promote the beneficent purposes of our Deputation, and we therefore with particular pleasure commit to you the Guardianship of our Valiant and able Knights who shall be received into our honourable and ancient Society, indulging ourselves in the flattering expectation of seeing our benevolent attention followed by the most signal effects, to the great emolument of the province and the general advantage of the Empire. We trust therefore that you will from time to time transmit to us an account of the Success of this our Royal favor and that you will see to the due observance of the Laws herewith sent. May your P[rick] and p[urse] never fail you! Farewell!

Signed John McNaughton Sovereign[13]

What Catherine the Great would have thought of Russia being a province of the 'Court of Anstruther' must be left to the imagination

– though her own exploits suggest she might have appreciated the ribald humour of the Benison. As sovereign McNachtane had generally issued correspondence from the chambers of the Benison at Anstruther. In addressing the duke of Cumberland in 1746 this had been reduced to an office. Now he wrote from his royal court.

After the presentation of the letter the knights (the founder-members) approached the Prince and, amidst complex ritual, kissed the emblem or medal of the order, and had their knighthood confirmed by having the medals put round their necks by the Prince. Quite possibly a supply had been sent from Scotland – and one example of a Scottish Benison medal survives in the Hermitage Museum in St Petersburg.[14] The sign which is referred to repeatedly in the rituals was a phallic gesture whereby the upper arm was extended horizontally, with the lower arm held pointing upwards at a sharp angle. Rather nauseatingly, the usher turns out to be the 'usher of the pink rod,' an obscene distortion of an office in the British parliament, the usher of the black rod.

Initiation rituals for new members are set out in elaborate detail. The candidate was brought into the hall of probation, where a speech by the chancellor emphasised the importance of the occasion and the honour he aspired to. The candidate was examined on his life, conduct and 'his qualifications'. On giving satisfaction (perhaps by masturbation), he was ushered into the presence of the most potent Prince and introduced as 'A man of *Uprightness*' worthy to be made a knight. An oath was then taken, the candidate swearing to show his zeal for the empire (Merryland has been promoted from the status of a colony) and to taste 'the most ravishing enjoyments', to watch over its interests, and assiduously cultivate its soil. If he breaks his oath, then all his undertakings should fail. The candidate declared 'that my wallet may be found empty – and that my *Piece* may miss fire and fail to discharge itself in the hour of Combat if I falsify the promise I have now made – so help me Rectitude and Love!' In other words, purse and prick will fail him if he broke his oath.

Installation then followed, with the new knight having the word and the sign demonstrated to him: the word being 'Uprightness,' the sign the raised forearm. Finally, before taking his seat, a newly admitted knight was taken to the chapter hall to give the last proof of their prowess by entering 'completely armed into the lists'. When fully armed, each knight was summoned to the jousting competition by the benison king at arms. The new knight declared himself 'ready to prove 'the prowess of my weapon' on any that denied that he was worthy to wear the medal of the society. He would prove such challengers 'traitors foul and dangerous to Venus to the Prince and me.' He then brandished his 'sword,' looked fierce, and if no one challenged his right to be a knight he was finally accepted into the order.

Further ceremonial accompanied a procession before the banquet, led by the usher of the pink rod. At the end of the procession came the Prince, flanked by the chancellor and the cup bearer, the 'Prince playing the Highland March viz in the Garb of old Gaul and the fire of old Rome'. The march had been composed by a soldier of the Black Watch and set to music by an officer, during or just after the Seven Years War (1756–63). The song had quickly become popular, and had been adopted as the regimental march. With its patriotic celebration of British victories over the French as triumphs in the fight for liberty and law, it evidently stirred the feelings of the British community in Russia. Scottish military prowess lies at the centre of the verse.

> In the garb of old Gaul, with the fire of old Rome
> From the heath-cover'd mountains of Scotia we come,
> Where the Romans endeavour'd our country to gain,
> But our ancestors fought, and they fought not in vain.[15]

The garb was Highland dress, banned after the '45 because of its Jacobite associations, but now adopted by Highland regiments recruited to fight in the Hanoverian cause. In the new Britain, safe from Highland threat now Jacobitism was dead, Scots were encouraged to direct their military ambitions towards the service of the state. But even the most pro-union Scots took pride in the fact that though the Romans had conquered what later became England, they had been unable to subdue Scotland. (The usual English response was that the Romans could have conquered Scotland if they had wanted to, but had not thought such a wretched country worth the trouble).

After marching once round the banqueting hall to the stirring military music, the knights of the Russian Beggar's Benison moved to their places and stood with their arms raised in the phallic salute until the signal to sit down was given.

Patriotic phallic pride duly asserted and the Prince seated on his throne, the banquet commenced. Afterwards, the Beggars settled down to drinking toasts, accompanied by much mumbo-jumbo. There the notes in Allen Fitzherbert's papers end. They were probably compiled shortly after the events of 1773 which they purport to describe – though it may be that they detail Porter's plans for the grand inauguration of the St Petersburg Benison rather than recording actual events. Nonetheless, that they indicate the ethos and ambitions of the club may be assumed. The basic similarity of obsession with the Scottish Benison is obvious, but Porter felt free to devise new rituals and elaborations according to taste.[16]

Nothing further is known of the Russian Benison. It may, like so many clubs, have died in infancy, but equally it may have existed for many years to serve the more disreputable tastes of the British community. It is possible that the Benison was the 'spouting' club which Samuel Bentham recorded Porter addressing in 1780, though that sounds a much more sober body. Porter is the only member of the Russian Benison who is named – with the partial exception of one 'John' —, the usher of the pink rod. The fact that a version of the candidate's oath in French is given suggests that foreigners as well as Britons became members. The British patriotism of 'In the days of old Gaul' might be off-putting for the French, but their language was the most common medium used by Russians in communicating with westerners.

Nearly two generations later, in 1816, William Arnot, merchant in St Petersburg, was recruited as a member of the Beggar's Benison by Sovereign James Lumsdaine of Innergellie, who issued a standard diploma with no reference to a Russian 'province.' Did the Russian Benison still exist, or did Arnot get a diploma from Anstruther because the Russian branch had disappeared? And what is to be made of the claim, made in the early twentieth century, that in 1817 the Archduke Nicholas of Russia (later Tsar Nicholas I) joined the Benison, along with three of his staff officers? Canch Kavanagh, who made the claim (see chapter ten below) is notoriously unreliable and cites no sources. Yet when Archduke Nicholas visited England in 1817 his host was the Prince Regent, a member of the Benison, and in spite of Kavanagh's extravagant claims as to Benison membership, Nicholas and his colleagues are the only foreigners he lists. How did he come up with their names? It seems apt to end the story of the Russian Benison with yet another unanswerable question.

Notes

1 A.G. Cross, 'The Order of the Beggar's Benison in Russia. An unknown episode in Scots-Russian relations in the eighteenth century,' *Scottish Slavonic Review*, no. 3 (Autumn 1984), 45–63; Derbyshire County Record Office, D239M/0478 Fitzherbert. This was a very active period in Scottish trade with Russia. By the 1790s Scotland was importing more from Russia than from any other Continental country, D.S. Macmillan, 'Problems in the Scottish trade with Russia in the eighteenth century,' in A.G. Cross (ed.), *Great Britain and Russia in the eighteenth century* (Newtonville, Mass., 1879), 169–72.

2 A.G. Cross, *By the banks of the Neva. Chapters from the lives and careers of the British in eighteenth-century Russia* (Cambridge, 1997), 31–4.

3 B. Gip, *The passions and lechery of Catherine the Great* (London, 1971). All these items were evidently destroyed in World War II. I am grateful to Dr Tim Hitchcock for this reference.

4 Cross, *Neva*, 99–102. It is the obituary of Porter in *Gentleman's Magazine*, lxxxv (May 1815), 474 that associates Porter with Dumaresq.

5 A.T. Milne (ed.), *Correspondence of Jeremy Bentham*, iv (London, 1981), 31; *Gentleman's Magazine*, lxxxv (May 1815), 474

6 Cross, *Neva*, 35, 233, 264–5.

7 T.L.S. Sprigge (ed.), *Correspondence of Jeremy Bentham*, ii (London, 1968), 501–2.

8 Milne, *Correspondence*, iv, 314.

9 Cross, *Neva*, 89.

10 J.R. Dinwiddy (ed.), *Correspondence of Jeremy Bentham*, vii (Oxford, 1988), 442.

11 Cross, 'Beggar's Benison in Russia,' 63; *Gentleman's Magazine*, lxxxv (May 1815), 474.

12 *Archaeologia Scotica*, iii (1831), appendix, p.22.

13 Cross, 'Order,' 55–6.

14 Appendix 3, no. 1.3 Larissa Dukelskaya (ed.), *The Hermitage. English art – sixteenth to nineteenth century* (Leningrad and London, c. 1979), plates 62–3, cited in Cross, 'Order,' 49, 62.

15 D. Herd, *Ancient and modern Scottish songs and heroic ballads* (2 vols., Edinburgh, 1973. 1st edn, 1769). The song is often attributed to Henry Erskine, but see D. Stewart of Garth, *Sketches of the character, manners and present state of the Highlanders* (2 vols., Edinburgh, 1822), i, 360–1n. To this day the Grand Lodge of Antient, Free and Accepted Masons of Scotland uses 'In the Garb of Old Gaul' as its ceremonial march.

16 Cross, *Neva*, 35 states that the notes 'significantly amplify what has hitherto been known about the actual ceremonies' of the Benison in Scotland. I think this most unlikely. The St Petersburg Benison might claim legitimacy through the link with Scotland but the rituals it describes appear to be Porter's own inventions.

CHAPTER NINE

The Wig Club, 1775–1827

The Allure of Pubic Hair

Some in eighteenth-century Scotland revered locks cut from the head of Bonnie Prince Charlie. Objects of less sentimental and more earthy devotion were the locks of pubic hair culled from the mistresses of King Charles II and King George IV, venerated by the Wig Club and the Beggar's Benison respectively. Female pubic hair is an obvious symbol of male sexual ambition or token of achievement. Doubtless the history of collecting such trophies is long – an English pornographic work of the 1660s features female pubic hair as a trophy of sexual conquest, a young man wearing a sample 'as a Bravido in his hat,'[1] and there is a 1709 reference in England to a fop having a 'Patch-Box of divers … Reliques collected from the subliminary Banks'.[2]

Traditionally, however, possession of samples of pubic hair was sometimes regarded as more than just a souvenir. They were a source of power. Through sympathetic magic, they could bring a man the willing sexual services of the donor. The theory was that physical samples collected from individuals, or their belongings such as clothes, could be used to control of their behaviour or destiny. Pubic hair would make a reality of the male fantasy of being able to make a desired woman co-operative. The trouble with this particular type of sympathetic magic was of course that obtaining a sample from a desired but rejecting female was likely to be difficult.

The belief had surfaced in Scotland in the infamous North Berwick witch trials of 1591. Prominent among the accused was John Feane or Fian, a schoolmaster, who according to a contemporary pamphlet acted as the devil's clerk at witches' sabbaths. One story of his activities told how, when serving as a schoolmaster at Prestonpans, he was enamoured of a gentlewoman who rejected him. Her younger brother was one of Fian's pupils, and on discovering that the boy 'did lie with his sister' — in the sense of sharing a bed with her — he ordered the boy to get 'three hairs of his sister's privities.' The boy's reward was to be that he would be taught 'without stripes,' being spared the beatings by his schoolmaster that were otherwise a normal part of the educational process.

However, the boy's attempts at the nocturnal plucking of his sister were noticed, and she complained to their mother that the boy wouldn't let her sleep. Mother — herself a witch — realised what the boy was up to, and after he had been beaten (he got his 'stripes' after all) he confessed that Fian had instigated his action. Being of a mischievous disposition, mother-the-witch then clipped three hairs from the udders of a virgin cow, and had these delivered to Fian. The story ends in farce — Fian pursued into church and through the streets by a seriously besotted cow that won't take no for an answer. It was this that first made folk suspect he was a witch.[3]

Folk-belief in the power given by possession of pubic hairs emerges again in England in 1705. A Norwich woman, having been repulsed in an attempt to instigate a three-in-a-bed session with a married couple, gave the husband some pubic hairs wrapped in a paper. He assumed that they were her hairs, and that she was thus indicating that she was available for sex, but she told him that she had had her maid held down and trimmed the hairs from her.[4] Thus the message seems to have been that not only was she herself available to him, but she was ready to supply him with hairs which would enable him, through sorcery, to have access to other girls. A variant on this theme of the sexual powers of pubic hair was displayed by the Scots mystical quack James Graham in the 1780s. The mattress of his famous electrical-celestial bed, which would help couples to conceive, was partly stuffed with 'springy Hair' of the best English stallions.[5]

The Wig Club's veneration of a wig reputedly made from women's pubic hair may have been inspired partly by knowledge of the traditional belief that possession of such hairs could provide magical power, but their wig was primarily an erotic memento, battle-honours won in sexual warfare. The myth-making obsession of clubs of the age made providing the wig with a venerable history a priority. As with the Beggar's Benison, a Stuart legacy was favoured. The Beggars had favoured James V, but the Wig preferred Charles II. Given the fashions prevailing in his reign, the choice of a wig to symbolise his sexual prowess was particularly fitting, for men's wigs had reached a peak in size. Portraits of Charles II display copious masses of hair tumbling down to the chest. That Charles could have reaped a female harvest sufficient to create such a wig was an awe-inspiring tribute to sexual stamina. There was no longer a danger of the veneration of one of the last of the Stuarts being seen as subversive – the absolutist tendencies of Charles II were a century in the past, and Jacobitism as a political cause was so dead that its senti-mental legacy was being adopted by he Hanoverian establishment, kilted Highlanders changing from being threatening barbarian hoards into patriotic soldiers of the Empire. The records of the club make no references to Jacobitism, but it is hinted at in a toast, said (admittedly on dubious authority) to have been drunk at Wig meetings. As well as drinking to the wig displayed before them on its stand, members drank 'To the Wig that's awa''.[6] Surely this hirsute absent friend was symbolic of 'the king over the water.'

Pubic hair was both magic and symbolic, and it was also central to an obscenely entertaining mock-epic poem published in Edinburgh in 1760, and it may be more than a coincidence that this, the first bawdy work in Scotland to exploit the erotic potential of pubic hair, was circulating in the years before the Wig Club's foundation.[7] The author was John Maclaurin (the son of the famous mathematician Colin Maclaurin) who was a young lawyer and would eventually become, as Lord Dreghorn, a judge in the court of session. The anonymous *The Keekeiad* was the first of several pieces of satirical verse that Maclaurin published[8] and it claimed to be based on a true episode in the life of an Edinburgh citizen, one John Jolly, which had earned him ridicule and branded him with the nickname 'the Keeker' or peeper. The drama concentrates with bawdy enthusiasm on Jolly's wedding night. At first all goes well, but then Jolly gets over inquisitive.

> After some hours of matrimonial Play,
> Languid, in bed, the happy Couple lay,
> When Jolly put his Finger, Heaven knows where

and demanded to be allowed to enjoy that 'where' with sight as well as touch. In the end he gets his way, and pursues his anatomical investigations with the help of a candle. But

> ... his Hand, which bears
> The Taper, dropt it on his Consort's Hairs,
> Her Hairs in dreadful Conflagration burn,
> And blaze, and crackle, like a lighted Thorn.
> ...
>
> The Dame, in Anguish bounces from the Bed,
> And breaks the Candle o'er her Husband's Head:
> ...
>
> 'Is it the Bus'ness of the nuptial Torch,
> A wife's obedient Nudities to scorch?'

She anguishes over the humiliation, and how to restore her lost 'decorous shade.' That pubic baldness was regarded as disastrous is confirmed by a verse Robert Burns enjoyed enough to record, 'Nae Hair On't,' which ends:

> It vexed me sair, it plagu'd me sair,
> It put me in a passion,
> To think that I had wad a wife,
> Whase c[un]t was out of fashion.[9]

Jokes about repairing such deficiencies with suitable wigs had long provided coarse entertainment,[10] and Jolly's wife contemplates such an expedient. Could she

> From each Acquaintance, beg , what she can spare,
> And hide my Nakedness with borrow'd Hair?

She rejects this plan, but Jolly urges her to go ahead

> 'The Temporary Baldness to repair
> Why not, from Friends, beg their superfluous Hair;
> No nubile Virgin, howe'er small her Dow'r,
> But of such hairs possesses ample Store.

Women already added false tresses to their hair to lengthen it, and padded their hips to improve their figures, so there could be no objections to a pubic wig. Jolly, it seems, finds the idea erotically stimulating.

The poet, turning from narration to speaking in his own voice, offers his support for the plan and reports that some maintained that in the long run the wife would benefit from the experience. Improving landlords burnt off the vegetation of barren ground, and reaped rich harvests as a result, so Mrs Jolly's pubic hair should grow back in double strength and thickness. The poet claims credit for his sensitive treatment of the unfortunate incident.

> 'Twas Veneration for the modest Fair,
> 'Twas the Protection of their precious Hair,
> That me impelled to tune my humble Lay,
> And try in Verse Instruction to convey.

The moral is that that husband's should not pry and thus endanger such feminine glories. Having proclaimed himself the champion of ladies' pubic hair, Maclaurin humbly suggests that he deserves a reward from those whose cause he has championed.

> This is the Present that will please me best,
> And this to you my Passionate request;
> Let each fair She, of Age compleat and full,
> From certain Hairs a choice Proportion cull,
> The rough Collection on your Bard bestow,
> And grateful bind 'em round his honour'd Brow.

Thus the poet, instead of the usual laurel or ivy, would be crowned with a wreath of pubic hair.

> Bearing the bushy Trophies on my Head,
> Parnassus' Top I will triumphant tread.

Even kings, who had golden crowns to wear, would be jealous.

Five years after Maclaurin's verse an English poet touched on the same theme. The rambling *The wig. A burlesque satirical poem by the author of more fun* claims that the first invention of wigs was inspired by the sight of the 'fair seat of love' of the 'queen of charms'.[11]

It cannot be proved that either *The Keekeiad* or *The wig* played any direct part in inspiring the Wig Club, but it is tempting to assert that they ought to have. The celebration of pubic hair and its roles as both a symbol of the genitals and a screen for them, and the themes of harvesting such hair from a variety of sources to provide erotically charged headgear for men are all highlighted, and all have prominence in the Wig Club's activities. According to one tradition, each member of the Wig Club had to provide locks of pubic hair suitably harvested to be added to the wig, as proof of having triumphed sexually.[12] Whether this proof of ability in matters sexual is more or less distasteful than the Benison's masturbation may be debated.

The Foundation of The Wig Club

In many respects the Wig Club is an easier subject for the historian than the Benison, as minutes and membership lists survive. But there is confusion about its origins. At first sight there seems to be no problem. The minutes show a new club being founded in 1775, and sanctified by the donation of the venerable wig that gave the club its name. But as already noted the *Records* of the Benison claim that the wig was originally in the possession of that club: 'one renowned Wig worn by the Sovereign composed of the Privy-hairs of Royal courtezans'.[13] Even allowing for the fertility of obscene invention clearly current in Scotland, it would be extravagant to postulate the existence of two royal pubic wigs. An explanation of how the wig passed from one club to the other only appears in writing in the early twentieth century, and the author of the story was the eccentric Canch Kavanagh, whose dabblings in club history mix recording traditions with fantasy.

The wig, as the minutes of the Wig Club record, was donated to the club by the earl of Moray. But nothing is said as to its origins or why it was held in reverence. Kavanagh's story fills the gap. The wig of pubic hair harvested from Charles II's mistresses had been given by him to his friend, the then earl of Moray. His grandson and successor as earl in due course lent this valuable heirloom to the Beggar's Benison, of which he was a member. But there was some disagreement in the Benison after the 6th earl of Kellie was elected sovereign which led Kellie to resign and the earls of Moray and Aboyne to leave. Moray took with him the wig, two drinking glasses and an ivory statuette of Venus. He and others proceeded to found the Wig Club, with the wig as its presiding relic.[14]

The story is plausible if it is understood as referring to the Edinburgh Branch Benison, not the Anstruther parent body. Neither Moray nor Aboyne are known to have members of the Benison, but hardly any names of the Edinburgh branch members have survived, and the evidence suggests that it was much more aristocratic in membership than the Anstruther Benison. A scenario emerges in which Moray lent his fabulous wig to the Edinburgh Benison to enhance its sexual fantasies but withdrew it after some quarrel. Then Moray and a few friends founded a new club in which the wig held centre stage, and quickly recruited other aristocrats – while the Edinburgh Benison declines and vanishes.

Ways in which the Wig differed from the Benison provide clues (apart from clash of personalities) as to why a new club might have been formed. The two differed notably in administration and membership. The Benison had had the same sovereign, John McNachtane, for nearly thirty years. On his death in 1773 James Lumsdaine of Innergellie took over, and embarked on what was to be a similar life-presidency. Robert Lumsdaine had been life-sovereign of the Edinburgh Benison, and his successor, Kellie, presumably looked to serving a similar term. It is entirely possible that those who formed the Wig wanted a club in which members had more control – and in which there was no dependency on a 'parent' in Anstruther. The Wig went, organisationally, to the opposite extreme from the Benison, rotating the chairmanship among members at each meeting. Moreover, the Benison may have been too broad-minded when it came to membership for the men who formed the Wig. The Benison was diverse in its membership, ranging from obscure East Neuk figures to nobles, in this reflecting the common feature of the club ethos, the idea that a club was a place in which the rigidities of social distinctions could, to some extent, be eased by good fellowship. But the Wig throughout its life was highly exclusive. Its social élite of members wanted a club in which they did not have to socialise with town and country bumpkins from the East Neuk and others admitted according to the personal whims of sovereigns.

How strong political issues were present in the forming of the Wig Club is uncertain, but undertones can be detected. Though not a political club, Wig was a club for the Tory political élite which was now dominant. This being the case, at first the club's name seems paradoxical. The similarities to of 'wig' and 'Whig' made puns inevitable. An English caricature of 1784 purports to show a meeting of the political Whig Club (founded in 1780) with its members wearing enormous Charles II-period wigs.[15] The Whigs, in power for most of the first half of the eighteenth century, traced their origins back to Charles's reign, when the name had been given to English politicians opposed to his absolutist tendencies and pro-Catholic policies. This sought to discredit them by imposing on them the name already contemptuously used for the king's most fanatical Presbyterian enemies, but when the Stuart dynasty was overthrown in 1688–9 the name Whig had come to be accepted by its triumphant enemies. Now the Tories (heirs to the Stuart-Jacobite cause – in so far as there were any) were back in power in the late eighteenth century, and the Whigs could be mocked – with huge wigs based on the whig / wig pun demonstrating how out of date they were, in terms of politics and fashion, an irrelevant party based on the fanaticisms of the previous century.

How was it, then, that a Tory-dominated club chose to call itself Wig and revere a vast wig as antiquatedly out of fashion as those in the caricature imposed on the Whigs? As with the Benison, wit rather than serious politics is involved. The Restoration period, symbolised by the massive wig, should not be seen entirely in negative terms, as the age of fanaticism and persecution of the whigs. Instead it should be celebrated as a libertine golden age, the equivalent of the James V age to the Benison. Don't let the Whigs steal the great wig. Proclaim it as a symbol of sexual ambition. This argument, it must be said, has no hard evidence to support it: but it does provide a solution to the paradox of the Tory W[h]ig.

On 6 March 1775 eleven men assembled in Fortune's Hotel or Tavern in Old Stamp-Office Close, off the High Street in Edinburgh[16] and formed the Wig Club. The meeting-place immediately indicates that this was a club for an élite. The tavern, formerly the town house of the earls of Eglinton, was the most prestigious in Edinburgh. When the nobles of Scotland met to elect the sixteen representative peers who would represent the country in the House of Lords, they dined at Fortune's. The lord commissioner, representing the king in the General Assembly of the Church of Scotland, began his formal procession to the assembly at Fortune's. Many of the more select clubs had chosen it as their meeting place: both the Poker and the Friday moved there from other taverns.[17]

Founders of the Wig Club, present 6 March 1775

Francis Stuart, 9th Earl of Moray
Charles Hamilton, 7th Earl of Haddington
Colonel Robert Campbell of Finab and Monzie
Captain Alexander Campbell younger of Finab and Monzie
John Scott of Gala
Sir James Baird
Captain the Honourable John Gordon
Captain the Honourable — Stuart
Captain Gray
Alexander Stuart
Sir Henry MacDougal[18]

Campbell of Finab chaired the meeting. Reputed to be extremely wealthy, Campbell had served as an MP in 1766–71 and been appointed joint receiver general of the customs in Scotland in 1771. But the initiative for the meeting probably came from Moray – after all, it was his wig – and Haddington, son of the earl noted earlier in the century for his bawdy verses. He was to cause great scandal in 1786 by marrying, as his second wife, a girl forty years younger than he was.[19] Proceedings began with the earl of Moray formally surrendering the wig to the club which was now being formed, though it was specified that if the club dissolved the wig would revert to him. To this generous gift of a treasured family heirloom he added 'The Box and other Apparatus, appertaining to the Wig.'[20]

The Order of the Knights Companion of the Wig then proceeded to devise ceremonies appropriate for making the wig a focus for veneration. On admission to the club, members were 'to kiss the wig, standing,' and each was to wear it during the ceremony of 'Drinking the Wig.' The president in proposing the club toast was 'to Desire the Knights to give a Wig'. The Wig was to have its own personal servant, 'Lord North' (nicknamed after the prime minister of the day) being appointed 'Cady to the Wig'.[21] To increase the size of the club, new members were elected. Among them is the only certain link between the new club and the Beggar's Benison. Sir John Whitefoord was admitted, ten years after receiving his Benison diploma. Until his death in 1803 he was one of the Wig Club's most regular attenders. Like Haddington, he was also a member of the Poker Club.[22]

Further elaboration of rules and rituals soon followed the initial meeting. On 13 March subscriptions and other payments were defined. The earl of Haddington presented the wig with a purse. A newly elected member gave it a comb, and 'Wilson the shoemaker is ordered to make a pedestal for the wig'. This was Gavin Wilson, himself a member of the most un-exclusive Cape Club (where he was known as 'Sir Macaroni') and the author of a collection of masonic songs.[23] The knights of the wig also resolved to consider a suitable badge, and arrangements were made for members of the club to meet and dine regularly (fortnightly during the winter). The venerable wig, it was ruled, was to be treated with due respect:

> As it is impossible to support the Honor of the Wig, if Drinking to exces Prevails, It is agreed that after each Knight has had one Bottle of Wine, the President to call for a Bill, and the Wig is to be put in its Box.

One key of the box was to be given to the knight who was to preside at the following meeting and one to the perpetual secretary, an office bestowed on the Hon. Captain Stuart.

The 'one bottle, call for the bill, put away the wig' rule suggests that proceedings ended at that relatively sober point.[24] This seems unlikely in such a hard-drinking age (though other clubs can be found which bound themselves to moderation), and possibly what was meant was that the locking up of the wig represented the end of the formal part of the meeting, but that carousing continued in its absence. After all, the wig represented woman, and after dinner the ladies retired, so gentlemen could get down to drinking, smoking and talking on matters unsuitable for them. The wig was the ideal woman. Lust after her, venerate her, then put her away in a box until she is next needed.

The president of meetings was known as the lord protector of the wig. This was a nice jibe at Oliver Cromwell. He had of course been lord protector of England, Scotland and Ireland, a despised puritan with the short, 'roundhead' haircut. On the restoration of monarchy in 1660 the vast chest-length wig had come into fashion partly in reaction, as a symbol of a new libertine age. Now a new lord protector would guard the famous wig, potent symbol of the legacy of Charles II. Associating Cromwell with indecent concepts had long caused amusement, and some member of the new club in 1775 may have recalled that nearly a century before a poet had written of the pego (the term for penis favoured by the club) that 'would fain have rul'd as Lord Protector' – that is, dictatorially.[25] What more suitable, in the context of the club, than a phallus / protector for the feminine wig?

After a summer recess (common to nearly all clubs) the defining of the Wig Club continued in the autumn of 1775. Membership had originally been set at twenty-five, but this was raised to thirty. Though the club was turning out to be a success, in that there were plenty of suitably aristocratic candidates hoping to be elected, attendance at meetings was a problem. In December one meeting was abandoned as only three members turned up, and at another only six were present.[26] In the decades that followed this was to be a continuing difficulty. Meetings had to be cancelled through poor turnout, even though membership was repeatedly raised, eventually to sixty-five. What most members wanted, it seems, was the was the *caché* of membership, not regular dinners. For most, it was a matter of getting elected, perhaps attending a few times to be initiated and entertained by the ritual, and then ignoring the club. Repeated demands that members attend or be fined or expelled did little good; and getting subscriptions paid was a nightmare. Still, a tenacious few kept the club going. Sometimes the minutes make a joke of the attendance problem, as on 6 July 1785: It was usual to start by noting who was presiding 'in the chair.' But on this occasion it was 'Sir John Whitefoord in one Chair and Sir Archibald Hope in another, who recommended it to the Members of the Club to be more punctual in their attendance.' No one else was present. On 11 January 1792, 'The Protector dined by himself,' with 'the hardest drinker of the Company in the Chair.'

By the end of 1775 the club had agreed to have a seal cut, bearing its motto, and badges had been ordered. The motto adopted was *Spolia Opima* (English or Scots were good enough for the Benison, but the noble knights of the wig wanted Latin), which was to appear on the seal around a representation of the pubic-hair wig. 'The choicest spoils' (of war) would be a literal translation, but the accepted meaning had come to be 'how sweet it is'.[27] Both would be appropriate. No trace of this intended club seal has been found, but a single impression of another seal is attached to a draft minute of a meeting in 1805. It is classical in inspiration (and, indeed, may have been an ancient seal re-used), like the Benison badge. A cock and a hen face each other, but in place of their heads are human genitals, phallus and vulva[28]. The phallus-bird had originally, in Greece, been based on a swan, the long neck being thought apt, but it had evolved into a cock,[29] and the obvious pun made it irresistible to English speakers. The message of the seal is plain. What rules is not the head and its perceptions, but the genitals and theirs. The sentiment is certainly suitable for the Wig Club, but the seal may have been the private fancy of Lord Doune, the earl of Moray's son, who signed the minute.

Further elaboration of ritual came in 1776. The first Monday of each February was to be celebrated as St Pego's Day. Here the penis is canonised, a status already accorded it for at least a century in bawdy literature – an English work of the 1670s fantasised the orgy that took place when the 'C[un]ts of Christendome' 'on pilgrimage to St Pego come'.[30] At the same Wig Club meeting it was ordered that all members were to drink 'to the Wig out of the Prick Glass'. Two such phallic glasses survive,[31] perhaps inspired by Juvenal's reference to how a drinker 'in a Glass-Priapus swills'.[32] These Wig glasses stand on glans and scrotum, with oval mouth above the scrotum, perhaps intended to suggest female genitals, and it has been suggested that they were trick glasses, designed so that part of the contents would be released suddenly when the glass was raised to a certain angle, so drenching the drinker.[33] This may explain the ruling made (rather ungrammatically) a few weeks earlier, that 'No Members who have once Drank the Wig Glass to be obliged to Drank it again.' Once caught by an unexpected soaking, members did not want to risk it again. Other anecdotes suggest that the 'ordeal' of initiates in drinking the toast concerned not where the wine splashed unexpectedly but the quantity drunk. One account suggests a quart of claret without stopping,[34] – but it may be that initiates were told they had to drink the whole prick-glass full at one go to ensure they raised the glass high and the trick worked satisfactorily. And at another meeting shortly after the mention of the single prick glass, Haddington 'presented the Wig with a Pego Glass':[35] perhaps this is the second of the surviving glasses. After starting with ritual concentrating on the female pubic wig, the Wig Club was turning to the phallic symbolism typical of the Benison. A cheerful little delftware drinking vessel on the same principal has been discovered recently in London, and an opening in the end of the penis meant that it could be used either by drinking from the cup, a finger being held over the end-opening, or from the jet from that opening, according to taste.[36] If, as is thought, the London piece dates from the late seventeenth century, then the Wig Club glasses draw on an old tradition of cheerful obscenity. A stoneware phallus from Doncaster shares with the London phallus an end opening, but though it also has a large opening on top, it lacks a cup to be filled with liquid: perhaps this was manufactured separately – or possibly a bottle was meant to be inserted there.[37]

That meetings could be boisterous, with due respect to the wig being abandoned, is suggested by the fact that the wig's pedestal or stand got broken. Mr Wilson had to be ordered to make a new one 'immediately'. It is presumably this second effort by Wilson, a *papier mâché* human head, that still gazes, bald and gaunt, from the wig box when the door is opened. The exaggerated length of chin and nose result in a Punch-like face, and may have been inspired by the old legend that these organs reflect the size of the penis, thus bestowing a compliment on the endowments of the original wearer of the wig, Charles II. Still, it is to be hoped that Gavin Wilson was better at making shoes (and artificial limbs, in which he specialised) than heads, for the effect is distinctly sinister.

Rise and Fall

After the formative first year, the minutes of the club record very little except routine business. Those attending are listed, new members are elected, there are continuing problems of attendance and subscriptions. The minutes are silent about ritual, except for a few references to new members going through 'the forms' or ceremonies.[38] In 1779 a croupier was appointed,[39] and references to cards and bets make it clear that betting was a popular activity (no doubt after the wig has been boxed for the night). The following year there was an innovation. It was decided 'to speak a Play': there was to be a club visit to the theatre, and the secretary was ordered 'to bespeak the Comedy of the Clandestine Marriage, and Fortunatus'.[40]

Like the Benison, though the Wig Club was secretive about quite what went on in meetings, it was happy to have its existence known. Doubtless much of the fun of being elected to such an exclusive club was being able to boast of membership. The press was sometimes used to advertise meetings. In January 1780 Mr Fortune was ordered to remind members in 'the News Papers' to attend the St Pego's Day meeting,[41] and other such advertisements followed. Drawing public attention to the existence of the club (and even being explicit about its dedication to St Pego) led to gossip, and this inspired publication in the *Scots Magazine* and the *Edinburgh Courant* in February 1781 of an item mocking the new Society of Antiquaries of Scotland by suggesting that the Wig Club was about to present its valuable wig to the earnest antiquarians. An elaborate mock history is detailed. Cleopatra had had the wig made for her lover, Mark Anthony, as he was going bald. All her handmaidens had contributed 'ringlets from their beautiful tresses'. Wearing the wig rejuvenated Mark Anthony in ways 'which agreeably surprised Cleopatra,' but it was captured at the battle of Actium by Julius Caesar and carried in triumph to Rome. Eventually Constantine the Great, on converting the empire to Christianity, gave the wig to the pope, and the church created a new history for it: the Queen of Sheba had given it to Solomon, and it had miraculous powers. The tale then leaps forward more than a millennium. Pope Clement III gave it to Charles II, who was so delighted that he secretly became a Catholic. When visiting his Catholic mistress, the duchess of Portsmouth, he always wore it. Thus the propaganda, active in Charles's own day, linking Charles's licentiousness with his Catholic sympathies and mistresses, is perpetuated. The wig was also worn at times, according to this satire, by Charles's more pious brother, James II, but he considered it a holy relic rather than an aphrodisiac. When he fled into exile he took the wig with him, and it descended to his grandson, Bonnie Prince Charlie. It was among his regalia when he landed in Scotland in 1745 – and presumably was abandoned after his defeat.[42]

These absurdities are worth relating because it is likely that they are not purely journalistic satire about the tendency of antiquarians to be fooled by the most ludicrous stories about musty relics. They are probably based on the sort of tales of the antiquity and adventures of their relic that the members of the Wig Club enjoyed inventing as the claret circulated, mock-heroics on which to base mock-rituals and reverence.

Satire did not deter the club from further advertising its activities. 1783 saw another summons to a meeting appear in the press. Those in the neighbourhood of Edinburgh were reminded that it was a standing rule that they should attend or resign and have their places filled by others. The meeting would be held on 4 February, 'St P—'s Day.' A later antiquarian failed to identify this saint and concluded that this 'must have been some joke known only to the club'. This was surely tongue-in-cheek innocence as pego was a well-known term, but it wouldn't do for a respectable author in Victorian times to reveal knowledge of such a coarse word. The report that at the meeting on 2 December 1783 the earl of Haddington presided wearing a wig 'of extraordinary materials' also pretends ignorance of grizzly details. So common were the club's advertisements that a commentator referred sarcastically to 'the virtuous and dignified wig [club] who so much to their own honour and kind attention always inform the public of their meetings'.[43]

Between January 1792 and April 1801 no minutes of the Wig survive. As with the Beggar's Benison, the coming of the French Revolution was an almost fatal blow to a club devoted to defiance of respectability and conventional sexual behaviour, even though in the Wig's case there was no element of political subversion present. It was time for the aristocracy to sober up, to fight to preserve the social order – and to behave in a way which demonstrated that that social order in which they held privileged positions was worth saving. After the turn of the century, when the threat of revolution had receded, the Wig showed faint signs of life. A vain attempt at revival in 1801 was so unsuccessful that in January 1802 Lord Elcho (Francis Charteris of Amisfield)[44] recorded attending a meeting on his own: 'No members attending me this day I have only to regret their loss of *Power* to do justice to *The Wig* and assign the Key of the Box and the Precious Jewells it contained into the hands of Lord Doune – The Rightful Heir to this Valuable Property.'[45] Absent members were stigmatised as impotent, unable to do service to the wig.

The club had been declared dead, but it wouldn't lie down. It twitched back into life in 1805, in 1810, in 1823, and in 1825–6, its meeting place frequently changing. In 1805 it met in the Royal

Exchange Coffee House; in 1810 it moved restlessly from Fortune's Tontine Tavern (in Princes Street) to Maceanas Tavern to Mr McEwen's Tavern; then in 1823 back to the Coffee House. The last recorded minute is dated 15 March 1826. Of course there were meetings of which no record survives, but it seems that the club was moribund, with a few stubborn members repeatedly dragging it back to life and recruiting new members. There were still aristocrats willing to join, indicating that the old name still had some *caché*, but willingness of members to actually meet and dine together seemed to be lacking. A final attempt at resuscitation saw the publication of a *List of members of the Wig Club, with the rules abridged*, dated from the Royal Exchange Coffee House, Edinburgh, December 1827. The rules as printed evidently represent a recent reworking. Membership was to be seventy and there were to be six regular meeting a year, including meetings immediately before the Caledonian Hunt and on the Tuesday of Race Week. Members were all to be 'Caledonians' (a point perhaps emphasised as the marquis di Riario Sforza had slipped into the club the year before) and were to pay two guineas entry money.[46] Not a hint of sexual interests appears in the rules, and it is possible that in its last days the dining club had dropped such elements from its social activities, or at least toned them down. Optimistically, six candidates for membership were listed along with their proposers and seconders, but the fact that different combinations of five individuals did all the proposing and seconding suggests that support for revival was limited. Certainly it was unsuccessful.

The Wig Club died for much the same reason as the Benison died a decade later. Both had been born in an age of liberation from past constraints through drunken sociability and sexual licence. Both were crippled by changing sensibilities which altered definitions of what was permissible among gentlemen even in a private club. As with the Benison, the 1820s might have seemed an auspicious time for revival. The revolutionary threat was over, the Bourbons and other vestiges of the *ancien régime* restored on the Continent, and George IV was on the throne. That true successor to the licentious royal tradition of James V and Charles II had come into his own, and perhaps the good old days of promiscuous aristocratic conduct fashionable under Charles II could be restored. But the world had changed. The aged rake on the throne was a left-over from a past most preferred to forget, and the scandal surrounding George's marriage brought him contempt. Belonging to clubs known to be concerned with sex, even if only in words and playful ritual, was increasingly likely to earn ostracism rather than jealous admiration of naughtiness.

Apparatus Appertaining to the Wig

The descent of the relics of the Beggar's Benison can be traced back to the death of Matthew Conolly in 1877. Those of the Wig Club only emerge at the beginning of the twentieth century, when they were briefly described.[47] Somehow in the 1920s they came into the possession of Canch Kavanagh, who mixed them up with the Benison relics in pursuit of his conviction that the two bodies were really a single organisation. The central relic, though it survived until the twentieth century, did not pass to Colonel Kavanagh. Louis Jones in the late 1930s heard a story that the wig was held in a lawyer's office in Leith, but failed to trace it.[48] Perhaps it still lurks there, among mouldering parchments, a ghastly record of ancient sexual conquests, some day to be located by the horrified hand of some unfortunate clerk groping for mislaid papers.

Also lost, though once in Canch Kavanagh's possession, is the ballot box. Made of wood and over two feet high, it was in the form of the lower half of a male body, with 'organs of generation [that] are detachable and of disproportionate size,' as Louis Jones described it. In manuscript as opposed to print he was rather less formal, referring to the 'detachable phallus, a noble piece that'.[49] The figure was hollow, and divided into 'aye' and 'nay' sections, though quite where votes were inserted remains (perhaps mercifully) unclear.

The relics that do survive give some support to the accounts in the minutes of proceedings. The wooden wig box has a door on the front which swings open to reveal inside the wig stand and the *papier mâché* head.[50] The stand occupies one side of the box, and the other has felt pockets fitted to the woodwork to house such 'apparatus' as the comb. The two prick glasses have already been mentioned, and a third similarly shaped object (though with a circular opening on top) is made from soldered sheet metal – brightly painted. Presumably it too is a drinking vessel, though whether it belonged to the Wig or the Benison is unknown.[51]

The Knights of the Wig

The overall social composition of the Wig Club has already been indicated: nobles, rich lairds (many of them baronets) and members of their families predominated. Nearly all members were men whose careers combined wealth and privilege with service to the state. From the fragmentary minutes about 155 men can be named with certainty as members during the club's half-century of existence, and about another 45 were proposed though subsequent admission cannot be proved. Of these 200 or so men, at one time or another in their careers the following approximate numbers can be identified as having served as, or held rank as[52] –

Nobles (lord, viscount, earl, marquis, duke)	c.38
Knights and baronets	c.32
Army or navy officers	c.55
Members of the House of Commons	c.26

These men were Scots, but they were Scots fully integrated into the élite of the British state. Though membership was limited to Scots there is no trace in the club of the sort of Scottish patriotism detectable in the Benison. A great many members were men as at home in English as Scottish society, and as time passed increasing numbers were men born in England, married to English women – and destined to die south of the border.[53] It is notable that the most powerful of the surviving distinctively Scottish élites – the legal profession – is represented in the Wig by only a few individuals. Was it that Scottish lawyers were seen as provincial – or that being paid professionals placed them below the Wig's social circle? (Military service was of course different – though sometimes called a profession it was honourable, and indeed a matter of duty, for a gentleman).

Some Wig members rose to high military office (though rank tended to be inflated by promotions continuing to be made after retirement) but few attained high political office. Involvement in politics was part of the life of a landed gentleman, but though one might spend some time in parliament it was not a career. The outstanding exception to this generalisation was Henry Dundas, later Lord Melville, who joined in 1782 when he was lord advocate of Scotland. In the years that followed he came to exercise a dominant position in the political management of Britain, especially Scotland.

But it may be significant that though Dundas was first proposed for membership in 1776 he was only admitted in 1782, having been proposed without admission more times than anyone else recorded in the club minutes. Socially he came from the right circles for admission, but perhaps there was a suspicion that he was too dedicated and ambitious a politician really to fit in. Moreover his presence might be divisive, for though all members were Tories some supported factions which favoured Dundas, others ones which were hostile. Dundas, it may have been feared, would be too much the professional politician and cause strife.

A few other individual members can be identified who won distinction beyond that they were born to. John Kerr, 3rd duke of Roxburghe (1784), won a lasting place in Scottish cultural history through the great library which he formed. Thomas Bruce, 7th earl of Elgin, has found controversial immortality by the purchase of the Elgin marbles. James Maitland, 8th earl of Lauderdale (1823), was a distinguished politician and economist. However, it was not their distinction but their blood that brought them to the Wig. No member was ever elected for intellectual or literary achievement. That is not a condemnation, but a simple reflection of the type of club it was. The judgement that 'hardly any of the members shone in literary, legal or political circles; they were perhaps more gifted with high spirits than brains'[54] would probably not have caused insult. The club was about good fellowship, not ambition or achievement.

As with the Benison, new members were recruited at a surprisingly wide range of ages, as the following table shows

Ages of members on being admitted to the Wig Club

Dates of Joining	Size of Sample	Age Bands					Average Age
		20s	30s	40s	50s	60s	
1775	9	3	2	2	2		37
1776–92	26	11	6	5	3	3	38
1802–26	24	6	9	5	3	1	36

Recruits ranged in age between twenty-one and sixty-eight years of age, the former probably being regarded as the earliest age at which it was suitable to admit youths to so 'adult' a club. For over half a century the average admission age remained in the late thirties, but obviously as the years passed the average age of those attending meetings must have become much higher, as some of those present would have been members for decades. As in the Benison, talk of sexual exploits must often have been a matter of nostalgic reminiscence or fantasy rather than current news.

Notes

1 R. Thompson, *Not for modest ears. A study of pornographic, obscene and bawdy works written or published in England in the second half of the seventeenth century* (London, 1979), 69.

2 Williams, *Dictionary*, ii, 638–9.

3 R. Pitcairn (ed.), *Ancient criminal trials in Scotland* (3 vols., Bannatyne Club, 1833), i, pt. 2, 219–21.

4 L. Stone, 'Libertine sexuality in post-Restoration England: Group sex and flagellation among the middling sort in Norwich,' *Journal of the History of Sexuality*, ii (1992), 513–14

5 B.B. Schnorrenberg, 'A true revelation of the life and career of James Graham, 1745–1794,' *Eighteenth Century Life*, , xv (1991), 62.

6 BBWCC, Kavanagh letter 20 Sept. 1922, quoted in Jones, *Clubs*, 193. Jones takes 'The wig that's awa" to be a Benison toast, referring to the wig that had been lost to the Wig Club, but he accepts the Jacobite allusion to the Stuarts who were also 'awa'.'

7 A number of English poems toy with pubic hair, but they are concentrated in the 1720s (with one in the 1730s), D.F. Foxon, *English verses 1701–1750. A catalogue of separately printed poems* (2 vols., Cambridge, 1975), i, B26, C372, C546, J34, P141, S51, W552.

8 J. Maclaurin, *The Keekeiad* (London, 1760, reprinted 1824); *DNB*; Smith, 'Sexual mores,' 60.

9 J. Barke & S.G. Smith (eds.), *The merry muses of Caledonia* (Edinburgh, 1959), 149.

10 Williams, *Dictionary*, ii, 877.

11 *The wig* (London, 1765), 15.

12 Jones, *Clubs*, 192–3.

13 *Records*, 8.

14 BBWCC, Kavanagh letter 20 Sept. 1922; Jones, *Clubs*, 190.

15 M.D. George, *Catalogue of political and personal satires preserved in the Department of Prints and Drawings in the British Museum*, vol. vi, *1784–1792* (London, 1935), 178–9. G.J.B. Benfield, *The Culture of sensibility. Sex and society in eighteenth-century Britain* (Chicago, 1992), 92 refers to the Wig Club as the Whig Club in error.

16 R. Chambers, *Traditions of Edinburgh* (Edinburgh, 1996: 1st edn 1824), 161–2,

192. There is a good (though inhibited) account of the Wig Club in HA Cockburn, 'Friday Club,' 135–41, including a list of many of the members.

17 W.M. Stuart, *Old Edinburgh taverns* (London, 1952), 55–6, 171.

18 Two lists of those who founded the Wig Club appear in the minute book, each containing ten names. But Alexander Stuart only appears on the first list (where he is named first), and 'McDugal' only on the second. I have assumed 'McDugal' to be the Sir Henry MacDougal listed as a member at the back of the minute book.

19 *CP*, vi, 235–6.

20 BBWCC, minutes. See also. J. Grant, *Old and new Edinburgh* (3 vols., Edinburgh, 188–2), iii, 1240.

21 Lord North served the club for over quarter of a century, being last mentioned in the minutes on 14 Dec 1790.

22 Cockburn, 'Friday Club,' 148,149, 154. Jones, *Clubs*, 190, 193–4 indicates that considerable numbers of Wig Club members were also members of the Benison, but the only evidence for this is the dubious word of Colonel Kavanagh.

23 Cockburn, 'Friday Club,' 160; D.D. McElroy, *Scotland's age of improvement* (n.p., 1969), 145–6.

24 Jones, *Clubs*, 194.

25 E. Ward, *Poet's ramble* (1691), quoted in *OED*, 2nd. edn; E. Partridge, *A dictionary of slang and unconventional English* (3rd edn, London 1949), 616.

26 BBWCC, minutes, , 20 Nov., 4 Dec., 18 Dec. 1775.

27 E. Ehrlich, *A Dictionary of Latin tags and phrases* (London, 1987), 209.

28 BBWCC, original minute, 8 April 1805. Possibly Doune was using the 'Seal Ring' that George Douglas of Cavers (the son-in-law of the 9th earl of Moray) had presented the club with in 1790.

29 J. Boardman, 'The phallos-bird in Archaic and classic Greek art,' *Revué Archéologique*, ii (1992), 234–6, 242.

30 Thompson, *Modest ears*, 123.

31 Appendix 3, nos. 16.1, 16.2; F.P. Lole, 'Priapic wine glasses – a new find,' *Glass Circle News*, no. 83 (June 2000), 9–10.

32 Williams, i, 388, quoting a 1693 translation.

33 Lole, 'Priapic glasses', 83–4.

34 Chambers, *Traditions*, 155. Chambers adds that the normal fare of the Wig Club was bread and ale but this seems pretty unlikely. The minutes show much concern for the safety of the club's wine cellar.

35 BBWCC, minutes 20 Nov. 1775, 5 Feb., 29 Feb. 1776.

36 Museum of London. *The Times*, 15 February 2001, with illustration.

37 Doncaster Museum.

38 BBWCC, minute, 15 Jan. 1776.

39 BBWCC, minute, 28 Jan. 1779.

40 BBWCC, minute, 14 Feb. 1780.

41 BBWCC, minute 17 Jan. 1780.

42 Jones, *Clubs*, 190–2; HA Cockburn, 'An account of the Friday Club,' *Book of the Old Edinburgh Club*, 1910, 136–7

43 Grant, *Old and new Edinburgh*, iii, 124. Grant takes much of his material from Chambers, *Traditions*, 154–5, 161–2.

44 In Jones, *Clubs*, 197 an unfortunate misprint gives the reading 'Charteris of Anusfield.'

45 Jones, *Clubs*, 198.

46 There are copies of the *List* in the NLS and BBWCC.

47 Cockburn, 'The Friday Club,' 138.

48 Jones, *Clubs*, 193.

49 Appendix 3, no. 14.1: Jones *Clubs*, 197, 209, and ms inventory in NMS.

50 Appendix 3, nos. 13.2 – 13.4.

51 Appendix 3, nos. 16.1 – 16.3.

52 These approximate figures are not based on full analysis, but on the club minutes and standard works of reference. There was of course considerable overlap between the categories listed – gentlemen who were also army officers, etc.

53 This is an impression given by the evidence rather than an analysis of it.

54 Cockburn, 'Friday Club,' 138, 141.

CHAPTER TEN

The Twentieth Century

The Wanderings of the Relics

Chapter two traced the surviving relics of the Beggar's Benison from Matthew Conolly to J.B.S. Gordon, in whose hands they were at the time of the publication of the *Records* and *Supplement* in 1892. By 1897 Gordon had lent them to J. MacNaught Campbell, who worked in the Kelvingrove Museum in Glasgow and had shown interest in buying them. After Campbell had had them for some time without making a bid, Gordon pressed him for their return.[1] Though the correspondence surviving is fragmentary, it seems that MacNaught Campbell was very reluctant to part with the relics – perhaps relying on the fact that the elderly priest would be unlikely relish a public dispute about the ownership of such items and was anxious not to leave them as an embarrassing legacy to his heirs. In the end, it seems, Gordon gave way. He wrote to Campbell saying 'Just take the Beggar's Benison in your own hands, and do as you opine best.'

Whatever the circumstances, MacNaught Campbell retained the relics, and indeed flaunted them. Many items were lent by him for exhibition at the great Scottish Exhibition at Kelvingrove Museum in 1911. How some of the objects listed as exhibited could have been publicly displayed without causing gross offence is mystifying. Presumably they were carefully arranged, with some motifs tactfully concealed.[2] Two items from Gordon's collection, however, did not pass into the hands of MacNaught Campbell. One was the 'Dinner Sentiments, Bon-Mots, Toasts, etc., collected from Scraps in Ink and Pencil dated from 1732 to 1820.' It had been printed in the 1892 *Supplement*[3] and was back in Gordon's possession in 1897, when he was trying to sell it separately, but no trace of it has been found since then. The Beggar's Benison Bible was also known to Gordon, and it was probably in his possession in 1892 when a description of it appeared in the *Records*.[4] It was bought, presumably from Gordon, by William Hunter, a Glasgow flour merchant, and after passing through the hands of a number of collectors is now privately owned.[5]

The main collection of Benison relics was sold by MacNaught Campbell in 1921 to Lieutenant Colonel M.R. Canch Kavanagh 'a gentleman of Fife' who, it was said had two major interests in his life – 'military camouflage and the Order of the Beggar's Benison'.[6] Louis Jones, the American scholar who thus described Kavanagh, may have only intended this as a casual aside, but equally it may be a discreet warning that Kavanagh was not to be trusted too far. This would have been appropriate, for Kavanagh was eccentric, totally unscholarly and obsessed with the idea that the Benison and the Wig were not only related but were one and the same club.

Kavanagh died in 1936, and the relics passed into the hands of his widow. There Louis Jones stumbled on them while studying eighteenth century clubs, and he was the only person among the many who had possessed or seen the material to take the trouble to list it, and he moved on from that to studying the Benison seriously.[7] His essay on the subject is by far the most scholarly and enlightening work on the Benison, though he was hindered by the fact that the conventions of his age meant that he could not even mention masturbation.

Not only did Louis Jones study the relics, he showed concern for their preservation, and tried to persuade the National Museum of Antiquities of Scotland to buy the collection from Kavanagh's widow.[8] This proved impossible. In 1938 Arthur Edwards, the director of the museum, ruled that it could not buy the Kavanagh Collection because it could never be displayed in public. As some of it had been displayed in Glasgow in 1911, and anyway most museums contain far more material than they can ever display, the argument was a peculiar one. Mr Edwards evidently did not want anything to do with such disreputable objects, and he suggested that the Wellcome Historical Medical Museum in London should be urged to buy them. Sex, it seemed, or at least the Benison's interest in it, was a pathological condition, best left to doctors. The influence of the eighteenth-century 'medicalisation of sex' was still dominant.

Mrs Kavanagh would have liked to have given her husband's material to the National Museum as a gift, but his death had left her 'rather badly off' so she needed to sell it, and this spared Edwards the embarrassment of refusing a free offer of her husband's beloved collection. But Mrs Kavanagh had her preferences as to buyers. A 'good offer' from an American was turned down, for she was patriotically determined that the relics (however disreputable) should remain in their homeland. A buyer was eventually found, in the person of Mr J. Gordon Dow, an Anstruther man with antiquarian interests. After his death his niece and her husband donated the collection, still in its original mahogany chest, to St Andrews University.[9] There it remains, still with the power to shock at first sight through the explicit celebration of sexuality that inspired the Benison.

The Benison Restored

The Benison had died in 1836, though gossip as late as 1861 claimed that 'chapters subordinate' to the club still existed.[10] On 4 July 1921 a 'small gathering of gentlemen' convened, place unknown, summoned by Lieutenant Colonel M.R. Canch Kavanagh, late of the Black Watch, member of the Conservative Club and the United Services Club in Edinburgh. They met to discuss the advisability of re-starting, or continuing, the Order of the Beggar's Benison. Those assembled unanimously agreed that this should be done.

Secondly, it was ruled that Scottish parentage should not be essential to membership. Then came agreement that Canch Kavanagh should be sovereign of the restored order, he having gained possession of its relics and arguing that the sovereign had always had possession. He thus had already acquired legitimacy as sovereign through holding the relics, and the vote merely confirmed his position. Kavanagh was then 'installed', though what the process consisted of is not recorded, and a number of Knights Companion (all the other men present) were then chosen:

Herbert Hugh Douglas Withers, Brevet Major, Prince of Wales Volunteers.
Basil John Douglas Guy, VC, DSO, Commander, RN.
Algernon Lee Ransome, DSO, MC, Brevet Lieutenant Colonel, Dorset Regiment.
Gerald Carlmill Harrison, Commander, RN.
David Logan Gray, MC, Captain, Cameronian Regiment.

'Sir' David Gray then proposed, and 'Sir' Basil Guy seconded, a motion that 'Sir' Herbert Withers should be Recorder. The motion was carried unanimously, and the meeting was them adjourned *sine die* – that is, without setting a date for a further meeting.[11]

In what sort of atmosphere did these proceedings take place? Were they all drunk, giggling as they played their game but managing to restore mock seriousness to propose and pass motions? Or were they all solemn, really believing that they were doing something significant? Phallic funsters or daft zealots? One of those present was certainly serious: 'Sir' Canch Kavanagh, the sovereign. Perhaps the others were friends, sadly humouring an eccentric friend – or were they, with suppressed giggles, co-operating with a wild-eyed nutter for a laugh. Perhaps the laugh was on them, and he had presented the Benison in a sanitised form as a boisterous convivial club – perhaps a bit rude but no real harm in it – and they believed him.

Who was Kavanagh? Only a brief outline of his career has been constructed. His name was his own invention. He had been baptised Maxwell Robert Canch, being born about 1871. His death certificate described his father as a 'landowner' – factually accurate, but giving an impression of social status which is misleading. Thomas 'Cansh,' owner of only one acre of land (worth £100 *per annum*) in Cathcart, Renfrewshire,[12] is the only landowner at the time in Scotland who had a name remotely like 'Canch,' and he may be assumed to have been 'Kavanagh's' father. At some point in his life Maxwell Robert Cansh or Canch adopted 'Kavanagh' as his surname and made Canch a forename. There is no obvious family connection (Kavanagh was not the maiden name of his mother or of either of his wives), and the choice of the name thus appears to have been simply a matter of personal taste and the image he had of himself. 'Canch Kavanagh' sounds a gritty, chunky, macho sort of man – it would well suit a film-star seeking a tough image. He joined the army, served as an officer in the Royal Garrison Artillery, and his death certificate describes him as a lieutenant colonel in that formation. But he preferred in later years to describe himself as 'late of the Black Watch,' having been, on the outbreak of World War I in 1914 appointed a captain and adjutant of the Fife or 7th Battalion, Black Watch, Territorial, a unit of the army volunteer reserve. A detachment from the Royal Garrison Artillery at Leith was sent to reinforce the battalion, and Kavanagh probably commanded it. He was promoted to major (territorial) in 1915 and to major (regular) in 1916. The battalion was allocated to coastal defence in Fife, as German landings were feared, and it is tempting, in view of the interest in the Beggar's Benison which he acquired around this time, to associate Kavanagh with the 'Left half' of G Company, 7th Battalion, which was stationed in Anstruther. In the Black Watch records his name appears in the double-barrelled form 'Canch-Cavanagh, M.R.'[13] After 1916 there is no mention of Kavanagh in the Black Watch's records: perhaps his interest in military camouflage (as referred to by Louis Jones) had led to him being transferred to work in that field. He died in 11 February 1937 in Edinburgh, being survived by his second wife, Wilhemina Turner Peddie.[14]

Canch Kavanagh was about fifty when he revived the Beggar's Benison, and his fellow knights companion were probably of similar vintage, friends he had made during his military service. Commander Guy, for example, was born in 1882, and had won his VC in 1900 and his DSO in 1917.[15] How long the revived club lasted after the refoundation of 1921 is unknown. 'Minute I,' as it is hopefully annotated, is also minute last. However an intriguing anedote relating to 1923 indicates that the revived club still existed then. D.N. Brackenburg, an English gentleman visiting Edinburgh who had an interest in the occult and arcane, asked Arthur Edwards, assistant keeper at the National Musuem (who long afterwards was to refuse the relics) about the Beggar's Benison. Edwards apparently had no information to offer, but then by chance Brackenburg met, in the library of the Society of Antiquaries of Scotland, a gentleman of about sixty who solemnly assured him that the Benison still existed and flourished in

Edinburgh. Indeed, it held annual fertility rites on the banks of the Forth. Finally, this informative gentleman revealed that he himself was sovereign of the Benison.[16]

Brackenburg, it seems, had stumbled on Canch Kavanagh – and the terms in which the sovereign spoke of his revived organisation (if he can be trusted) may indicate something of what he saw the new Benison as being about. The eighteenth-century founders of the club had liked snug rooms, wine or punch flowing freely. They would have thought the idea of frolicking on the chilly banks of the Forth (probably at dawn, which seems a favourite time for such antics) performing fertility rites crazy, if not downright perverted. It sounds as as though Kavanagh was trying to make the Benison into some sort of mystical male fertility cult, perhaps with the ex-army and navy officers concerned bound together by military service and concepts of masculinity and honour.

Kavanagh had notepaper printed with the heading

THE KNIGHTS COMMANDERS
OF THE ORDER OF
THE BEGGARS BENNISON[17]

but he didn't see fit to include any of the Benison's symbolism. The draft of one letter that he wrote as sovereign survives, headed 'Beggar's Benison and Wig Club.' – '20 Sept 5922, 3rd year of Sovereignship.' The letter outlines a version of the relationship between the Benison and the Wig Club which has no provenance but (as indicated in chapter nine) some plausibility. The intended recipient of the letter was apparently someone who had access to the relics of the Wig Club, and also to a glass which Kavanagh was trying to have returned to him as it rightly belonged to the Benison (several glasses are described, but in a confused way). Kavanagh urged: 'Your glass would indeed be a highly prized addition to the Mother Society for such it undoubtedly is and as for the old Wig you can have the very best Blessing as I the present Sovereign can bestow.' The Benison toast 'To the Beggar-Maid and Joy', he urged, had the same origin as 'your Wig Club toast'. The Wig should re-unite with the Benison to form again a single organisation.

Was there really at this point a revived Wig Club as well as Benison haunting twentieth-century Scotland? 'Perhaps your directors before considering our request would like to know more of the Society,' mused Kavanagh. But the only details he then gives are bizarre in the extreme. The Benison's oath forbade cheating at hazard, duelling without the sovereign's permission – and 'it's provisions are so strong against sodomy that one must believe that at some date the society's aim was the subversion of this vice'. He would not reveal who the members of the revived Benison were, 'but I can assure you that the social standard has not been lowered'. As a prospectus to those who might consider a merger, this is not very revealing – or rather what it reveals is muddled eccentricity.[18] Yet, whoever the letter was addressed to, and whoever 'the directors' may have been, Kavanagh did eventually track down some relics of the Wig Club and gain possession of them.

The historian may incline to excuse Kavanagh for his daft determination to revive the Benison/Wig Club in view of the fact that by purchasing their relics he helped to preserve them. Other aspects of his conduct were less helpful. Firstly, he mixed up the relics of the two bodies in a way which makes it impossible to be sure of the origins of some items. Secondly, he appears to have been unable to distinguish between the products of his fertile imagination and evidence. He makes statements on the history of the societies and their membership, without quoting any sources, that may have been based partly on oral traditions passed down to him but may equally have been invention. He had the Wig Club minute book in his possession, yet he largely ignored it because it made nonsense of his conviction that Benison and Wig were the same organisation. He wrote that more than half the members of the Wig Club belonged also to the Beggar's Benison but cited no evidence. He claimed many nobles belonged to the Benison, but to prove this refers to a betting book the existence of which is otherwise unknown. Probably he meant that many nobles had belonged to the Wig – which was true – though it is conceivable that he had access to some list indicating extensive noble membership of the Edinburgh Benison. Kavanagh devoted much time to compiling membership lists, but they are very confused, incomplete, and without any provenance. It would be folly to trust them.

The complications caused by Kavanagh's behaviour form an appropriate epilogue to the history of the Beggar's Benison and the

Wig. Instead of throwing light on the many obscurities involving the clubs and their activities, he added to them. The last laugh rests with the clubs, which delighted in combining publicising their existence with mystification about what went on in them.

Notes

1 This and the following paragraphs are based on correspondence in the BBWCC.

2 *Scottish exhibition of natural history, art and science: Palace of history: catalogue of exhibits* (2 vols., Glasgow, 1911), ii, 753. Exhibits include 'various articles' of 'arcana' – 'Pewter platter, a horn, a brass plate for box, two sashes, three medals, two diplomas. Lent by J. MacNaught Campbell.'

3 *Supplement*, 17–32.

4 *Records*, 10–11. See also *Supplement*, 89–91.

5 L. Hutchison, 'The Beggar's Benison,' *Scottish Book Collector*, i (1987–9). no. 4, pp.25–7.

6 Jones, *Clubs*, 205.

7 C. Jones, The *Clubs of the Georgian rakes* (New York, 1942), 205–7.

8 This and the following paragraphs are based on correspondence in the BBWCC and the National Museums of Scotland.

9 BBWCC; Stevenson, *Anstruther*, 182–4.

10 H. Fairnie, *The Fife coast from Queensferry to Fifeness* (Cupar, [1861]), 181.

11 BB, towards the back of a notebook in which Kavanagh transcribed historical notes on the Benison in 1921.

12 *Scotland: Owners of lands and heritages… 1872–3. Return of the name and address of every owner of one acre and upwards of land in Scotland* (Edinburgh, 1874), 174.

13 A.G. Wauchope, *A history of the Black Watch in the Great War* (3 vols., 1925–6), ii, 239–40, 247; N. McMicking, *Officers of the Black Watch* (2 vols., Perth, 1953–61), ii, 23.

14 Register of Deaths, New Register House, Edinburgh.

15 *The V.C. and the D.S.O. A complete record* (3 vols., London, *c*. 1934), i, 121. This work does not record Algernon Ransome's DSO.

16 Brackenbridge ruminated for over forty-five years before letting his curiosity about what he had been told in 1923 spur him into action. He then wrote to the National Museum asking for further information, NMS, letter of 1969.

17 There are several sheets of the notepaper in the BBWCC.

18 BBWCC, Kavanagh's draft of 20 Sept. 1920.

EPILOGUE

The Jezebel Club

Near some lamp-post, wi' dowy face,	*withered*
Wi' heavy een, and sour grimace,	*eyes*
Stands she that beauty long had kend,	*once had known*
Whoredom her trade, and vice her end.	

Robert Fergusson, d. 1774.[1]

The Benison and the Wig catered for male sexual obsession and fantasy. The object of such obsessive fantasy was the female, woman, but there are no individual, identifiable women in the evidence that survives. Two of the girls who displayed their bodies to the Benison in the 1730s are named, but their individuality is not important. They are samples temporarily focusing male lust for the female in general.

The Jezebel Club also catered for male obsession – but with real sex, not fantasy, for the club's members were women – prostitutes. The club itself, however, was a fantasy, created by an Edinburgh journalist in the 1780s. Benison and Wig members dreamed of sexual freedom, of free sex, but one of the most obvious consequences of the spread of libertine ideas was the growth not only of free sex but of paid sex. Mercury, god of the commerce of sex, balancing purse and penis, becomes a pimp-god. The growth of commercial sex, based on giving high priority to sensual pleasure, had its drawbacks, and most of those were experienced by women.

Urbanisation and the increasing ineffectualness of social control by both kirk sessions and burgh authorities brought both customer and supplier of commercial sex decreasing risk of detection and punishment, and decreasing guilt as acceptance of the legitimacy of the pursuit of pleasure grew. The result was a boom in prostitution. Increasing numbers of women found there was a commercial market in which they could sell themselves, full-time or part-time, in the absence of other forms of employment – or sometimes because the only other types of work available seemed so unattractive that prostitution was preferable. Increasingly for men with the money, relations with prostitutes became an accepted part of life.

William Creech, Edinburgh bookseller and journalist, drew attention to the spread of prostitution when he contrasted the Edinburgh of 1763 with that of 1783. He hailed some glories, but also emphasised the price of 'progress'. Population had grown fast, but the numbers of brothels and prostitutes had grown many times faster. His sensational figures were doubtless exaggerated (he was, after all, a journalist),[2] but the trends he highlighted were real enough. Prostitutes, ranging from the destitute to the almost respectable publicly flaunted by rich customers, were much more part of the city scene than ever before. In 1775, Creech might have added, Edinburgh had acquired its first published guide to what was on offer, though it only described a small number of 'voluptuaries of Venus' in a few establishments.[3]

The ready availability of prostitutes in Edinburgh for casual encounters is attested by one of their most experienced customers, James Boswell, whose journals reveal that they were a commodity as easily obtained in Edinburgh in the 1760s and 1770s, on the streets or in brothels, as in the many cities across Europe in which he had sought out their sisters. His tastes, or recurring guilt, led him to patronise the lower end of the market, contributing to his seventeen bouts of gonorrhoea. The picture is not an edifying one, and the conclusion is conventionally moral. Wracked with guilt but unable to control himself, the libertine descended into a nightmare of drunken sexual debauchery.[4] The horror of his decline is saddening – but his life was longer and happier than those of the women whose sexual services he bought.

Boswell's guilt was personal. Creech sought to instil guilt in his fellow-citizens by drawing attention to the fate of those providing commercial sexual services, but chose to do this not by heavy moralising but by satire. In the *Edinburgh Evening Courant* in the 1780s he created the Jezebel Club, as a symbol of the thriving profession and as a parody of male societies dedicated to professional self-interest. All trades and professions had their societies, so should not the whores have one too? The humour is sometimes light-hearted, sometimes horrible.

The Jezebel Club was introduced by Lydia Harridan, 'in the Chair,' writing to the newspaper's editor:

> You are daily announcing New Clubs to the Public; but you have not yet thought proper to give ours a place. Allow me to inform you, that our Club is one of an old establishment, and at present the most numerous in this city …. It hath made a more rapid progress of late years than any other society whatever. Besides, the visible effects which our Club has had on the manners of the metropolis entitles it to some attention.

A gala meeting was to be held the following Sunday, 'after evening service'. Supper would not be served until a few minutes after midnight, to prevent censures 'from the superstitious'. Thus the prostitutes after their 'service' (possibly not religious) in the evening, would avoid the sin of holding a sociable dinner on the Sabbath so as not to offend the pious. The latter, Creech implies, would make more fuss about social activity on Sunday than about the women's profession.

At the forthcoming meeting, Lydia Harridan announced, it would be proposed that the Jezebels should arrange suppers or dinners with other clubs,

> *The Wig – the Jeroboam – the Borachio – the Cape – the Hum-drum – the Antimanum – the Pandemonium – the Skink – the Spunge – the Free and Easy – the Gin – and the &c. Clubs.*

This would be done in order to preserve a 'friendly intercourse.' Clearly the sexed-up members of the Wig Club were appropriate targets for the jezebels, and presumably the members of the other clubs Creech lists were also thought to have pertinent interests.

Pointed satire but light in tone: let's get together with some of the bawdy male convivial clubs and have some fun. Then, next item. There were vacancies in the Jezebel Club as some members were dying, '*decayed*,' at the age of twenty. To prevent this, in future new members would not be accepted into the club – into prostitution – under the age of ten, and they would not be permitted to drink gin until the age of twelve. A most enlightened reform, again presenting a topsy-turvy world of moral priorities: girls could become prostitutes at ten, but were righteously to be restrained from drinking gin at that age. Further, Lydia Harridan revealed, problems were caused by parents complaining that their children and servants were joining their club. The response was that the fault lay at home. If girls became prostitutes, it was because they had not been brought up properly.

A proposal for the encouragement of circulating libraries at first seems odd in the context of the Jezebel – until it is realised that promotion of pornography is meant, as well perhaps of books containing 'facts of life' information. 'It will be recommended to all parents to give an unrestricted licence to draw knowledge from the *pure* fountains of information.' Sexual awareness in children was to be encouraged – and after all, information and useful knowledge were enlightened ideals. Exploiting the published word would increase business.

The jezebels were resolved to oppose a plan for a new prison in Edinburgh, the Bridewell, as 'shocking to female delicacy,' and members with the right connections were urged to campaign against it.[5]

> Many of the Club having been in intimate habits with Members of the august houses of Parliament, it is to be hoped they will use their influence to strengthen opposition.

Magistrates, ministers and the city guard were to be thanked for their 'great lenity and indulgence'. It was proposed that boxes in the theatre should be booked for the year 'by way of show-box' in which jezebels could flaunt their attractions, the theatre manager being obliging in such matters. Walks or pitches for members were recommended, including ones on the new Princes Street. But the poorest members of the profession were requested to keep to decaying, poverty-stricken areas of the Old Town. In respectable parts, people were complaining loudly of being 'blasted with gin and obscenity' by these creatures. The better off would evidently tolerate well behaved, attractive prostitutes on their streets, but not the 'decayed'. Dancing schools were to be encouraged, as they taught youths to abandon 'sheepish modesty' and become manly – become clients for prostitutes.[6]

Such was the agenda of the Jezebel Club, amusing and shocking, a comment on some of the effects of Enlightenment which are usually overlooked by those extolling the intellectual achievements of the age. In the phrase that Smollett had coined in *Humphrey Clinker*, Edinburgh was a 'hotbed of genius.' But also increasingly a hotbed of sensual pleasure, where practical application of crude simplifications of some of the ideas of the 'geniuses' about how humans should behave contributed to a boom in commercial sex.

The Benison and the Wig, two sleazy sex clubs reflecting the convolutions of male libido. Devoting a whole book to them can seem to be taking a sledgehammer to crack a nut, and for some perhaps it should have appeared as part of the book whose title Douglas Adams imagined – *Everything you never wanted to know about sex but have been forced to find out.* Yet examination of the clubs reveals that far from being disfiguring pimples that appeared randomly on Scotland's skin, they were remarkable in how they reflected their societies, changing ideas, and current controversies.

The Wig Club, perhaps, was no more indecent than many other club's, the veneration of the wig a fairly routine bit of ritual fun. The Benison, with not only real sex but taboo masturbation as its speciality, is harder to categorise. A few years ago Billy Connolly, renowned for shocking audiences with jokes on taboo subjects, said of masturbation that 'it's hardly a spectator sport.' 'You're wrong Billy' shout raucous voices from Fife nearly three hundred years ago, 'ha' ye no imagination man?' The Benison would have been proud to have pushed taboo-breaking even further that the comedian could contemplate. 'Evil, sick bastards' is a conclusion on Benison members recently urged upon the author by a correspondent in the club's Anstruther birthplace. On the other hand Gershon Legman, learned in erotic lore, was nonchalantly dismissive: 'a sexual initiation and penis-measuring club … what would nowadays be called a college fraternity'.[7] There is in fact no evidence of Benison penis-measuring, and though the club initiation was sexual in nature it was not, as the reference to college fraternities implies, an initiation *to* sexual activity – most members were married men. It may be, however, that Legman was more accurate in the implication that masturbation was – or is – part of some college fraternity associations. Evidence from, for example, France and the United States indicates that sexual activity can be involved in such initiations. But the Beggar's Benison seems unique in that the sexual activity involved men of widely differing ages rather than a young peer group.

Were a club practising Benison-type activities to be revealed today, the immediate media reaction would be to denounce – or hail – it as homosexual.[8] Benison members would have initially been bewildered at this categorisation, for the modern term and concept of homosexuality had not been invented in their day. Once it was explained to them, they would have been furious and appalled to find they were being accused of sodomy. Their sexual interests, they would have insisted, were entirely heterosexual (to use another term which is anachronistic). They were strongly opposed to sodomy. They would have perhaps admitted to arousal by the explicit sexual activities of their male colleagues, but their fantasies were about satisfaction with females. After all, they could have argued, men often talk together about women with lust, and such talk can be sexually arousing, but this hardly made those taking part in the discussion homosexuals. All they did in the Benison, the heterosexual case for the defence might run, was carry arousal inspired by group male dreaming of women a logical stage further than was usually done. They well knew that their behaviour would disgust many – but that was a major part of its appeal.

Inevitably it is the sex in the Benison that gets all the attention, but it proves to be far more than simply a 'sex club.' In some ways it may be argued that it was less sex-obsessed than the Wig Club. The Wig's only established interest was the celebration of sex – or lust – even if this was done entirely symbolically, whereas the Benison had for a time at least complex political and patriotic overtones half playfully, half seriously entwined by combining the commerce of sex and the commerce of the smuggling trade in double and treble entendres. Their myths played with Scottish history and, through the patronage of Mercury, with classical mythology. If many members might be dismissed as provincial bumpkins, there were men of some wit and education, however indecently employed, involved in inspiring it. Their advocacy of free sex might be largely theoretical, their activities largely confined to defiant masturbation, for they were no revolutionaries who wished to destroy social structures, and their defiance was private and combined with the maintenance of conventional and respectable outward lives. Nonetheless, in their rejection of sexual conventions as a sign of deep-seated rejection of the *status quo* of the prevailing culture they bear comparison with movements in many ages which have seen overthrowing sexual taboos as a way of expressing their alienation. The adepts of the Free Spirit in the Middle Ages had advocated promiscuity through 'an eroticism which, far from springing from carefree sensuality, possessed above all a symbolic value, as a sign of spiritual emancipation.' The Ranters of mid seventeenth-century England were not very different in attitude.[9] and the Restoration libertines of the following generation, while they would hardly qualify as spiritual in intention, also used promiscuity to demonstrate freedom, escape from a Puritan past. In the West in the 1960s, and after breaking sexual taboos was seen as a fundamental symbol of rejection of discredited values of existing society as well as a source of pleasurable activity.

Benison initiates might come out of the closet to perform their unseemly initiatory act before their colleagues, a demonstration of their prowess but also a symbol of their emancipation from prevailing morality and their disgust with the age they lived in. But in practice they contained their activities and fantasies within the closet, rather than trying to, by word or deed, persuade society to revolt against convention. Yet they were not entirely secret, as their widespread recruitment of members indicates. Many must have known of their activities, but there was no move to denounce them. Just as the national churches of Britain tended to turn a blind eye to the fornications and adulteries of the rich and landed while demanding conventional morality of the masses, so the weird things gentlemen got up to in clubs were generally ignored.

It is the fact that, as a club, the Benison's favoured activity was masturbation that has made historians so reluctant to research and write about it. Yet it can be argued that here the club was more in line with modern thinking than its contemporaries. Members asserted that the practice was natural, and rejected the irrational anti-masturbation health panic that had begun in their own day and was to last for centuries. In this they were more enlightened than the Enlightenment of their own age, even if their expressing their opinion by masturbating in each other's company may be seen as eccentric in the extreme. Historians have suggested that a distinctive feature of the Scottish Enlightenment was that new ideas were not just theories discussed by intellectual élites but tended to permeate down through society and be put into practical effect. If the Beggar's can claim to be 'enlightened,' then their enlightenment was certainly down to earth and practical.

Moreover their chosen sexual activity was harmless. If members had sallied forth to seduce they would have spread unwanted pregnancies, disgrace to girls and social disruption – and then might in retrospect be regarded as heroes like Robert Burns. But by being more responsible and confining themselves to masturbation in their libertine endeavours, they have tended to bring on themselves disgust. They might take heart from the fact that one modern government is on their side. South Africa has faced a huge epidemic of rape in recent years, and has launched an official campaign to persuade men to 'Masturbate! Don't Rape!' The violence has clearly grown partly from the brutalisation entailed in the 'Armed Struggle' fought against Apartheid. 'The other word for masturbation is Arm Struggle' urges a newsletter hopefully, 'Join the Arm Struggle and stop raping our mothers, wives, sisters and children'.[10] That is a desperate plea that puts the 'depravity' of the Benison in perspective in assessing sexual behaviour.[11]

The Benison was a club where men relieved political grievances and sexual frustration not by plotting violence against the state or aggression against women, but by resorting to drink, humour, goodfellowship, and the naughtiness of saying and doing of forbidden things. Nobles and gentry who became honorary members joined themselves in spirit to this Libertine brotherhood – and had more scope for putting ideals of 'free sex' into practice than the frustrated masturbators of Anstruther. The members of the Benison, on a charitable interpretation, may be regarded as a fairly innocuous, eccentric bunch of dirty old (and young, and middle aged) men.

Notes

1 Quoted in A Scott, *Scotch passion. An anthology of Scottish erotic poetry* (London, 1982), 148.
2 W. Creech (ed.), *Edinburgh fugitive pieces* (Edinburgh, 1791), 81 (2nd edn., Edinburgh, 1815), 105. At first Creech said there were six or seven Edinburgh

brothels in 1763, but by 1783 there were hundreds and prostitute numbers had risen by the same proportion. Later he rewrote his piece for Sir John Sinclair's *Statistical account of Scotland*, and made his claims more precise – and more extreme. Five or six brothels, increasing twenty-fold by 1783, while prostitute numbers {'women of the town') increased over a hundred fold.

3 [J. Tytler], *Ranger's impartial list of the ladies of pleasure in Edinburgh* (Edinburgh, 1775; facsimile reprint Edinburgh, 1981).

4 Stone, *Family, sex and marriage*, 572–99.

5 The foundations for the new Bridewell were laid in 1791, Creech, *Pieces* (2nd edn), 104.

6 Creech, *Pieces*, 48–52.

7 G. Legman, *The horn book. Studies in erotic folklore and bibliography* (New York, [1964], 77, quoted in L. Hutchison, 'The Beggar's Benison,' *Scottish Book Collector*, [i] (1987–9), no. 4, p.25. Legman, 251 cites an American Beta fraternity whose members became known as the 'Master Betas' – which recalls the character allegedly smuggled by scriptwriters into a British children's cartoon series – 'Master Bates'.

8 Legman, *Horn book*, 250, refers misleadingly to the Benison's 'solemn rite of homosexual initiation'.

9 N. Cohen, *The pursuit of the millennium. Revolutionary millenarians and mystical anarchists of the Middle Ages* (3rd edn, London, 1970), 151.

10 *Sunday Times*, 2 June 1997.

11 A recent alteration has been made to the Catholic Church's catechism, which has been interpreted as indicating that the church's attitude to masturbation is now that 'the act itself is still regarded as unsatisfactory ... We are not saying, fine, go ahead and enjoy yourselves. It is still objectively wrong, but subjectively it might not always be sinful' (*The Times*, 19 March 1999, p.5, quoting Father Terence Phipps, Allen Hall, London). The statement is hardly a model of lucidity, but the idea that the practice is mortal sin is clearly being discouraged.

Officials of the Beggar's Benison

The main source from which the lists have been compiled is the surviving diplomas. Dates for sovereigns indicate terms of office, those for recorders the years in which they are first and last known to have acted.

Anstruther or Parent Benison

SOVEREIGNS

1745/6–1773	John McNachtane
1773–1820	James Lumsdaine of Innergellie
1820–1828	Thomas Erskine, 9th Earl of Kellie
1834?–1836	James Black
1919–	Maxwell Robert Canch Kavanagh

RECORDERS

1746?, 1763–1766	Robert Hunter
1765	George Paton, 'for the Recorder'
1770	Shadrach Moyse
1773	James Durham
1775	Philip Anstruther, deputy
1781–1790	Patrick Plenderleath, deputy
1795	M. Hunter, 'the Recorder Hereditary'
1813–1816	John Grahame, deputy
1820–5	Archibald Johnstone
1836	Matthew Forster Conolly, interim recorder

TREASURER

pre-1820	Andrew Johnstone

AGENT AND STATIONER IN ORDINARY

1750–	George Paton

CONSERVATOR OF LIBERTIES, PRIVILEGES AND IMMUNITIES

1761–   William Bruce

Edinburgh Branch Benison

SOVEREIGNS

1752–1761?   Robert Lumsdaine of Innergellie
1760s?   Thomas Erskine, 6th Earl of Kellie?

GRAND MASTER

1755–1761?   Chambre Lewis

RECORDER

1755–84   Walter Ferguson

Glasgow Branch Benison

RECORDER

1792   William Elliot

Russian Branch Benison

CHANCELLOR

1773   William Porter

USHER OF THE PINK ROD

1773   John …

Beggar's Benison Diplomas: Known Copies

The following list includes all diplomas admitting members which survive, all blank texts of the diploma, and all diplomas now lost of which some details are known. Some diplomas are hand written, some engraved, with a copper-plate text with blanks to be filled in. Some are on parchment, others on paper.

The 'Anstruther' and 'Edinburgh' seals referred to are those described in Appendix 3, nos. 3.4 and 3.5.

? 1739.
Fictitious? E. Hawkins (ed.), *Medallic illustrations of the history of Great Britain and Ireland*, (British Museum, 2 vols., 1885), ii, 527 states that the earliest known date on a Benison diploma is 1739, but the source given for this information is Fergusson, *Henry Erskine*, which never mentions the date.

12 December 1746. George Paton.
Granted by John McNachtane in the 8th year of his sovereignty. Recorder: R. Hunter.
Seal, Appendix 3.3.1.
Paton was certainly a member of the Benison but the diploma conflicts with many others in suggesting that NcNachtane became sovereign *c*.1738. Moreover under the diploma's text, written at the same time and in the same hand, is the appointment of Paton as agent for the society, dated 1750 and the 10th year of McNachtane's guardianship. A possible explanation is that this was written later in an incompetent attempt to claim that McNachtane's sovereignty dated from the Benison's 1739 reorganisation, rather than from the 1745–6 date that many other diplomas indicate. The fact that the seal matrix is unfinished, perhaps because the engraver's error in assigning three testicles to the genitals displayed, adds to the seeming irregularity of the diploma.
British Museum, Department of Medieval and Later Antiques, M.567.

Formerly in the possession of Edward Hawkins (1780–1867), keeper of antiquities in the British Museum. It was presented to the museum in 1880 by a Mr Blackstone.

1750.
Referred to in a letter, BBWCC, 6 Dec. 1911, Anstruther, T.D. Murray to MacNaught Campbell: 'I could give you a good deal of information regarding the history of the society but not on paper. There are several parchments and seals in this district. The earliest I have seen is 1750 and the latest 1825.'

6 Nov 1755. Thomas Brown of Braid.
Granted by Robert Lumsdaine of Innergellie in his 3rd year as sovereign and by Chambre Lewis in his 1st year as grand master. Issued in Edinburgh. Recorder: Walter Ferguson.
'Edinburgh' seal on a broad pink ribbon. NLS, kept with NLS copy of the 1892 *Records*. Sent to W.K. Dickson at the Library on 9 Sept. [no year] by Henry (surname illegible) of the Department of Forensic Medicine, University of Edinburgh.

1756.
Referred to in a letter, BBWCC, 21 Nov 1911 by T.D. Murray, Anstruther, as being in the possession of a friend who was descended from a member of the Benison.

28 Nov 1758. William Gibson, Esq., of the city of Edinburgh.
Granted by Robert Lumsdaine, in his 6th year as sovereign and by Chambre Lewis as grand master. Recorder: Walter Fergusson.
Parchment, with 'Edinburgh' seal on broad brown ribbon in a metal box. Edinburgh City Library, George IV Bridge, Y DA1820 G44 (Accession no. 70638A).
Uniquely, this diploma limits the rights to 'free trade' etc. to sixty years.

1761.
Granted by Chambre Lewis ('Lewis Chamber') as grand master.
'Edinburgh' seal attached. Described in J.A. Dulaure, *Histoire abrigé de differens cultes* (2nd edn., 2 vols., Paris, 1825), ii, 299.

15 March 1763. The Hon. David Steuart Erskine, Lord Cardross.
Granted by John McNachtane 'In the 3rd year of his 4th election' as sovereign. Recorder: R. Hunter.

'Anstruther' seal attached on pink ribbon. NAS, GD103/2/416, Society of Antiquaries of Scotland Collection.

5 Aug. 1763. John Duddingston yr. of Sandford, Lieutenant, 1st Regiment of infantry.
Granted by John McNachtane 'In the 3rd year of 4th Election' as sovereign.
Recorder: R. Hunter.
No seal. SAUL, Ms Deposit 26, Bundle 31.

14 May 1764. Mr Thomas Mathie.
Granted by John McNachtane in his 19th year as sovereign. Recorder: R. Hunter.
Pink ribbon but no seal. Murray Library, Anstruther: Kilrenny and Anstruther Burgh Collection. Bought in 1982, having been found behind layers of wallpaper in a house in Edinburgh, Stevenson, *Anstruther*, 187.

16 July 1764. John Bruce Stewart of Symbister, Esq.
Granted by John McNachtane in his 19th year as sovereign. Recorder: R. Hunter.
Formerly had a seal attached depicting an erect penis, but this had been cut off. NLS, transcript kept with NLS copy of the 1892 *Records*. Sent to W.K. Dickson at the library by a descendant of Stewart, R. Stuart Bruce, Symbister House, Whalsay, Shetland, with an accompanying letter dated 18 September 1926.

23 Nov. 1764. Ensign Colin Campbell of the 35th Foot.
Granted by John McNachtane in the 19th year of his sovereignty.
In possession of Mr Gascoigne of Lotherton Hall, Aberford, Yorkshire, in 1911, and described in a letter by him to Lord Scarsdale which is now in the archives at Kedleston Hall, Derby.

1765.
According to MacNaught Campbell, T.F. Donald, of Donald & Co., chartered accountants and stockbrokers, Glasgow, who was the secretary of the Hodge Podge Club, had a copy of a diploma of this date. BBWCC, letter of 12 May 1897 annotated by Campbell.

21 Feb. 1765. Sir John Whitefoord, Bt.
Granted by John McNachtane in his 20th year as sovereign. Recorder: 'G. Paton for the Recorder.'
No seal. EUL, La. Charters 3222 (802 Box 22).

30 Apr. 1765. Andrew Ramsay Esq., of Glasgow.
Recorder: 'G. Paton for the Recorder.'
Seal attached but type not recorded. BBWCC, described in a letter dated Philadelphia 16 March 1897 from Charles H. Krumbhaar, who was descended from Ramsay.

30 Dec. 1766. Duncan MacDougall, Esq., writer in Lorne.
Granted by John McNachtane in his 22nd year as sovereign. Recorder: R. Hunter.
'Anstruther' seal on a pink ribbon. EUL, kept with a copy of the 1892 *Records* at JA.3648.

7 Aug. 1770. James Stewart, esq.
Granted by John McNachtane in 24th year as sovereign. Recorder: Shadrach Moyse.
Pink ribbon but no seal. NAS, GD50/214, John MacGregor Collection.

27 May 1771. Rev. John Nairne.
Described as having 'certain Isernian symbols' 'on its engraved surface'.
Transcript in Rogers, *Social Life*, ii, 417; *Scottish Notes and Queries*, vi (1892–3), 44. Both sources wrongly misinterpret the date '5771' as 1767, and Rogers omits some of the double entendres from the text.

8 Mar. 1773. Mr Thomas Rennie, writer in Edinburgh.
Granted by John McNachtane in his 28th year as sovereign. Recorder: not named.
'Anstruther' seal on a pink ribbon. NLS, Ch 915. The diploma was given to the Society of Antiquaries of Scotland in about 1920 by A S. Carnegie, 6 Abercromby Place, Edinburgh: *PSAS*, liv (1919–20), 214. Transcript in Jones, *Clubs*, 186–7 and A. Macnaghten, *In search of two kinsmen* (1979), 50–1.

1773 (no day or month given). Sir William Nairne of Dunsinane, Bt.
Granted by James Lumsdaine in his 1st year as sovereign. Recorder: James Durham.
Pink ribbon but no seal. NAS, GD103/2/435, Society of Antiquaries of Scotland Collection.

30 Aug. 1775. The Honourable Nathaniel Curzon, Kedleston, Derbyshire.
Granted by James Lumsdaine in his 3rd year as sovereign. Recorder: Philip Anstruther, dep.

'Edinburgh' seal on a pink ribbon, in a metal box. Scarsdale Papers, Kedleston Hall, Derby.

18 Aug. 1781. William Douglas Clephame, captain, 2nd regiment of guards. Granted by James Lumsdaine in his 9th year as sovereign. Recorder: Patrick Plenderleath.
'Anstruther' seal on a pink ribbon. NAS, GD1/49/135, Clephame of Garslogie.

2 Aug. 1783. George, Prince of Wales.
Granted by James Lumsdaine in his 12th year as sovereign. Recorder: P. Plenderleath.
Described in *Records*, 13 (which misreads the Recorder's initial as 'R'). The diploma was then (1892) 'in the possession of a well-known Antiquary,' and was dated '5783,' that is 1783. V. Lunardi, *Five aerial voyages in Scotland* (London, 1786), 52, states that the prince became a member a few months before he himself did. In 1922 it was stated that the diploma was still in existence (though this may have been simply a repetition of the statement in the *Records* thirty years before) and was dated 1785, BBWCC. Jones, *Clubs*, 193, wrongly states that George visited Scotland in 1783.

15 Nov. 1784. Alexander Strachan of Tarrie.
Granted by James Lumsdaine in his 10th year as sovereign. Recorder: Walter Ferguson.
'Edinburgh' seal on pink ribbon, in a metal box. NLS, Ch 916. The diploma was given to the Society of Antiquaries of Scotland in about 1920 by A.S. Carnegie, 6 Abercromby Place, Edinburgh: *PSAS*, liv (1919–20), 214.

28 Apr. 1785. Sir Thomas Dundas, MP.
Granted by James Lumsdaine in his 13th year as sovereign. Recorder: Patrick Plenderleath, D.R. (deputy recorder).
'Anstruther' seal on a pink ribbon, in a watch case inscribed 'Alex Gardner Jeweler to his Royal Highness the Prince of Wales medalist Edinr.' North Yorkshire County Record Office, ZNK X 2/22/87.

10 Oct. 1785. Vincent Lunardi, amigarum lucaensis.
Granted by James Lumsdaine in his 13th year as sovereign. Recorder: Patrick Plenderleath, D.R. (deputy recorder).
Transcript in V. Lunardi, *Five Aerial Voyages in Scotland* (London, 1786), 53–4.

10 Jan. 1786. Capt. William Robertson of Lude.
Granted by James Lumsdaine, in the 12th year of his sovereignty. Recorder:
P. Plenderleath, deputy recorder.
'Anstruther' seal on pink ribbon. NAS, GD38/1/58, Dalguise Muniments.

1786. 'A young nobleman aged 20.'
Granted by James Lumsdaine in his 13th year as sovereign. Recorder: Patrick
Plenderleath.
'Anstruther' seal. Summary in *Notes and Queries*, 8th series, x, 156 (22 Aug.
1896).

11 May 1788. Hugh Cleghorn, Professor of Civil History in the University of
St Andrews.
Granted by James Lumsdaine, in his 15th year as sovereign. Recorder.
Patrick Plenderleath, DR (deputy recorder).
'Anstruther' seal. SAUL, Cleghorn Papers, Box 1, Envelope 2, item 12,
cited in A. Clerk, *An enlightened Scot. Hugh Cleghorn, 1752–1837* (Duns,
1992), 23.

7 July 1788. Sir William James Cockburn, Bt., lieutenant, First Battalion
Royal.
Granted by James Lumsdaine in his 15th year as sovereign. Recorder:
Patrick. Plenderleath, D.R (deputy recorder).
Seal on a pink ribbon, but the wax is blank. NAS, GD216/266, Cockburn of
that Ilk Muniments.

30 Nov. 1790. David Parkhill, Esq., lieutenant in the 16th Regiment.
Granted by James Lumsdaine in his 16th year as sovereign. Recorder: P.
Plenderleath, deputy.
'Anstruther' seal on pink ribbon. SAUL, Pittenweem Papers.

24 Jan. 1795. Hon William Maule.
Granted by James Lumsdaine in his 19th year as sovereign. Recorder: M.
Hunter, 'the Recorder Hereditary'.
Pink ribbon with fragment of seal. NAS, GD45/15/83, Dalhousie Muniments.

Post-1800. Blank.
Printed transcript. Records, 6–7

Post-1800. Blank.
BBWCC.

18 Sept. 1812. David, Lord Ogilvie, captain, 42nd Royal Highanders.
Granted by James Lumsdaine in his 39th year as sovereign. Recorder: James Grahame, deputy.
'Anstruther' seal on a pink ribbon. NAS, GD16/25/36, Earls of Airlie.

30 Nov. 1813. Andrew MacVicar Esq., of Edinburgh.
Granted by James Lumsdaine in his 41st year as sovereign. Recorder: John Grahame, deputy.
Pink ribbon but no seal. SAUL, BBWCC.

4 Mar. 1816. William Arnot, Esq., merchant in St Petersburg.
Granted by James Lumsdaine. Recorder: John Grahame, deputy.
'Anstruther' seal on a pink ribbon. The diploma was found in 1997 folded inside the copy of the *Supplement* held in SAUL (St A. HQ462.A6). Now transferred to BBWCC.

Post-1816. Blank.
'Lighthouse' seal (see Appendix 3 no. 3.6) at top left corner.
Inserted in the Beggar's Benison Bible (Appendix 3, no.8.1).

30 Nov. 1820. Thomas Marshall Gardner of Hillcairnie Esq.
Granted by Thomas Erskine, Earl of Kellie in his 1st year as sovereign. Recorder: Archibald Johnstone.
Text printed on paper, in a decorated border. At the top left is Kellie's coat of arms, and at top right the 'Anstruther' Benison badge. 'Anstruther' seal on a broad green ribbon. 'Designed and engraved by Charles Thomson 204 High Street Cross, Edinburgh.' The day and month are printed, only the year being left blank.
BBWCC. Facsimile in *Records*.

1820. Colonel William Wemyss.
Granted by Thomas Erskine, Earl of Kellie, in his 1st year as sovereign.
Probably printed like Thomas Gardner's – it is described as 'highly enriched with classical and other devices'. Described in Ferguson, *Harry Erskine*, 149–50.

1825. John Cleghorn.
See p. 175 above.

1825. Peter Cleghorn.
See p. 175 above.

1825.

Mentioned in a letter in BBWCC, 6 Dec. 1911, Anstruther, T.D. Murray to MacNaught Campbell: 'I could give you a good deal of information regarding the history of the society but not on paper. There are several parchments and seals in this district. The earliest I have seen is 1750 and the latest 1825'.

1834. James Rodger, merchant, Anstruther.

Granted by James Black in his 1st year as sovereign. Recorder: David John Roger, A.R.(Assistant Recorder?).

Printed from the same plate as the Gardner diploma of 1820, but on parchment and with Black's coat of arms printed on paper and glued over (presumably) the earl of Kellie's arms. 'Anstruther seal' on green ribbon

This is the 1834 diploma mentioned in *Medallic illustrations of British history*, ed. E. Hawkins (3 vols., British Museum, 1907), ii, notes to plate cliv, and in *Catalogue of the Montague Guest Collection of badges, tokens and passes* (British Museum, London, 1930), 120.

British Museum, Department of Medieval and Later Antiquities, George Witt Collection (gifted 1865), W315.

APPENDIX 3

Relics of the Beggar's Benison and the Wig Club

Most of the items listed below are in the Beggar's Benison and Wig Club Collection of St Andrews University. The artefacts are held in the University Collections, the manuscript material in the University Library as MS 38351.

Only original material relating to the two organisations is listed here, the correspondence and notes (1890s-1930s) which form the majority of the manuscripts being excluded.

THE BEGGAR'S BENISON

1 Medals and Dies[1]

1.1 Oval, 62mm x 39mm, silver gilt with suspension loop.

> Obverse: BE FRUITFUL & MULTIPLY. Naked male and female figures standing facing front and holding hands. The male, on the left, gestures to the left as if to lead the female off. Behind him a lion walks to the left.
> Reverse: MAY PRICK & PURSE NEVER FAIL YOU. Draped male and female figures. The female is seated on the left, with a tree behind her, with her legs wide apart. With her right hand she holds a purse aloft, while with left she points to the genitals of the male figure, who stands on the right with arms spread. Behind him a hound runs to the right.

The Adam and Eve of the obverse are contrasted with the cruder scene on the reverse. If the figure there is the beggar-maid, the male is James V. The association of purse and genitals may suggest that Mercury is also alluded to – but the hound suggests Adonis, who appears on 1.3 – 1.6.

Glendennings. Historical medals, tokens and numismatic books (Sale catalogue for 17 November 1988), lot 287 and illustration. Noted as unpublished and 'Extremely fine and extremely rare.' (a copy of the catalogue entry is held in the NMS).

Either 1.1 or 1.2 is probably the oval medal recorded as 'noted by a well known firm of London numismatists,' *Notes on the records of the Beggar's Benison Society and Merryland of Anstruther, Fife*, 1739–1836 (This work consists largely of notes and extracts from the *Records* of 1892, published c 1932), 10. Full details of the medal are not given, but it is described as oval, 'much larger' than 1.2 below, and bearing the legend MAY PRICK AND PURSE NEVER FAIL YOU. Thus both medals 1.1 and 1.2 described read 'prick and purse' rather than 'prick nor purse' which is standard on the other medals.

1.2　Oval,. 51 mm long. Silver.
Obverse and reverse: legends and subjects as for 1.1 above.
Montague Guest, 120, no. 998. Badly worn.

1.3　Oval, 35mm x 28mm, silver, silver gilt or gold, with suspension loop.

Obverse: BE FRUITFULL AND MULTIPLY. Naked male, a lion moving left behind him, holds naked female by the hand, gesturing towards a bower to the left.
Reverse: LOSE NO OPPORTUNITY. Naked female figure lies asleep in foreground with cupid behind her. Behind him, naked male figure approaches, holding spear, accompanied by dog (seated). A tree stands to the left.

Adam and Eve on obverse, Aphrodite (Venus) and Adonis on the reverse. The medal is perhaps earlier than 1.4 and 1.5, being rather cruder in execution.
BBWCC, 2 copies (silver gilt), on a loop of red ribbon. NMS, H.M200, in original oval wooden case lined with velvet and covered in shagreen, presented in 1929 by J.C. Dunlop, FRCP, Drumbeg, North Berwick: 'Donations to the museum,' *PSAS*, lxiii (1928–9), 311. See *Glendennings. historical medals, tokens and numismatic books* (Sale catalogue for 17 November 1988), lot 286. For an example struck in gold 'with high points smoothed by wear' see Larissa Dukelskaya (ed.), *The Hermitage. English art – sixteenth to nineteenth century* (Leningrad and London, c. 1979), plates 62–3. Davis, *Tickets*, 107, no. 57; Hawkins, *Medallic*, ii, 526, no. 87; *Medallic illustrations*, iii, plate cliv, no. 6; *Montague Guest*, 119.
Cochran Patrick, *Medals*, 172 appears to have believed that this was not a Benison medal, as he thought all of the latter had the legend 'Beggar's Benison Anstruther' inscription found on 1.4.
The die for the reverse is at NMS, QN163, Hocking, 'Notes,' 327–8.

1.4 Round, 33mm, silver or silver gilt, with or without suspension loop.

Obverse. As in 1.3.
Reverse: THE BEGGAR'S BENISON ANSTRUTHER, with date '5826' below. A scroll reads LOSE NO OPPORTUNITY. Otherwise as in 1.3 except that the dog is running to the left and the tree is omitted.

'5826' is the Benison date for 1826.
BBWCC. 3 copies, all gilt and all attached to plain green satin ribbons ending in rosettes, 24 cm x 4.5cm. Illustrated in *Records*. Cochran Patrick, *Medals*, 172 (silver gilt). NMS H.M102 (white metal); Davis, *Tickets*, 107, no. 59; Hawkins, *Medallic*, ii, 527, no. 89; *Medallic illustrations*, iii, plate cliv, no. 8; *Montague Guest*, 119, no. 997.
The dies (early 19th century) for both the obverse and reverse are at NMS, III.15.474 & 475, Hocking, 'Notes.'

1.5 Round, 30mm, silver gilt, with suspension loop.

Obverse: BE FRUITFUL AND MULTIPLY. Theme as in 1.3 except that the bower lies to the right and the figures turn that way.
Reverse: LOSE NO OPPORTUNITY. Theme as in 1.3, except that both figures are partially clothed, the dog is omitted, the male stands at the feet of the female rather than behind her, and Cupid flies overhead holding draperies. Tree in centre.

NMS H.M201 (silver gilt, with plain green sash with rosette attached). Presented by Lt. Col. M.R. Canch-Kavanagh, late of the Black Watch, Grimblethorpe Hall, Lincoln. 'Donations to the museum,' *PSAS*, lvii (1922–3), 297; BBWCC, wax impression, presumably made from the die; Davis, *Tickets*, 107, no. 58; Hawkins, *Medallic*, 527, no. 88; *Medallic illustrations*, iii, plate cliv, no. 7; *Montague Guest*, 119, no. 996
The die for the reverse is at NMS, QN 164, Hocking, 'Notes.'

1.6 Round, no suspension loop.

Obverse: legend and theme as in 1.2, except that there is no specific bower, trees being scattered all across the background, and male figure leads female to the right.
Reverse: legend and theme as in 1.3, except that the male figure stands to the left of the reclining female, cupid holds draperies above her head, and there is no dog or spear. The male's hands cover his genitals.

Photograph in NMS, sent with letter from A.H. Baldwin & Sons 18 Nov. 1988.

1.7 Round. Silver. Round, 31 mm

> Obverse: THE BEGGAR'S BENNISON on scroll. Vertical anchor, crossed by horizontal phallus with testicles, facing right. A purse is tied onto the phallus with a ribbon.
> Reverse: monogram (not deciphered).

Presumably a badge or medal made for an individual member of the Benison, whose initials comprise the monogram.
Photograph in NMS, sent by A.H. Baldwin & Sons, 1988, and still in the possession of the company in 2001.

2 Sashes

2.1 90 cm x 9.4 cm. Watered silk.

> Green watered silk with painted legend SOVEREIGN BEGGARS BENISON, with a crown after the first word.

The decorative finials on the crown may represent ships' sails and end-on views of ships. Looks considerably older than 2.2 below.
BBWCC. Illustrated in *Records*.

2.2 98 cm x 9.2 cm. Watered silk.

> As 2.1

BBWCC

3 Seals: Matrices and Impressions

3.1 Rectangular with rounded corners, 12mm x 15mm.

> ANSTRUTHER / BEGGAR'S / LOVE'S CAVE / BENISON. / 1732

Impression in NMS; Jones, *Clubs*, 187.
Matrix (brass, with mahogany handle) in BBWCC.

3.2 Round

> MAY PRICK NOR PURSE NEVER FAIL YOU / 17 / B.B. / A. / 32

Illustrated in *Records*, but the matrix is not in the BBWCC and no impressions are known.

3.3   Rectangular with rounded corners, 14mm x 18 mm.

> SIGHT IMPROVES DELIGHT / B.B./ A. Heart in centre, with vulva within it.

Impression in NMS, probably from BBWCC. Illustrated in *Records*. Jones, *Clubs*, 187–8.
Matrix (brass, with mahogany handle) in BBWCC.

3.3.1 Round. 31mm

> THE BEGGAR'S BENNISON, on horizontal phallus, facing right, with purse tied onto the phallus with a ribbon. The top of the ground is left empty, while below is an anchor.

The seal matrix may have been left unfinished – perhaps when it was realised that the engraver had provided three testicles. The seal is attached to a diploma dated 1746, though an addition written in the same hand at the same time is dated 1750.
The diploma was acquired by Edward Hawkins, whose collection of British medals included a Benison medal. He sold his collection to the British Museum (where he was keeper of antiquities) in 1860, but the diploma evidently passed to a Mr Blackstone, who presented it to the museum in 1880.
British Museum, Department of Medieval and Later Antiquities, M.567.

3.4   Round, 32mm.

> THE BEGGAR'S BENNISON on scroll. Vertical anchor, crossed by horizontal phallus facing right. A purse is tied onto the phallus with a ribbon.

The phallus and purse are symbolic of Mercury, the anchor is the coat of arms of Anstruther – as well as symbolic of sexual intercourse ('dropping anchor'). Illustrated in *Records*. Impressions in NMS, and on diplomas dated 1786 and 1788. Jones, *Clubs*, 187.
Matrix (brass, with mahogany handle) in BBWCC.

3.5   Round, 32mm.

> THE BEGGAR'S BENNISON, with NISI DOMINUS FRUSTRA on a scroll. Horizontal phallus facing right, with purse tied onto the phallus with a ribbon. An anchor is it above and a castle below.

The castle and motto are from the coat of arms of Edinburgh.
Illustrated in *Records* (and see pp. 12, 20). NMS, impressions; BBWCC, impressions, including one in lead; Jones, *Clubs*, 187.
Matrix (brass, with mahogany handle) in BBWCC.

3.6 Round, c.22mm.

> RECTUS / 18 16 / INS MAI / B.B.A. A lighthouse with cleft on the side. Two birds (pelicans?) face the lighthouse and support it.

Commemorates the lighthouse built on the Isle of May. The lighthouse is clearly intended as phallic, and the combined phallus and vulva motif is evidently based on the *lingam* and *yoni* symbol of the Hindu god Shiva.
Illustrated in *Records*; Jones, *Clubs*, 188; Impressions in NMS, probably from BBWCC, and in the Beggar's Benison Bible.
Matrix (brass, with wooden handle) in BBWCC.

4 Test Platter

4.1 Round, 32.1 mm diameter x 2.9 deep. Pewter.

> Top: THE BEGGAR'S BENISON ANSTRUTHER 1732 / THE WAY OF A MAN WITH A MAID / TEST / PLATTER. Phallus in vulva.
> Bottom: Two stamped makers' marks. One reads GRAHAME AND WARDROP, the other shows a ship with the legend round it SUCCESS TO THE UNITED STATES OF AMERICA. A rough scratched inscription reads N.B. MANY A SIX INCH LONG / PRICK, IN FULL BLOOM / AND STATURE OF FIERY / BEGOT IN SUITABLE / CUNT, DRIPPING WITH JUICE / HAS BEEN BRANDERED HEREUPON

'Brandered' presumably has here some relation to the usage of the verb 'to brander' meaning 'to be on heat.' The reference to the United States indicates a date of manufacture after 1783.
BBWCC. Top illustrated in *Records*; Jones, Clubs, 184–5.

5 Breath Horn

5.1 27.4 cm long x 7.3 cm across mouth. Silver plate.

> Legend, in diamond-shaped panel enclosed in vulva, MY / BREATH / IS / STRANGE, LEV. X5, 16, 17, 18 / 1739 / B.B./ A.

The name 'Breath Horn' is given in *Records*, 9.
The date in the legend commemorates the reorganisation of the Benison in 1739 rather than being the date of manufacture. The initials B.B.A. distinguish the Anstruther branch of the Benison, which would not have been necessary in 1739 as the separate Edinburgh branch was not established until the 1750s.
BBWCC. Illustrated in *Records*. Jones, *Clubs*, 183.

6 Punch Bowls

6.1 25.9 cm diameter x 11.3 cm high. Chinese porcelain.

> *c.*1765. Painted, on the outside decorated with two bouquets of flowers and two medallions surmounted by pink ribbons, with legend THE BEGGAR'S BENNISON and anchor, above horizontal phallus with testicles, facing right, with purse suspended on a ribbon. A similar medallion is at the centre of the inside.

The bowl has been broken and repaired, though it was complete when the photograph now in the Records was taken. Records, II noted that 'A box with a Punch Bowl having Insignia is still in existence in Glasgow' but the box has disappeared.
BBWCC. Information on dating from David S. Howard.

6.2 Chinese porcelain bowl

> *c.* 1765. Evidently identical to 6.1.

Nathaniel Curzon of Kedleston (1751–1837) became a member of the Beggar's Benison in 1775, but the bowl is of earlier date.
Kedleston Hall, Derby, in possession of Lord Scarsdale. Information from David S. Howard.

6.3 Chinese porcelain bowl

> *c.* 1765. Evidently identical to 6.1 and 6.2 except that the two Benison medals on the outside are here replaced by the coat of arms of the Wentworth family.

The common design suggests that 6.1, 6.2 and 6.3 were part of the same order sent to China. The service was almost certainly made for Sir Thomas Wentworth, 5th baronet (1726–92), who succeeded his father in 1763.
D. S. Howard, *Chinese armorial porcelain* (London, 1974), 263 (description and illustration), and information from Mr Howard.
The bowl was sold in Harrogate in the 1970s and is now believed to be in the United States.

6.4 33cm diameter. Chinese famille rose porcelain.

> *c.* 1770–5. 'Enamelled on two sides of the exterior and in the centre of the interior with a large circular medallion inscribed in gilt on a blue ground THE BEGGAR'S BENNISON, divided on the exterior with two tied floral bouquets, the interior rim with a wide band of fruit and flower

sprays' (Catalogue description). The medallions are identical to those on 6.1, 6.2 and 6.3, bearing the Benison 'Anstruther' phallus and anchor badge.

Auctioned at Christie's, London, 16 November 1999, the seller being anonymous. The catalogue date ('*c.*1800–1810') has been revised by David S. Howard. *Christie's: Fine Chinese export ceramic and works of art*, 16 November 1999, p. 84 (description and illustration).

6.5
Described as a 'specially made [Benison] punchbowl, with its phallic decorations' which 'eventually passed into the hands of another McNaughton to be preserved in discreet privacy today,' Duncan McNaughton, 'John MacNaughton and the "Beggars' Benison." An eighteenth century character,' *Scottish Genealogist*, xiv, no. 3 (1967), 58. It is evidently this which has also been described as 'a magnificent porcelain punchbowl, decorated with the erotic insignia of the club,' A. Macnaghten, *In search of two kinsmen* (1979), 51. It is possible that this is identical with 6.4.

7 Wine Glasses

Though 7.1 to 7.3 are very similar, minor differences suggest that they may not all be from a single set of glasses.

7.1　13.3cm tall x 7.2cm base diameter x 4.8cm bowl diameter. Lead glass, bucket-shaped bowl, with opaque twist in stem. Enamelled, with legend round the bowl: THE BEGGAR'S BENNISON, with motif of anchor, castle and phallus as on the 'Edinburgh' Benison seal (3.5) and the punch bowl (6.1), except that the horizontal phallus faces left rather than right. The enamelling is white, except that the purse is green and the ribbon attaching it red.

The glass has been broken at the base of the stem and repaired, and may have had a new foot attached, accounting for it being larger than the foot of 7.2 below.
Enamelled glass was fashionable in Britain in the 1760s and 1770s, and one group of pieces has been identified which has particularly strong Scottish links. In addition to the Benison glasses it includes a number of wine glasses with polychrome family crests. A pair of wine decanters having similarities to this group bear the enamelled legends 'SIR JNO ANSTRUTHER FOr Ever' and 'LADY ANSTRUTHER FOr Ever.' These presumably commemorate some parliamentary election of the period. The British centre of glass enamelling was

Newcastle upon Tyne, but it is possible that this group was enamelled in Scotland.

BBWCC. Illustrated in *Records*. S. Cottle, 'The other Beilbys: British enamelled glass of the eighteenth century,' *Apollo*, 124 (1986), 315–27, especially 318–20.

7.2

13.3cm tall. x 6.7cm base diameter x 4.8cm bowl diameter Similar to 7.1

Private Collection, London. Cottle, 'The other Beilby's,' 318–20 (including illustration). Formerly in the Alexander Collection, and in possession of Asprey plc in 1980. Sold at auction at Sotheby's, London, in December 2001.

7.3

presumed similar to 7.1 – 7.2.

Scotland, private collection. Displayed on loan at Broadfield House Glass Museum, West Midlands, in 1999, and earlier in Glasgow.

7.4 Red wine glass 'with the insignia of the Order on the side.'

Jones, *Clubs*, 208. Present whereabouts unknown.

8 Bible

8.1 Bible (Edinburgh 1744). Leather bound, with new spine with title THE BIBLE. BEGGAR'S BENISON, ANSTRUTHER. Brass hasp plates engraved P.B.B.A. on front cover and B.B.B.E. on rear cover. The lock on the hasp has crossed vulva round the keyhole with LIGNUM SCIENTIAE above and BONI & MALI below.

The initials refer to the Parent benison of Anstruther and the Branch in Edinburgh. The hasp legend translates as 'The tree of knowledge of good and evil.'

Inside the front cover is the bookplate of John Alexander Stewart. Two sheets with miscellaneous comments about love and sex follow, perhaps written in the early nineteenth century. In between them another, smaller, sheet has been glued with a typed description of the Bible transcribed from *Records*, 10–11. An inscription on the title page reads 'Beggar's Benison, Castle of Dreel, Anstruther. Given for use by Thomas Earl of Kellie, at the Initiation of Standing Members. Kept defiantly by Andrew Johnstone, and discovered in 1823 in a Pawn Office, Canongate, Edinburgh.' On the back of the title page are glued printed copies of the coats of arms of twenty-nine leading Scottish nobles, evidently cut from some early nineteenth publication on the peerage, and a biographical notice relating to Charles Erskine, 8th earl of Kellie (1797–9). In this notice the name of Thomas, 6th earl of Kellie (1756–81) is underlined, and a manuscript note reads 'Thomas was the Sovereign'. This is evidently in the same hand as the inscription on the title page itself, and thus may be dated to around 1823.

Between the title page and the beginning of the text nine sheets of lined paper have been inserted. Both their sizes and the handwriting on them varies. The first sheet bears a note 'A number of Leaves are here torn out. The fresh papers inserted are collected from fragments & loose slips found in the "B.B." chest.' The second sheet is blank except for the bookplate of James Alexander Stewart. The manuscript notes on the rest of the sheets are probably early nineteenth century, and comprise attempts at bawdy wit and inane obscene profundities. These sheets are followed by a blank diploma – not just a transcript, but a diploma drawn up for use, already sealed, then later glued into the Bible. The seal is the 1816 'lighthouse' type (3.6), applied to the top left corner of the diploma. At the end of the text of the Bible two further sheets of paper (unlined) are glued, and contain miscellaneous anecdotes and reflections relating to sex. In the text of the Bible there are a few annotations, and on the back of the title page of the New Testament printed notices are glued relating to early biblical manuscripts and to statistics concerning the Bible.

A volume which binds together copies of the *Records* and *Supplement* is kept with the Bible and contains a typed statement concerning the Bible's provenance, signed by John Alexander Stewart on 23 March 1954. This relates that it was bought by William Hunter, a Glasgow flour merchant, who left it to his nephew D.M. Hunter. On the death of the latter the Bible was bought from his widow by Stewart, from whom it passed to a lady. She sold it to Larry Hutchison, Dunfermline.

L. Hutchison, 'The Beggar's Benison,' *Scottish Book Collector*, [i (1987–9)], no. 4, pp.25–7; D. Foxon, *Libertine literature in England, 1660–1745* (New York, 1965), 16n states that the Bible was offered for sale by Hugh Hopkins, Glasgow (catalogue 98) in 1962.

9 Snuff or Tobacco Box

9.1   Oval, 7 cm long x 5.2 cm broad x 2.3 cm deep, Silver plate.
      Inscribed decoration. Indecipherable monogram on lid. Makers' initials inside lid 'J. B. & Co.'

The box probably dates from the mid or later nineteenth century. It is tightly packed with ginger hair, with a card with a ms note, 'Hair from the

Mons Veneris of a Royal Courtesan of George IV. His Majesty was introduced to the Sovereign and Knights of the B.B. when he visited Scotland and arrived at the [harbour?] of Leith for the first and last time'. BBWCC; Jones, *Clubs*, 193, 208.

10 Drinking Vessel

10.1 *c.* 21 cm long x 15.3 cm. Metal sheets, soldered together and painted. Phallic, resting on testicles and glans, with cone-shaped mouth on the top.

This may be either a Benison or a Wig Club relic.

11 Pandora's Box

11.1 68.3 cm long x 41.5 cm broad x 34 cm high. Mahogany.

Plain brass corners and lockplate. Brass carrying handles on either end, one broken.

11.2 Brass plate (12.3 cm x 7.6 cm, with scalloped corners), now separate but formerly attached to the top of 11.1. Engraved vulva with the legends PANDORA'S BOX FOR CHAMPIONS BOLD and OPEN SESAME, with BEGGARS BENNISON CASTLE OF DREEL ANSTRUTHER within.

The earliest use of the term 'open sesame' noted in *OED* is 1785. BBWCC. Illustrated in *Records*.

12 Miscellaneous

12.1 'Book of Sentiments etc.'

In possession of J.F.S. Gordon in 1897. This presumably is identical with the 'Dinner Sentiment, Bon-Mots, Toasts Etc. collected from Scraps written in Ink and Pencil, dated from 1732 to 1820,' printed in *Supplement*, 17–32, and evidently collected by Matthew Conolly.
Whereabouts unknown. Mentioned by J.F.S. Gordon in a letter in BBWCC dated 18 Oct. 1897.

12.2 Bell.

Said to have existed in 1892, *Supplement*, 16, but this is more likely to have been a relic of one of the Anstruther burghs.

12.3 Hour Glass.

Said to have existed in 1892, *Supplement*, 16, but this is more likely to have been a relic of one of the Anstruther burghs.

THE WIG CLUB

13 The Wig and its Accessories

13.1 Wig.

This appears to have originally been in the possession of the Beggar's Benison of Edinburgh: 'one renowned Wig worn by the Sovereign composed of the Privy-hairs of Royal courtezans,' *Records*, 8. The earl of Moray gave the wig to the Wig Club in 1775. According to H.A. Cockburn, 'An account of the Friday Club,' *BOEC*, iii (1910), 138, the wig still existed in 1910, and in the 1930s Louis Jones heard that it was in a lawyer's office in Leith, *Clubs*, 193.
Whereabouts unknown.

13.2 Wig Box, 44 cm long x 26 cm broad x 48 cm high. Mahogany, with brass carrying handle on top. The hinged door on the front has a brass lockplate. Inside, a base for the Wig Stand is fitted on the left, and on the right felt pockets are fitted to the back and side for the comb and other paraphernalia that the wig acquired.

BBWCC.

13.3 Base of Wig Stand. Mahogany, circular base c.20 cm in diameter, c.18.2 cm tall.

Shaped to slide into a fitting in 13.1.
BBWCC.

13.4 Wig Stand. Painted life-size human head, 26.5 cm high. *Papier mâché.*

Made by Gavin Wilson, shoemaker.
BBWCC.

14 Ballot Box

14.1 'Shaped like the lower half of a man, about two feet high, but hollow and divided into "aye" and "nay" sections.' 'The organs of generation for this statute are detachable and of disproportionate size,' Jones, *Clubs*, 197, 209.
'The naked body of a man (unnecessarily proportioned), from the waist to the knees,' H.A. Cockburn, 'An account of the Friday Club,' *BOEC*, iii (1910), 138.

Jones assigned the ballot box to the Beggar's Benison. But the Benison is not known to have held ballots to elect members, whereas the Wig Club did have a system of balloting.

Whereabouts unknown.

15 Seal Impression

15.1 Oval, 30mm x 22mm, Cock and hen facing each other, each with head replaced by human genitals.

Impression on original Wig Club minute of 8 April 1805. The minute is signed by Lord Doune and the seal may have been his rather than the club's. Louis Jones believed that this was the seal ordered by the club in 1775, but that seal had been supposed to bear the wig and the club's motto.

BBWCC; Jones, *Clubs*, 159.

16 Drinking Glasses

16.1 21 cm long x 12.5 cm tall. Clear glass, probably lead glass.
In the shape of phallus and scrotum. The mouth or cup, placed over the scrotum, is a pointed oval, doubtless vulvar in reference. Left testicle broken.

This and 16.2 are presumably the 'prick glasses' mentioned in the minutes of the Wig Club. The inspiration may have come from the Roman *priapus vitreus* referred to by Juvenal, but 10.1 above is obviously a crude attempt at a similar drinking vessel, and may have been a more immediate inspiration. Kavanagh (BBWCC) claimed that the Beggar's Benison had had phallic-shaped glasses (said to have been made in Antwerp) but said that none survived, so 16.1 and 16.2 are here assigned to the Wig. Ceramic examples of 'drinking phalluses' can be found in Doncaster Museum and the Museum of London.

E.P. Lole, 'Priapic glasses – a new find,' *Glass Circle News*, no. 83 (June 2000), 9–10.

16.2 21.3 cm long x 10.4 cm tall. Clear glass, not lead glass.
Similar in overall design to 16.1, but produced by a different glass house. Both testicles broken.

BBWCC.

17 Manuscript and Printed Material

17.1 Minute Book of the Wig Club, 1775–1826.
Bound in calf skin. Decorated title page reads 'The Knights

Companion of the Wig, Being Assembled at Fortune's, March VI, MDCCLXXV.'

The minutes are nearly all in the same hand, and were probably written up from original loose minutes many years after the dates of meetings.
BBWCC.

17.2 Original minutes of the Wig Club. Loose sheets containing signed minutes of meetings on 3 Apr. 1801, 18 Jul. 1801, 9 Jan. 1802, 20 Mar. 1805, 8 Apr. 1805, 28 Mar. 1810, 11 Apr. 1810, 31 Jul. 1823, 15 Mar. 1826, and 8 Mar. [no year given].

BBWCC.

18.3 Loose betting slip, 1805, Lord Doune etc.

BBWCC.

18.4 List members of the Wig Club, with the rules abridged. Dated Edinburgh, Royal Exchange Coffee House, Dec. 1827.

Printed. The list is very incomplete. It represents neither a full list of members admitted since 1775, nor a list of members alive in 1827.
Copies in NLS and BBWCC.

1 Abbreviations used in references to Benison medals:

Cochran-Patrick, Medals	R.W. Cochran Patrick, *Catalogue of the medals of Scotland*, (Edinburgh 1884)
Davis, *Tickets*	W.J. Davis & A.W. Waters, *Tickets and passes of Great Britain and Ireland* (Leamington Spa, 1922)
Hawkins, *Medallic*	E. Hawkins (ed.), *Medallic illustrations of the history of Great Britain and Ireland*, (British Museum, 2 vols., 1885)
Hocking, 'Notes'	W.J. Hocking, 'Notes on a collection of coining instruments in the National Museum of Scotland,' *PSAS*, xlix (1914–15), 327–8
Medallic illustrations	*Medallic illustrations of the history of Great Britain and Ireland*, (3 vols., British Museum, 1904–11)
Montague Guest	*Catalogue of the Montague Guest collection of badges, tokens and passes* (British Museum, London, 1930)

Index

(BB) and (WC) indicate members of the Benison and the Wig. Names of officials concerned in the issuing of Benison diplomas, as listed in Appendix 2, have not been indexed. Nor have place-names which occur repeatedly scattered throughout the book (Fife and the East Neuk burghs).

Index